Universalism and
the Doctrine of Hell

Universalism and the Doctrine of Hell

Papers presented at the Fourth Edinburgh Conference in
Christian Dogmatics, 1991

edited by
Nigel M. de S. Cameron

Carlisle, U.K.
Paternoster Press

Baker Book House
Grand Rapids, U.S.A.

British Library Cataloguing in Publication Data

Universalism and the Doctrine of Hell:
Papers Presented at the Fourth Edinburgh
Conference in Christian Dogmatics, 1991
  I. Cameron, Nigel M. de S.
236

  ISBN 0–85364–552–3

Library of Congress Cataloging-in-Publication data
Universalism and the doctrine of hell / edited by
  Nigel M. de S. Cameron.
     p. cm.
   ISBN 0–8010–2576–1
   1. Universalism—Congresses. 2. Hell—
Congresses. 3. Future life—Congresses. 4.
Salvation—Congresses. I. Cameron, Nigel M.
de S.
BX9941.2.U55   1993
236'.25—dc20   93–16689
                                   CIP

Typeset at Rutherford House, Edinburgh
and printed in the UK by
The Guernsey Press Co. Ltd., Guernsey, Channel Islands
for the publishers

Contents

v

*When all is done, the hell of hells, the torment of
torments, is the everlasting absence of God, and the
everlasting impossibility of returning to his presence...
to fall out of the hands of the living God, is a horror
beyond our expression, beyond our imagination.... What
Tophet is not Paradise, what Brimstone is not Amber,
what gnashing is not a comfort, what gnawing of the
worme is not a tickling, what torment is not a marriage
bed to this damnation, to be secluded eternally,
eternally, eternally from the sight of God?*

John Donne
Sermons IV, 86

Contributors

Henri Blocher is Dean and Professor of Systematic Theology in the Faculté de Théologie Évangelique, Vaux-sur-Seine, Paris

John E. Colwell is pastor of King's Church, Catford, London and author of *Actuality and Provisionality: Eternity and Election in the Theology of Karl Barth*

Kendall Harmon, an Episcopal priest, is a doctoral student in Theology at Keble College, Oxford

Trevor Hart is Lecturer in Systematic Theology at the University of Aberdeen

Paul Helm is Professor of the Philosophy of Religion, King's College, London

Frederick W. Norris is Professor of Christian Doctrine at Emmanuel School of Religion, Johnson City, Tennessee

David J. Powys is vicar of St James the Less, Mount Eliza, Australia

Professor Daniel A. Du Toit is Professor of Systematic Theology and Ethics in the Faculty of Theology, University of Stellenbosch, South Africa

Thomas F. Torrance is Professor Emeritus of Christian Dogmatics in the University of Edinburgh

John W. Wenham is the former Vice Principal of Tyndale Hall, Bristol and Warden of Latimer House, Oxford, author of *The Goodness of God.*

Introduction

The once confident claim of Christians that Jesus Christ offers the only way to God – surely the most characteristically *Christian* of assertions – is found today at the centre of a series of disputes. Not only are there Christians who deny it, and affirm the legitimacy of other ways and, ultimately, their success; in a world increasingly self-conscious in its pluralism it is a claim which fails to meet the standards of mutual respect and cultural decency demanded of those who would engage in public religious discourse. In a shrinking world of competing religious claims the one principle urged upon all is that of relativism, which while it may leave the community's conscience untroubled by the need to decide between A and B denies absolutely to all pretenders to religious truth any kind of ultimacy at all; except, of course, to the liberal, whose illiberality toward those who disagree in something which matters (rather than something which doesn't) is nowhere more obvious.

As so often, the fog of war covers a series of engagements. Does the one God have many names, many masks, such that all roads lead to Jerusalem? If not, are there then anonymous Christians, saved by and living for a Jesus whose name they have never heard? There are both more and less orthodox versions of that thesis, driven alike by a concern for the fate of the unevangelised, those to whom the gospel has never been preached. An earlier generation could read in their fate the supreme motive for mission without losing sleep over its justice or, in turn, letting such concerns feed back and begin to question their theological understanding. Justifying God's putative ways to questioning women and men has become very hard; and the patent fact that some questions, at least, are unanswerable on remotely orthodox criteria has in no way diminished the questioning nor the growing desire, for better or worse, to give answers.

Again, to pick up a question which affects the shading, if not the colours, of the credibility of orthodoxy: when the books are opened, will the number of the saved greatly exceed that of the lost (a view which has been held by some very conservative Calvinists), or are they few that be saved? And then we move to the second focus, that of, as it were, the eschatological demonstration of the bankruptcy of relativism. On that as on the uniqueness of Christianity these writers are at one: God's way of reconciling us with him and himself with us is solely through Jesus Christ; and there will come a day when all the world, the very cosmos, will know. But what then? If there is a final division into sheep and goats, are the goats consigned to unending conscious torment or rather to a firing squad? And, of course, where does Scripture line up on each of these and other questions; and where the tradition of the church?

These essays bring together contributions from Britain, France, the United States, Australia and South Africa. Contributors share a common adherence to the evangelical faith, once delivered to the saints. On some of these key questions they agree, on others they agree to differ. Some directly engage issues of controversy; others reflect on historical and theological contexts. We hope these papers convey something of the vigour of their original presentation over three sunny Edinburgh days in August, 1991, though the reader's imagination will have to supply the interaction they sparked.

And finally: thanks to Vivienne Goddard, publishing manager at Rutherford House, whose final project this represents; Janella Glover, house manager, who supervised the conference; and Sarah Chambers, doctoral student here at Trinity, who helped with proofing and compiled the index.

Nigel M. de S. Cameron
Trinity Evangelical Divinity School
Deerfield, Illinois
June 1992

Universalism: Two Distinct Types

Trevor Hart

1. By Way of Introduction

'The creeping paralysis of universalism is rapidly gaining ground throughout Christendom. This dangerous doctrine minimizes the seriousness of sin, impugns the righteousness of God, emasculates the doctrine of the atonement and denies final judgement, [and] finds no support in the Scriptures.'[1] So wrote J. Oswald Sanders in 1966. Thirteen years later Edwin Blum[2] laid the following charges firmly at the door of universalist doctrine: that it 'trivializes sin by effectively denying that sin deserves punishment'; that it undermines Christian morality since 'The choice of good or evil loses its cutting edge when the results are ultimately a good destiny in either case'; that it denigrates the central Protestant doctrine of justification by faith by denying that faith in Jesus Christ is in fact necessary for salvation; and that it erodes any true sense of missionary zeal, since the significance of the future judgement is altogether lost if all will ultimately be saved without distinction.

Some such catena of charges is to be found rehearsed in many evangelical treatments of universalism. This reflects the fact that the ultimate scope of divine salvation is an

---

1   J. Oswald Sanders, *What of the Unevangelized?* OMF, 1966, p.9.

2   See *Themelios*, Vol. 4, No. 2, (1979), pp. 59-61.

issue lying at the dogmatic heart of the gospel, and not
merely a fascinating side show on the eschatological
fringes of theological concern. Christology, the doctrine of
atonement (both its necessity and its means), justification
by faith, natural theology, the nature of biblical authority,
human freedom in relation to divine sovereignty, and the
Christian doctrine of God itself are all potentially at stake
in any discussion of this subject. Undoubtedly some
universalist eschatologies take a shape which has
problematic repercussions in these other areas. The
purpose of this paper, however, is to suggest that such
sweeping charges as those outlined above are as unfair
and unjustified in relation to some universalist theologies
as they are fair and justified in relation to others. Basic to
the argument, therefore, is the recognition that (as Richard
Bauckham notes) 'Only the belief that ultimately all men
will be saved is common to all universalists. The rationale
for that belief and the total theological content in which it
belongs vary considerably.'[3]

The universalist conclusion, then, is a variegated
species some types of which root and grow in theological
soils where others would only wither and die. If the
continuing evangelical critique of what has apparently
become an unquestioned dogma of more 'liberal'
theological perspectives and a secretly cherished hope of
many whose more 'conservative' stance will not allow
them to accord it any dogmatic status is to be taken
seriously, then it must ensure that it engages in a careful
study of the origin of species, and addresses the problem
of universalisms rather than universalism. Otherwise it
will find itself guilty precisely of sweeping and general
charges which will have little real impact. In what follows
we shall identify and consider two broad types of
universalistic doctrine, a classification intended to be

---

[3]   'Universalism: a historical survey' in the aforementioned
       volume of *Themelios*, p. 49.

neither exhaustive nor satisfactory, but simply to enable comparisons and contrasts to be drawn helpfully within the scope of our treatment.

2. Pluralistic Universalism

In *The Absolute Validity of Christianity*[4] Ernst Troeltsch addressed an issue that had come increasingly to impinge upon the Christian consciousness since the emergence of historicism with its view of history as the sphere of the contingent, the relative and the transitory; of knowledge of the past as a fragile commodity discoverable only through careful and critical sifting of the data, and then generating results which were at best approximate. The precise dilemma faced by Troeltsch was how to reconcile this essentially sceptical spirit with the claims of the Christian religion to provide a set of universal values and truths, values and truths rooted inevitably in that very same historical flux. In what sense could claim any longer be laid to a universal, absolute or normative status for an historically and culturally particular set of religious beliefs, whatever their hold may have been over the civilised world in the pre-historicist past?

In his recent work *Atonement and Incarnation*,[5] Vernon White reminds us that the past ninety or so years have served rather to heighten than to alleviate this difficulty for Christian apologists. New vistas of the human and pre-human history of our planet which, he notes, 'appear to be untouched and untouchable by the Christ Event'[6] have been uncovered by recent scientific and historical endeavours. The shrinking of our world to a 'global village' has been matched by the relentless expansion of the dark recesses of space beyond it. Troeltsch's perception of

---

4   1901. Reissued as *The Absoluteness of Christianity*, London, 1972.
5   Cambridge, 1991.
6   *Ibid.*, p. 2.

human existence as but 'a breath on a cold window pane'[7] has been reinforced rather than undermined, therefore, by the continuing march of human discovery. In view of this irreversible broadening of our perspective, White argues, the challenge to the Christian theologian is to explore *how, if at all, an historically particular event or set of events might be said to effect something of universal significance for the human race.*

That the death of a man on a cross outside Jerusalem in the first century is somehow constitutive of reconciliation on a universal scale has formed a central part of Christian soteriological doctrine through the centuries. Yet it is clearer now than ever before that many millions of human persons have and will pass through their own brief portion of universal human history without any serious opportunity of hearing or responding to the supposed soteriological claim made upon their lives by this man. The current state of our knowledge, White suggests, militates against the traditional perception of Christianity as truly offering good news to all human persons, and makes any such claim to salvific universality or absoluteness essentially scandalous. Certainly for many in our day the effect of our ever receding epistemic horizon is precisely 'to relativize all claims to universal spiritual significance of any particular historical event.'[8]

Whether it is the alleged significance of particular events, or entire systems of value and belief that are under critical scrutiny, the question of the relationship of Christianity to other historical, cultural and (especially) religious contexts is clearly raised by considerations such as these. Whether or not sense can any longer be accorded to claims of religious or salvific absoluteness or

---

7   Cited in White, *op. cit.*, pp. 107-8.
8   *Ibid.*, p. 2.

universality is, as Troeltsch saw, a matter of vital concern to the contemporary theologian.

While Troeltsch's own response to this question in the aforementioned work was to defend the absoluteness of the Christian religion, by 1923 he had moved to a more radical stance which, as McGrath notes, endorsed the infamous observation of Rousseau that religion is 'une affaire de geographie'.[9] Thus in his essay, 'The Place of Christianity Among the World Religions',[10] written shortly before his death, he argues for what Hick calls a 'relative absoluteness' for Christianity.[11] Troeltsch's research into the history of Christianity in the intervening years had led him to form the view that it, just as surely as the other major religious traditions of the world, is inextricably linked to the particular social and cultural patterns within which it has developed over the centuries. It stands or falls indeed with elements of the ancient and modern civilizations of Europe. Thus the question of a claim to some sort of absolute or universal validity recedes into the background, as closer examination in fact reduces that which is genuinely common to humankind and universally valid to the vanishing point. Thus the traditional understanding of Christianity as a religion to be carried to the furthest corners of the globe, enlightening the heathen nations with its truth, falls prey to a general cultural and philosophical pluralism in which truth and falsity are but functions of specific societal contexts rather than transcontextual absolutes. If Christianity is in any sense absolute, then it is so only for those belonging to the

---

[9]   See McGrath, *The Making of Modern German Christology*, Oxford, 1986, p. 84.

[10] Reprinted in Hick and Hebblethwaite (eds), *Christianity and Other Religions*, London, 1980, pp. 11-31.

[11] See Hick and Knitter, (eds) *The Myth of Christian Uniqueness*, London, 1988, p. 16.

culture of Europe.[12] For other races in other temporal and spatial contexts other religious traditions will serve in a similar way. In others words 'Christianity is "absolute" for Christians, and the other world faiths are likewise absolute for their own adherents,'[13] and we must understand this as part of the divinely ordained purpose of bringing human beings to salvation. What is important, therefore, is that each culturally bound tradition should strive to fulfil its own highest potentiality, and not be distracted by the misguided attempt to make converts of others.

This pluralist approach has gained considerable intellectual ground in the period since Troeltsch's death. For many today who would count themselves firmly within the Christian tradition the concomitant conviction is self-evident; since the death of Jesus can no longer be viewed as relevant to every context, salvation (whatever that might now mean) must be held to be available apart from it, and *via* many different religious (or indeed non-religious) routes.

Universalism as such – *i.e.* the view that ultimately all human persons will enjoy salvation – is, of course, no necessary component of the pluralist thesis. Many ways to salvation can be missed or rejected just as readily as one universal way. In fact, however, the two do often seem to fall together in contemporary theologies, supporting one another quite conveniently as they do.

---

12   Christianity 'is God's countenance as revealed to us; it is the way in which, being what we are, we receive, and react to, the revelation of God. ...It is final and unconditional for us, because we have nothing else, ... But this does not preclude the possibility that other racial groups, living under entirely different cultural conditions, may experience their contact with the Divine Life in quite a different way.' Troeltsch, *op. cit.*, p. 25.

13   Hick, *op. cit.* p. 16.

Clearly a conviction that all *must* ultimately find salvation is helpfully bolstered by the view that their empirical refusal or failure to embrace faith in Jesus Christ makes no necessary difference to their eternal destiny. If the pluralist thesis seems to make the ultimate salvation of all more probable than the exclusivist insistence upon faith in Jesus Christ, so too the belief that God will ultimately save every human person apparently makes the pluralist thesis infinitely more reasonable. Many ways would seem to be much more efficient than just one in the accomplishment of this divine task.

This intimacy between dogmatic universalism and pluralism is to be found, for example, in the more recent writings of John Hick. Hick's starting point appears to be on the one hand a conviction drawn ultimately from the Christian tradition that God's nature is love, and on the other a passionate concern with the theodicy question and the issues of divine justice posed by it. His attempts to resolve the tension generated by the juxtaposition of these two led him to the hypothesis[14] that all will ultimately achieve salvation through a gradual, and at times painful, therapeutic and purgatorial process continuing beyond this life (according to Hick's later works,[15] perhaps through several others), and leading eventually to the conformity of the person to what Christian tradition has called the 'divine likeness'. The suffering and pain of this present existence is thus justified on the grounds not only that each individual will ultimately be received into a glorious salvation, but that this same darkness and pain is a necessary part of the road which *leads* to salvation.

While in Hick's earlier writings this optimistic universalism seems still to be wedded to a relatively

---

14   See *Evil and the God of Love*, London, 2nd ed., 1977.
15   See, *e.g.*, *Death and Eternal Life*, London, 1976.

orthodox Christian theology, in due course a number of factors drove him to embrace the pluralist thesis propounded by Troeltsch.[16] Chief among these was the sort of apparent moral contradiction already mentioned. Can we seriously believe that a God of love, whose salvific purpose is genuinely directed towards all human persons, should ordain that salvation be contingent upon factors restricting it almost inevitably to a small minority of the race? Hick's response to this unease with traditional soteriological doctrine was to call for a Copernican revolution in theology; a shift, that is to say, away from a 'Ptolemaic' view in which Christianity and its gospel are inevitably at the centre, to a view in which God is at the centre, and Christianity is recognised for what it truly is: one among many religious satellites orbiting this common deity, one way among many to the salvation which the God of love will ultimately effect in all. For Hick this theological crossing of the Rubicon is the only satisfactory response to the scandal of the particularity of Christianity.[17]

There are, of course, mediating positions between traditional exclusivism and Hick's pluralism. Thus there are those who address the scandal of the historical and cultural particularity of Christianity while yet ascribing to it a potentially universal saving scope. This they do by arguing that while the salvation of any person is utterly dependent upon God's redeeming action in the death and resurrection of Christ, access to the benefits of the same may be had apart from explicit allegiance to Christ. Hick refers us to the effective repealing of the *extra ecclesia*

---

[16]   This case is stated clearly in his *God and the Universe of Faiths* (London, 2nd ed. 1977) as well as in numerous subsequent articles on the topic.

[17]   See, *e.g.*, 'The Non-Absoluteness of Christianity' in Hick and Knitter (eds), *The Myth of Christian Uniqueness*, London, 1988, p. 22.

nulla salus doctrine in the teaching of Vatican II that Christ's sacrificial death 'holds true not only for Christians, but for all men of good will in whose hearts grace works in an unseen way. For, since Christ died for all men, ... we ought to believe that the Holy Spirit in a manner known only to God offers to every man the possibility of being associated with this paschal mystery.'[18] In similar vein the encyclical of John Paul II *Redemptor Hominis* insists that 'every man without exception... has been redeemed by Christ ... because ... with each man without any exception... Christ is in a way united, even when man is unaware of it.'[19] What is affirmed here, then, is that while none are in fact saved apart from that salvation effected by Christ, nonetheless enjoyment of this salvation will not in every case be contingent upon explicit epistemic awareness of its source.

A similar 'inclusivist' line is taken by Vernon White who writes: '*Knowledge* of the Saviour is not a necessary constituent of *being* saved, not, that is, in this life, and not in the sense that historical knowledge about the events of Jesus of Nazareth is required. What may be required is the kind of personal humility and responsiveness which will accept the anonymous Saviour's gift (a responsiveness which may not necessarily be found in everyone...): but then this could well be mediated and enabled through the positive values of another religious or humanitarian tradition. There is therefore no possible mandate for imposing historical knowledge on the non-Christian world as if it is a prerequisite for final salvation, nor for denying that it is a world through which God can bring its people to salvation (still, of course, through Christ).'[20]

---

18   Pastoral Constitution on the Church, para. 2.
19   *Redemptor Hominis*, London, 1979, para. 14.
20   *Op. cit.*, pp. 112-3.

What exactly, though, does 'through Christ' mean on this model? White is at pains here to insist upon the important distinction between effective action and knowledge of the agent. In the case of atonement, he argues, it is the former and not the latter which is determinative. It is Christ's death and resurrection for us which save, and not our knowledge or understanding or right belief. The western theological tradition since the Enlightenment has tended to over-intellectualize in its soteriology, to conceive of knowledge as of the *esse* rather than the *bene esse* of being saved. This can be seen as the root of both exclusivist and pluralist eschatologies. For if revelation (conceived of as saving knowledge) and belief (reception of the same) are our central soteriological categories, then we are faced with an awkward choice: either we must insist upon the uniqueness of Christ as Saviour, and thereby inevitably restrict salvation to those who in the final analysis can be said to have known about him and received that knowledge in an appropriate manner, or else we are forced to deny his uniqueness in an attempt to open up saving knowledge of God to a much broader and morally acceptable constituency.

If, however, we focus not on knowledge, but rather on effective action as the determinant in salvation, then new possibilities are opened up. 'For while particular events are only accessible *qua* knowledge to the limited number of people who cluster around them (or the preaching of them) in space and time, their effect could, in principle, be universal.'[21] This enables us both to proclaim the universal redeeming scope of Christ's death and resurrection, and at the same time to meet the moral dilemma of the empirical restrictedness of knowledge and faith of the same through the centuries. Thus to say that a person is saved by God *through Christ* is simply to affirm

---

[21]   *Ibid.*, p. 20.

that there is no salvation for any apart from his sacrificial self-offering on the cross and his glorious exaltation of our humanity in the rupturing of the tomb on the third day. It is not necessarily to say anything about the mental or emotional state of the person with regard to these particular salvific events.

White's insistence upon making this clear distinction between event and epistemic reception is one which in broad terms we must endorse in the soteriological context. Certainly we shall be well served by it if it helps to name and to cast out the demon of rationalistic pelagianism which enquires as to which doctrines must be believed if a person is to be saved. We are not accepted by God on the basis of our own feats of cognitive fidelity, but on the basis of Christ's death and resurrection.

This said, however, we must question the adequacy of his specific contention that a person may be 'saved' by an anonymous Saviour, quite apart from any knowledge of the same. There is a sense in which this must be true if it was indeed while we were yet dead in our sins that Christ died for us. Inasmuch as his redeeming act can be said seriously to have been *for us* we must acknowledge that we were to this extent saved by an anonymous redeemer quite apart from and prior to any knowledge of or faith in the same on our part. It must be asked, however, whether and in what sense we could be spoken of as in an existential state of *being saved* had such knowledge and faith not ultimately followed on. There is a question here concerning the very nature of the salvation spoken of in the gospel. What sort of salvation is it which occurs as a result of, yet *possibly in utter ignorance of* Jesus Christ's life, death and resurrection? Is it not of the very nature of biblical salvation that it consists in a conscious personal sharing in sonship; in embracing joyfully the knowledge of who God is, the Father who willingly delivers up the Son in the Spirit that we might share in the Spirit of sonship; in having one's life transformed by a thankful *metanoia* rooted firmly in this knowledge, and by the ongoing sharing in that trinitarian *koinonia* which is its ultimate end? Is it possible to share in *this* salvation, and yet to remain ignorant of the one who is not only its cause or source, but its very substance?

White's thesis makes a helpful distinction, but pushes it too far, driving a wedge between redemption and revelation in a way that is, biblically speaking, highly problematic. A salvation which consists essentially not in purely forensic or extrinsic relations between two agents, but in real personal at-one-ment, real reconciliation between persons, cannot come to fruition without our being drawn precisely into personal saving knowledge of the agent. As an objective fact it may be carried out behind our backs and without us: as one which cuts savingly into our existence it cannot remain so.

What is also clear from the passage cited is that this inclusivist model is by no means necessarily universalist in orientation. There may still be distinctions drawn between those who are being saved and those who are not. Another problem immediately raises itself here; for if it is not the knowledge of faith which indicates the boundaries of such a differentiation, what is it? The answers hinted at by White ('personal humility and responsiveness... which may not be found in everyone') and by others taking a similar line such as Rahner tend in fact to point towards some intrinsic moral or spiritual quality in the person concerned, and thereby to wrest salvation from its mooring in the sheer graciousness of God, casting those who have not heard of Christ back upon themselves at the crucial point. No doubt faith can easily be misconstrued as a condition of salvation; but it can also readily be seen in terms of pure response to the good news. It is not clear what other factor might fulfil the same role in those ignorant of their anonymous Saviour.

Hick utterly rejects all such inclusivist theologies, branding them the mere addition of irrelevant epicycles to a now outmoded theological astronomy. They, just as surely as their more traditional exclusivist counterparts, insist upon maintaining the real uniqueness of Christ for revelation of God, and for salvation, and thereby fail to grasp the nettle which presents itself to the serious-minded theologian. Inasmuch as this still lays claim to a truth possessed by Christians to which others must ultimately be drawn in order to be saved or to reach full spiritual maturity, it is patronising and a source of potential antagonism to the adherents of other religious traditions. If we are to see them as being saved in any sense (as we must) then it must be in terms proper to their own traditions. We must finally cast aside all hangovers from the old religious imperialism of the past, and enter realistically and fully into the new universe of faiths which the Copernican revolution opens up.

In all this, not much has changed since Troeltsch. The universalism which fits hand and glove together with it is thus one which proclaims not only that it is quite unnecessary for a person to know about or to believe in Jesus Christ in order to be saved, but, strictly speaking, quite unnecessary also for Christ to have lived or died. The significance of the Christ event is utterly relativized. A person can be saved apart from Jesus Christ altogether; although Hick, like Troeltsch, is content enough for Jesus to remain a figure of religious and 'salvific' significance for those who either through accident of birth or through conscious choice take the Christian route to their ultimate destiny in the hands of God.

This pluralistic variety of universalism, then, is one which is rooted in a context where most of the central doctrines of Christianity are indeed severely compromised. We may briefly enumerate the most obvious among them.

1. Christology. If the uniqueness of Christianity as a divinely ordained way to salvation is no longer to be taken seriously, then clearly traditional incarnational christology cannot be sustained either. For any one religion to lay claim to a unique incarnation of God himself is unacceptable. Thus it is not surprising to find Hick at the forefront of the attempts to 'move beyond' the 'myth' of the incarnation in the late 1970s. 2. Trinity. Since the doctrine of God as triune *koinonia* of Father, Son and Spirit stands or falls with some form of incarnational christology, the doctrine of God inherent in this brand of universalism also loses most of its recognisably Christian shape; although in 1988 Hick was still prepared to concede that the sort of 'inspiration christology' which he personally found tolerable was 'fully compatible with the conception of the Trinity as affirming three distinguishable ways in which the one God is experienced,... namely, as creator, redeemer, and inspirer.'[22] 3. Atonement. The cross of Jesus is no longer accorded any objective atoning significance. Rather salvation is to be had, *via* various religious traditions, within the context of a general divine-human relationship in which 'if we are truly penitent we can ask for and receive forgiveness and new life.'[23] The precise role of Jesus or his death in this, for those belonging to the Christian tradition, is reduced to that of an example of self-giving love. 4. Justification by Faith. To be absolutely fair to Hick here he nowhere suggests that any will be saved in spite of their rejection of God and his salvation, so there might be said to be a sense in which he adheres to some form of this doctrine. Rather he teaches that all will ultimately come to embrace God's salvation, his confidence being rooted in a propensity for God built into human nature itself. Yet inasmuch as he abandons quite decisively any need for faith in Jesus Christ in order for a person to be saved, we may say that the doctrine in

---

22   *The Myth of Christian Uniqueness*, p. 32.
23   *Ibid.*, p. 33.

its biblical form has altogether disappeared. Thus too the motive for evangelism and missionary activity is quite lost. As for Troeltsch, so also for Hick, what is needed is increased understanding between the religious traditions of our world, and not competing claims for allegiance or attempts to convert.

Here then we have a universalistic thesis the central contention of which is that all will ultimately be saved regardless of their attitude to Jesus Christ and his death; regardless, indeed, of the person of Jesus at all, or any alleged significance of his actions. This is not, and nor would it claim to be, in any sense a Christian universalism, but one springing naturally from the far more diverse and multi-textured soils on the far side of Hick's religious Rubicon.

3. Christian Universalism

There is, however, an altogether distinct brand of universalist doctrine the natural environment for which is the more familiar terrain of the Ptolemaic universe on this side of the stream. In as much as its eschatological vision is one determined (ostensibly at least) by concerns claiming to be proper to the inner logic of the gospel itself it must be accorded the epithet 'Christian'.

Most instances of this Christian universalism would appeal to some such list of factors as the following in support of their case: the central Christian conviction that love is the very nature of God, and that the most fundamental relation of this God to all his creatures must therefore be one of love if he is to be true to himself; the concomitant conviction that this same God must ultimately have the final good of all his creatures in view, that 'he desireth not the death of (any) sinner, but rather that he may turn from his wickedness and live'; the gospel stress on the utter unconditionality of the salvation wrought by Christ, and the rejection of any notion that some might be more deserving than others of redemption; the clear affirmations in Scripture concerning the universality of the scope of Christ's saving passion and resurrection and the completeness of the salvation effected by the same (*i.e.* in some sense God *has* saved all in Christ); and lastly an insistence that God, as Lord of all, must prevail, that the universal saving will springing inevitably from his nature must be fulfilled in his creatures. Clearly these are all considerations springing out of Christian theological concerns. The extent to which others are either sidetracked, eroded or treated in an unsatisfactory manner is a matter for our consideration.

From its focus on these biblical and theological issues the Christian case for universalism generally proceeds to a specific philosophical consideration of what has been called the omnipotence of divine love. The terms in which the discussion is normally couched parallel conveniently those of the so-called logical problem of evil. Here three elements are juxtaposed to create an unstable equilibrium: divine omnipotence, divine goodness and the fact of evil in the world. In its deductive form the logical problem proceeds as follows:
If God were good he would desire the well-being of his creatures, and would seek to eradicate suffering and evil from their experience.
If God were omnipotent or sovereign he would be able to bring about this desired state of affairs.
Evil is a painful reality in the experience of his creatures.
Therefore either God is limited in power, or in goodness, or both.
An important response to this syllogism has been the free will defense in its various forms, which insists that in a world populated by human beings the presence of moral evil at least is inevitable, since to be human is to be free to choose between good and evil courses of action. Thus the presence of evil in this moral form at least is the price of being human.

Turning now to the philosophical case in support of universalism we may identify a similar logical structure.

If God were all good (if his nature were truly love) then he would desire the eternal well-being (salvation) of all his creatures, since his natural relation to all would be fundamentally one of love.

If God were truly sovereign (omnipotent) then he would be quite capable of bringing about this desired state of affairs, *i.e.* the salvation of all. Empirically, at least, not all are participating in salvation, since not all have responded in faith to Jesus Christ. Therefore, either God's sovereignty or his love must be called into question; or else (the more acceptable option) we must conclude that in due course and by means currently beyond our grasp, God will indeed bring all to salvation.

This is the conclusion reached, for example, by J.A.T. Robinson who provides one of the most subtle and compelling instances of this type of universalism. Robinson insists that Christian universalism is a conclusion founded not upon some *a priori* rational or moral set of considerations, nor upon the sort of optimistic anthropology resorted to by Hick. 'There is,' he writes, 'no ground whatever in the Bible for supposing that all men, simply because they are men, are "going the same way" – except to Hell.'[24] Rather 'the sole basis for such a doctrine, as more than wishful thinking, is the work of God in Christ.'[25] There can be no other; nor is any needed. The gospel directs us unequivocally to the determinative nature of 'what has been, one decisive act of God, once and for all, embracing every creature',[26] and Christian universalism is simply the confident assertion that this same accomplished fact of which the Bible cannot say

---

[24]   *In the End God*, London, 1950, p. 108.
[25]   *Ibid.*, p. 108.
[26]   *Ibid.*, p. 99.

enough, the saving divine intervention in Jesus Christ which in some sense can be said objectively to have effected the salvation of all, will be translated into the future. 'The promise of universal restoration is assured by the past: there cannot possibly be any other outcome.'[27]

Clearly there are others aspects of biblical teaching which must be taken equally seriously, and which seem at first sight to point to an altogether different conclusion. We shall see presently just how Robinson incorporates these into his thesis; but for now we need simply note that his reason for according the universal statements of Scripture ultimate eschatological status resides in his understanding of the doctrine of God itself, and of God's nature as 'omnipotent love' in particular. Thus he writes: 'If God is what ultimately He asserts Himself to be, then *how* he vindicates Himself as God and the *nature* of His final lordship is at the same time the answer to *what* He essentially is. The truth or falsity of the universalistic assertion, that in the end He is lord entirely of a world wanting his lordship, is consequently decisive for the whole Christian doctrine of God.'[28] Thus the doctrine of God itself is at stake in the answer we give to the question 'will any finally be left outside the boundaries of redemption?' This, Robinson insists, is not an intrusive piece of natural theology, but rather a case developed philosophically from roots in the logic of divine self-revelation. It is 'what God ultimately asserts Himself to be' which is the driving force behind the argument, and not an abstract concept of deity obtained independently of God's saving action in Jesus Christ.

The God revealed in Jesus Christ, Robinson contends, is such a God as could only be considered to have failed in his saving purposes were any of his creatures finally to be

27   *Ibid.*, p. 99.
28   *Ibid.*, pp. 102-3.

lost. 'Judgment,' he writes, 'can never be God's last word, because, if it were, it would be the word that would speak his failure.'[29] And in this case, he concludes, 'God would simply cease to be God'[30] as Christians, in their obedient response to his self-revealing initiative, understand the meaning of this word.

One fairly obvious response to this dogmatic universalism is that the necessity which it posits for a direct correlation between the universality of God's love and of Christ's redemptive activity on the one hand, and the final scope of those enjoying redemption on the other, is unable to accommodate a vital factor: namely, the capacity of the individual person to reject his or her salvation in Christ. This is, in other words, a sort of free will defense for eschatological dualism. Only by robbing human persons of their freedom (and hence of their human integrity), it is argued, can the universalistic thesis be maintained. Men and women must be able to resist salvation: the omnipotence of love cannot be such that it triumphs at the expense of true human personhood, effectively depersonalising those whom it saves. This is a considerable objection to the universalist thesis, and it is for this reason that so much of Robinson's presentation is taken up with an attempt to demonstrate just how the ultimate salvation of all is indeed compatible (and *must be* so) with their freedom either to choose or reject it.

In order to suggest just how this might be the case he directs us to an analogy drawn from the sphere of human personal relationships. Lest he be thought guilty at this point of basing his universalist case on a piece of subtle anthropomorphism, simply transferring by univocal predication some general truth about human love and freedom to the divine-human relationship, Robinson is

---

[29]   *Ibid.*, p. 106.
[30]   *Ibid.*, p. 107.

careful to point out that his intention is 'not to substantiate the truth of universalism (which rests entirely on the work of God in Christ), but to make its truth less baffling for our imaginations to grasp.'[31] If, in other words, we can see something to be true at the human level, we can at least grasp more readily how something similar *might* also be true (whether in fact it is or not) with God. This clarified, Robinson proceeds to his task.

We can all testify from our own experience, he suggests, to occasions when some gesture of love towards us by another human person has constrained us to respond with love. At such times we find ourselves unable to do any other than make this response: our whole being goes out to the other person. Try as we might to resist, everything in us tells us not to do so. 'Our defences are down, the power of love captures the very citadel of our will, and we answer with the spontaneous surrender of our whole being. Yet, at the same time, we know perfectly well that at such moments we can, if we choose, remain unmoved; there is no physical compulsion to commit ourselves.'[32] In other words, while we are constrained by love to a loving response, we do not lose our freedom in making that response, but rather discover true freedom. For a brief moment we become conscious of being ourselves in an extraordinary way, and to resist the urge to love would be to lose and not to gain personal fulfilment. If, then, this occasional experience is known to us in our human relationships, surely we can see how it would be possible for God's love toward each person to be such that each would ultimately be constrained to respond to it, and in doing so to find true personhood rather than losing it in the choice to reject God? In fact, Robinson concludes, the testimony of Christians over the centuries

---

31   *Ibid.*, p. 110.
32   *Ibid.*, p. 110.

is precisely that it is here, in that submission to Christ and his gospel which takes place in unconditional response to the prompting of the Spirit, that *true freedom* is to be found.

The essence of Robinson's universalism consists in fact in the confident assertion that ultimately all will be saved because all will in time come to choose the salvation offered through Christ's atoning death and resurrection. Thus there is no suggestion that any will be saved other than through faith in Christ, since *salvation itself consists precisely in the free choice of life through the death of Christ and the rejection of that hell which is the deserved fate of human beings*. Thus, he contends, 'there could be no greater calumny than to suggest that the universalist either does not preach hell or does so with his tongue in his cheek.'[33] On the contrary, both hell and judgement must be preached with integrity as existentially real alternatives to salvation. 'Only the man who has genuinely been confronted by both alternatives can be saved. To preach heaven alone ... is to deny men the possibility of salvation. For salvation is a state of having chosen; and in the moment of choice..., both alternatives are existentially as real.'[34] It is thus that Robinson is able to make sense of the biblical dualism between the saved and the lost. This is, as it were, a perfectly true and necessary account for the person facing the choice between salvation and its alternative. 'From below' hell and judgement are indeed realities, since no person can reject Christ and face anything other than eternal death. Thus we must not be too dismissive of Robinson's 'kerygmatic hell' as it has been called. It is kerygmatic not in the sense that it belongs only to the *kerygma* and not to the real world (a view which would rob the *kerygma* of its integrity, turning its dark side into an empty threat), but

---

33   *Ibid.*, p. 119.
34   *Ibid.*, p. 118.

rather in the sense that it is absolutely necessary that the *kerygma* should present what is the only real alternative to choosing life in Christ. Being saved involves rejecting this dark alternative to life in all its fulness; and that which is rejected is indeed real enough. It is because Robinson is equally convinced that all will in fact make this choice under the compulsion of divine love that he speaks of universalism as the 'truth as it is for God' (*i.e.* from above), and biblical dualism as the all too real scenario facing human beings in their existential viewpoint prior to this decision of faith. All will choose life: but the choice is only a real and significant one precisely because neither the reality of hell nor the urgency of choice is in any way lessened. Thus Robinson concludes that the divine love 'will take no man's choice from him; for it is precisely his choice that it wants. But its will to lordship is inexhaustible and ultimately unendurable: the sinner must yield.'[35]

We turn now to an evaluation of Robinson's position, and begin by considering some of the charges laid at the door of universalism in the opening part of this paper to see how well they stand up in the context of Robinson's rather than Hick's version of the doctrine.

1. *That it trivializes or minimizes the seriousness of sin.* There is no suggestion of this in Robinson's thesis. Sin is presented in all its awfulness and deservingness of hell. The contention is not simply that in spite of their sin all will be saved; but rather that because of Christ's dealing with sin and because of their response to this atoning reality in faith, all will be saved. This no more trivializes sin than God himself could be said to have done by allowing any to be saved in spite of it through faith in Jesus Christ and him crucified.

---

[35]   *Ibid.*, p. 123.

2. *That it emasculates the doctrine of atonement.* Again this criticism presumably resides on the assumption that if all are to be saved regardless of their attitude to the cross, then the saving significance of the cross itself, and its necessity for salvation, is called into question. We have seen this to be a wholly legitimate charge in relation to Hick's pluralistic universalism. Again, however, it is not so in the case of Robinson. The atoning action of God in Christ is not marginalized, but is rather at very heart of his universalism, since it is precisely the universal scope of the cross which fuels his conviction that all will ultimately make theirs subjectively that which is already theirs objectively.

3. *That it denies final judgement and the reality of hell.* It is certainly true that the universalist conclusion logically entails the denial of a final separation of human beings into eternally fixed categories of redeemed and lost. But many universalists accord something like a purgatorial significance to hell, seeing it not as an end, but as a means to the end of ultimate redemption. As we have seen Robinson does not take this line, but he does accord existential reality to both judgement and hell as the inevitable outcomes of rejection of the gospel. Thus his universalism does not deny that judgement and hell are real: but simply that the judgement will find any wanting, and that hell will be occupied. And this is because he believes all will finally embrace Christ and be saved. If that is somehow a prospect which makes us feel uncomfortable, rather than one which fills us with joy, then we should ask some searching questions as to the reasons for this discomfort.

4. *That it denigrates the doctrine of justification by faith.* Clearly Robinson is not guilty of this. His case from beginning to end is rooted in the conviction that salvation comes by faith in Christ alone. It is universalist because he expects faith itself to be a universal phenomenon,

spreading out to match the universality of God's redeeming love in Christ. Thus faith is not simply a boundary marker, a convenient means of identifying the difference between those who are saved and those who are not; rather it is the form which salvation itself takes as it bites into our existence, forcing upon us the choice between life with God, and life without him. Understood thus, the significance of justification by faith is in no way lessened by the universalist conclusion. Whether few are saved in this way or all, the necessity for and significance of such faith remains the same.

5. *That it impugns the righteousness or justice of God.* It is commonly contended that such a stress on the love of God as drives one to universalism must in some way detract from what Scripture clearly teaches about divine justice. Again we should note that even were this to be the case, Robinson avoids the criticism by presenting a scenario in which none are in fact saved apart from faith in Christ, and in which judgement and hell remain the inevitable fate of those who reject the gospel. Thus logically at least it remains true that the demands of justice stand firm; even if there is finally no need to implement them. But we must pursue this issue further, since it is not clear that the criticism springs from an altogether satisfactory notion of the relationship between love and justice in God.

The danger here lies in the suggestion that love and justice are somehow two separable quantities within the character of God, and that the dynamics of atonement consist in some sort of power struggle between two distinct sets of claims within God himself. The concomitant suggestion follows on that men and women may thus be placed either under the love of God, or else under his justice; that the claims of the one may apply to them or not, depending upon their faith or lack of it; that God may be a loving Father towards some, and an arbiter of naked justice towards others. Robinson insists, quite correctly, that this will not do if we are to maintain the Christian doctrine according to which love is the very nature of God, and not an assumed attitude, or a principle to be matched against another equally ultimate and quite distinct from it. To see things in these terms is simply to transfer a Manichaean type dualism into the very doctrine of God itself. 'Rather,' he writes, 'is (God's) justice a quality of his love, a characterisation of its working. His is a love of cauterising holiness and of a righteousness whose only response to evil is the purity of a perfect hate. Wrath and justice are but ways in which such love must show itself to be love in the face of its denial.'[36] Thus God's relationship to the creature is ever one of love and grace, and simultaneously one of justice. On the one hand this means that human sin is to be understood as taking place in a filial and not simply a legal context: sin is always sin against our gracious Father, and never simply a transgression of some abstract legal code. On the other hand it means that a love which is satisfied only by the universalist conclusion would have to bring this conclusion about in a way that satisfied the holiness which is its obverse. This Robinson sees as having been done through the fact that Christ has paid the price for all, and that (he contends) all will receive this same salvation willingly.

6. *That it undermines Christian morality and erodes missionary zeal.* These two may be taken together since both spring from a common assumption that unless dualism can be preached confidently the motivation for evangelism on the one hand and Christian obedience on the other will be greatly reduced. Viewed from the perspective of unbelief it might also be suggested that a gospel with no hell lacks the existential teeth necessary to win converts. Thus Bauckham notes the somewhat disingenuous approach of some in the seventeenth and

---

[36]   *Ibid.*, p. 104.

eighteenth centuries who, while adhering firmly to a universalist eschatology, nonetheless treated this as an esoteric doctrine and continued to preach hell on the basis that 'the threat of eternal torment was a necessary deterrent from immorality during this life' for the masses.[37] Whether in relation to initial repentance and conversion, or subsequent repentance and holiness, then, the conviction here seems to be that it is necessary quite literally to 'scare the hell' out of people in order to secure results.

This is an assumption which must be examined carefully. Just what sort of repentance or obedience is it that can result only from sufficient exposure to the threat of the terrors of hell? True repentance and obedience, surely, are motivated by love, joy and gratitude at so great a Saviour, and by the desire to serve for the sake of the object of that service alone; 'repentance' motivated primarily by a concern for self-preservation, or obedience issuing from fear of the consequences of disobedience, these can find no place in a gospel of unconditional good news. Insofar as the darkness and awfulness of hell provides a necessary foil or context for the full appreciation of the significance of the unconditionality with which God redeems us, it may properly be spoken of as a necessary part of the proclamation of the gospel. It cannot become the focus of our proclamation unless we resort to a form of conditionalism which seeks an existential foothold in the fear and guilt of those who hear. The gospel's very purpose is to liberate from these things, and they cannot become its henchmen without it degenerating into a sub-Christian form. The only true motive for genuine repentance is that of the sheer goodness of the good news as it addresses the individual and proclaims him or her to be loved and forgiven: the same should furnish Christians with sufficient motive for evangelism.

---

37   *Op. cit.*, p. 50.

Certainly Robinson's universalism does nothing to undermine the sense of need to proclaim the gospel. His kerygmatic hell makes evangelism absolutely necessary, since, if all are to be saved not apart from faith but through it, then clearly they must hear the gospel preached. In fact a universalism such as Robinson's would seem no more likely to be guilty of these twin charges than certain forms of Calvinism in which the eternal destiny of all is equally fixed in advance by divine decree. In fact wherever the unconditionality of grace is preached faithfully, the spectre of antinomianism raises its head; but the answer is not a slide back into legalism *via* a threat-orientated gospel, but rather a new understanding of the logic of repentance and obedience as equally unconditional responses to divine grace. The essence of Christian repentance and obedience is its motivation in love; and as at least one prominent Scots theologian has observed, you can't frighten a person into love.[38] Only the essential goodness of the good news itself can generate this. Again, understood thus, the scope of this grace hardly seems relevant to the context of personal repentance or obedience: all that matters is its application to the individual at a given moment in time.

7. *That it lacks any foundation in biblical teaching*. This charge is made, of course, by those convinced in advance that the weight of biblical teaching is clearly in favour of some form of dualist eschatology. In this they are correct enough; but this is not at all the same as saying that the universalist such as Robinson can find no support whatever in appeal to the Scriptures. The reality of the situation would seem to be that there are both texts which appear to posit a universal redemption in Christ and

---

[38]   Thomas Erskine, in a letter to Lord Rutherford dated 8 November 1853, writes: 'If spiritual perfection consists... in the love of God, and of men, and of all righteousness, it is not easy to see how such a doctrine as the eternity of punishment can lead to it. Men cannot be frightened into love.'

others (rather more as it happens) which speak of a
division between the saved and the lost. Faced with this
seeming confusion the sort of analysis which would accord
dualism the victory on the basis of a clear statistical
majority is irrelevant. The task of theologians must be to
seek to provide a framework within which these
apparently contradictory sets of texts can both be afforded
satisfactory meaning in relation to the larger account of
Scriptural teaching. The strength of Robinson's
universalist account is precisely that it does accord sense
and significance to both the universalist and the dualist
texts in the New Testament taken at face value. It neither
treats Scripture lightly, nor ignores those parts which
present inconvenient obstacles to its case. If we would
reject Robinson's conclusions, therefore, then the onus is
very much upon us to provide an alternative framework
within which the 'universalist' texts can be accommodated
satisfactorily and without exegetical liberties being taken
in relation to them. It must be confessed that those
rejecting universalism on 'biblical' grounds have not
always achieved this.

At the root of Robinson's universalism lies his
understanding of God's omnipotent love, and it is to this
that we must return in seeking the real weakness in his
eschatology. Earlier we indicated the way in which he
utilizes the philosophical principle of non-contradiction in
favour of his case, insisting that if God is both all good and
all powerful, then universalism follows on logically as the
necessary conclusion. In logical terms this may be a valid
argument, but its soundness can certainly be challenged.
The notion of omnipotent love assumed in its premisses is
one which *must succeed* in bringing about its desired goal
or else it ceases by definition to be omnipotent love, and,
Robinson contends, God ceases to be God. Once one has
agreed this much, then the contention that God desires the
salvation of all his creatures, taken together with the claim
that he is omnipotent love, is sufficient in itself to secure

the logical conclusion of universalism. If this is how God is, then this is what must happen. It is on this basis alone that Robinson is both able and compelled to assert the absolute impossibility of any being lost. Here is the driving force which informs and shapes the way in which he interprets various New Testament passages, so that there is much more than simple *Sachkritik* going on. The doctrine of God as omnipotent love, understood thus, is the non-negotiable absolute around which all else revolves. The insistence, however, that the omnipotence of love cannot see its desires and purposes thwarted or rejected without ceasing to be omnipotent love seems to me to be highly questionable as an account appropriate to the biblical pattern of divine self-revelation. If the premisses of Robinson's deductive proof are not true, then the argument is unsound and must be rejected. If this is *not* how God is, in other words, then the logical necessity of his dogmatic universalist conclusion evaporates.

Robinson's avowed starting point is the Christian belief that love is what God *is*, and that love must therefore be constitutive of every divine-human relationship, whether it takes the specific form of mercy or judgement. Furthermore he contends on biblical grounds that this passion of God for his creatures desires their salvation in each and every case. Some would perhaps seek to avoid the universalist conclusion by challenging his argument at *this* point, by denying that God loves all or desires the salvation of all (since if he did all would undoubtedly be saved). This does not seem to me to be a live option, however, if we are to maintain anything resembling an orthodox trinitarian doctrine of God and to work out our doctrines of creation and redemption in that context. Thus, as Colin Gunton writes, *'to be part of the creation means to be related to the Father through the Son and in the Spirit*; sin is the denial of this basic truth in which we live as if it were not so, and redemption consists in the fact that the Son himself takes human flesh in order decisively to re-establish this relationship, to reorder, renew and redirect it to its original and eschatological destiny.'[39] To be human, therefore, is to partake in the Father-Son relationship proper to God himself. There can be no human person who is created unloved by this God, or for whom this same God has not sent his Son to die.

Rather, I would suggest, the fundamental flaw in Robinson's argument arises from the fusion of love with a notion of omnipotence as that which always and inevitably achieves its purpose. Must omnipotence always be successful in order to be omnipotent? Must omnipotent love, therefore, always achieve that which it desires? If we are to answer these questions in biblical terms, rather than borrowing answers from elsewhere, then the suggestion that it is so is highly problematic. Here we find ourselves compelled by a biblical and theological notion of personhood to lodge something resembling a 'free-will' defence in the face of the relentless deductive logic of Robinson's case for universal salvation. A God who freely creates persons in his own image that they might share freely in that life of fellowship and love which is his very nature may love them to the end; but it is not clear that, having created them thus, he can then guarantee the outcome of their personal relationship with him, without undermining the very personhood which is the image of God in them. We do not appeal here to any notion of supposed human autonomy over against God. Such is proper only to secular humanism and deistic theologies, and not to a truly biblical understanding of human existence. True freedom is not freedom from, but freedom for and under God, freedom only in relation to him. Yet while the personal freedom granted by God is fulfilled in love and obedience, it can, within the contingency granted it by his creative and redemptive love, resist and cling

---

[39]   See Gunton, *The Actuality of Atonement*, Edinburgh, 1988,
        p. 169. Italics original.

instead to the bondage of subpersonal existence, denying its own freeness. It need no longer do this since Christ has defeated that which binds it; yet it may choose, in a supreme denial of that which he has done for it, to do so. Again, the salvation pictured in Scripture is itself an essentially personal and relational phenomenon, and as such belongs to a sphere where the language of guaranteed and necessary outcomes seems strangely out of place. The logic of persons is simply not compatible with the deductive logic of Robinson's syllogistic reasoning; yet love is supremely a personal relationship, and it is precisely personal logic, therefore, with which we have to do in any attempt to think biblically about salvation.

Robinson, as we have seen, attempts to get around this difficulty with his analogy of freedom and constraint in human love as a paradigm for understanding how all might *freely* be constrained by God's love to embrace the gospel. The essence of the human analogy he cites, however, is precisely that it presupposes the genuine possibility of rejection of love. It could not be otherwise. Were this possibility to be absent, then the value of a loving personal response would be altogether undermined. Love cannot be caused; it can only be freely rendered. Thus this analogy cannot in fact serve to hold together the genuinely free and loving response to the divine love in which Robinson sees salvation as consisting, and the absolute necessity implicit in his statement that ultimately all *must* respond in this way to God. It founders precisely on that crucial difference between causal or deductive logic and personal logic which it is an attempt to disguise. Only deductive logic can secure the 'must' which dogmatic universalism requires. It is this 'must' which, however it is presented, makes such universalism an ultimate denial of the personal and relational character of creation, of salvation, and thereby of God himself. The most that Robinson's analogy, and his soteriology in which genuinely personal free choice is so vital a component, can sustain is the claim that all *may* eventually choose salvation in Christ (an inductive, rather than deductive form of the argument), and not that they must. Here there would seem to be a logical gap between his doctrine of omnipotent love with its necessary demands, and his understanding of salvation in supremely personal categories.

'Christ', according to Origen, 'remains on the Cross as long as one sinner remains in hell.'[40] Not literally on the cross, of course, but the metaphor makes its point. Robinson cites this approvingly adding that it is no mere matter of speculation, but 'is grounded in the very necessity of God's nature.'[41] For a God who loves his creatures with an infinite love, and who desires nothing more than their salvation it could not be otherwise. Hell for them must also entail a sort of private hell for him. Both Origen and Robinson proceed from here to insist that the necessity of God's nature also demands that this should not in fact be so. A love that continues to suffer rejection and separation from its object must be thought of as having failed, and omnipotence cannot fail in its purposes. But if love is understood in properly relational terms, rather than viewed as a unilateral force, then its omnipotence cannot entail its guaranteed success. For the reciprocal love which is its fulfilment cannot be guaranteed or coerced, but only offered in free response. H.R. Mackintosh writes that universalism 'has too much operated with a divine love which in reality is a thing, a nature force comparable to magnetic attraction, and advancing to its goal with overwhelming and previsible certainty.'[42] In the final analysis Robinson cannot escape this charge. Perhaps instead we must think and speak of the divine love as victorious in remaining love, concerned

---

40   Cited in Robinson, *op. cit.*, p. 123.
41   *Ibid.*, p. 123.
42   *Immortality and the Future*, Edinburgh, 1915, pp. 207-8.

eternally for the well-being of its object, even in the face of eternal rejection. This means, of course, endorsing the idea that God continues to suffer over the loss of those who reject him; but then suffering is not the failure of love but the form which it takes in the face of rejection. And some such notion would appear to be necessary in any account in which God is love by nature (eternally) and not by choice (or temporarily). That it should cease to be so, turning its back in due course upon the lost, or that it should resort to an impersonal coercion to satisfy its own desires, preserving but not 'saving' those who would reject it, these would be the true failure of love and not its victory.

4. By Way of Conclusion

Notwithstanding the serious weakness inherent in Robinson's universalistic thesis (on the grounds of which it must certainly be rejected) it remains true nonetheless that he works his position out within a theological context utterly distinct from the pluralist paradigm embraced by Hick and others in recent years. The major doctrinal landmarks in relation to which his eschatology is framed are ones which ought to provide few difficulties for those of a conservative theological persuasion, and in this he is representative of a respectable tradition in Christian theology which *has not generally been guilty of many of the charges laid enthusiastically at its door* by those rushing to reject its conclusions. This ought to concern us, for the bringing of false charges is not in the interests of good scholarship, or, indeed, of attempts to state the dualist case in a convincing manner. Only by addressing ourselves to the real weaknesses in Christian universalism will that be achieved. Furthermore, it may be that our theology shares genuinely similar theological concerns to that of some forms of universalism. The existential question poses itself to all of us: can we really believe that the God who gives his all on the cross for those who have rebelled against him for so long will finally allow them to damn themselves in spite of it? All too often defences of eschatological dualism appear to be glib and even self-satisfied in the statement of their conclusions. Occasionally one is given the impression that some Christians will be disappointed if, in spite of everything, God does indeed choose to 'save' all in spite of their rejection of him; as if they themselves will somehow have been robbed or upstaged were this to happen. Perhaps there is something of the elder brother in Jesus' story of the Prodigal Son in all of us. Certainly these are not Christian sentiments or attitudes. We cannot view the loss of any human person as anything other than a tragedy, or view his or her salvation with anything but joy and delight, however and whenever it might take place. Those of us who feel compelled (on whatever grounds) to give an affirmative answer to the question must, therefore, if we are firmly rooted in the New Testament doctrine of God, feel its force and perhaps even sense the theoretical attractiveness of the universalist answer. We should also remember the fact that Jesus' words about judgement and hell were intended primarily as a direct personal challenge to us to repent and believe, and not as fuel for speculation concerning the fate of others.

2

Universal Salvation in Origen and Maximus

Frederick W. Norris

Few would quarrel over the claim that the two most nimble, creative minds of the early church were Origen and Augustine. Each profoundly influenced those who followed him, both defenders and detractors. At nearly seventy years of age Augustine attempted to sort out his written legacy in the *Retractions* and put his own stamp of correctness or incorrectness on what he had claimed earlier.[1] In many instances that shape of his later thought became the mark of orthodoxy in the West; the synod of Orange in 529 offered twenty-five canons intended to make Augustine's views primary.[2] The bishop of Hippo had been opposed as an innovator by some significant figures in Gaul, not the least being Cassian who learned his theology at the feet of monks who treasured much they had received from Origen. But Cassian's wing of western tradition lost its official battle. Both in the textbooks and

---

1   Augustine *Retractions*, ed. Pius Knöll, '*Corpus scriptorum ecclesiasticorum latinorum*, 36' (Vienna: F. Tempsky, 1902).

2   The Council of Orange in Giovanni Mansi, *Sacrorum Conciliorum Nova et Amplissima Collectio* VIII (Florence: Antonii Zatta, 1762; Reprint Berlin: C. Reinecke, 1902), 711-724. For a still enlightening commentary on how these twenty-five *capitula* depend upon Augustine, see Charles Joseph Hefele, *A History of the Councils of the Church from the Original Documents*, Vol. IV, trans. by William R. Clark (Edinburgh: T. & T. Clark, 1895; Reprint New York: AMS Press, Inc., 1972), 155-163.

the encyclopaedias that group has become maligned as
Semi-Pelagian when it might as easily be called early or
Semi-Augustinian. Yet in the modern period not a few
insightful scholars have found Augustine's views and the
Council of Orange's dogmatic pronouncements to be
somewhat heavy-handed.

Origen of Alexandria

Origen also figured prominently in conciliar dispute. Within
his own lifetime, about 230, Demetrius, his bishop in
Alexandria, led a council that banned Origen from his
teaching post in the metropolis, and thus forced him out to
Caesarea in Palestine.[3] In 400 Theophilus, bishop of
Alexandria, annoyed by the views of Origenists in the
Egyptian monasteries, called a council and condemned
their source.[4] The Fifth Ecumenical Council, held in

[3]   The synod appears only to have insisted that since Origen was a
        priest ordained by bishops of Palestine, he should serve there in
        Caesarea. But Demetrius wanted his priesthood declared invalid
        and may have had other disagreements. He and some other
        Egyptian bishops later had the ordination for priesthood
        revoked and Rome made a similar declaration. See Eusebius
        H.E. 6.8.5. & 6.23.4; *Kirchengeschichte*, ed. Eduard Schwartz,
        '*Die griecheschen christlichen Schrifsteller 9.2.,*' (Leipzig:
        J.C.Heinrichs'schen Buchhandlung, 1908), 536 & 570. The
        apology for Origen, which Eusebius mentions in 6.23.4 and
        6.33.4; *Kirchengeschichte*, ed. Schwartz, GCS 9.2, 570 & 588,
        is most probably that of Pamphilus, five books of which
        Eusebius edited and then added a sixth. Eusebius says that he
        discussed Origen's problems about his ordination in the second
        book. All the books are lost except the first which is still
        extant in a translation by Rufinus. See Henri Crouzel, *Origen*,
        trans. by A.S. Worrall (San Francisco: Harper & Row, 1989),
        22.

[4]   Most of the information about Theophilus' views and those of
        the synod in 400 are to be found in the epistles of Jerome where
        he translates the letters of Theophilus into Latin. See Jerome,
        Epistles 92, 93, 96, 98, 100; *Saint Jérôme: Lettres*, ed. Jérôme
        Labourt (Paris: *Société d'Édition 'Les Belles Lettres,' 1954),
        Vol. IV, 148-157, 157-159, Vol. V (1955) 8-32, 35-67, 68-91.*

Constantinople during 553, appears to have named Origen among the heretics it condemned; the bulk of the anathemas suggested by Justinian and accepted by the 543 synod of Constantinople are rejections of what the synod saw as Origen's teachings.[5] The condemnation of Origen followed a bitter controversy about the meaning of his writings. Yet none of these controversies is in any way guided by a written, thorough self-assessment from Origen similar to Augustine's *Retractions*. Indeed much of the discussion of Origen's failings, specifically his view of *apokatastasis*, which is of concern to us in this debate on universalism and the doctrine of hell, arises from passages in Origen's most unusual yet fascinating treatise, *On First Principles*. Although written about 229 when Origen was in his mid-forties, it certainly does not represent a final re-evaluation of his previous writings, let alone a systematic theology. As we shall see it is not at all certain that Origen ever was a systematic theologian as we often use that term.[6]

During the twentieth century some patristic specialists have insisted that Origen was an elitist, not a deep Christian theologian, perhaps no Christian at all. At the same time a group of significant scholars has tried to refurbish Origen's reputation. Some of them have begun with the sense that condemning a person three hundred years after his death within a quite changed context is not fair. Certain historians have argued that the appearance of his name among the heretics listed by the Fifth Ecumenical Council is an interpolation. Others have noted how Origen tried to distinguish between the rudiments of

---

5   Justinian *Epistle to Menas* and the *Letter of 553* found in Eduard Schwartz, *Acta Conciliorum Oecumenicorum* III (Berlin: W. de Gruyter, 1940), 189-219.

6   Henri Crouzel has repeatedly warned against that error. See particularly his *Origène et la philosophie* (Paris: Aubier, 1962), 209-210.

faith and speculations, the *regula fidei* which could assist anyone toward salvation and the soundings which perhaps only the most gifted theologian could discern; he understood the importance of the pastoral approach to the teachings of the church. Still other scholars have noted the importance of the mystical life for Origen and how that root brought much of positive consequence to the church.[7]

Yet for this conference one of the more interesting aspects of the refurbishing of Origen's reputation by twentieth-century scholars concerns the concession of Origen's error on the doctrine of *apokatastasis* by an important defender of his work. Jean Daniélou, who insisted that Origen was a superior churchman, warned that his view of universal salvation was defective. Daniélou argued that Origen's doctrine concerning the pre-existence of souls and the rising and falling of those souls many times in order to be finally purified defeats two important parts of the gospel. In the end it neither takes seriously the tragic power of human free will to reject God nor properly weighs the sense that human choice is limited to this present life. Therefore the pre-existence of souls and the cycles of their return should be rejected because the Platonic doctrine of *metempsychosis*, not Christian tradition, guided Origen's speculations. Indeed without naming Origen, the first canon of the Fifth Ecumenical Council specifically forbade such views: 'If anyone teaches the mythical doctrine of the pre-existence of the soul and the *apokatastasis* that follows from it, let him be anathema.'[8]

---

7   Herbert Musurillo, 'The Recent Revival of Origen Studies,' *Theological Studies* 24 (1963), 250-263 noticed how the 1920s & 30s and the 1950s & 60s saw investigations of Origen that resulted in two vastly different pictures, one of the heretic who never understood Christian theology and the other of the faithful churchman who explained the faith for his age.

8   Jean Daniélou, *Origen*, trans. by Walter Mitchell (New York: Sheed and Ward, 1955), 288-289. On *metempsychosis* in Origen

What then was Origen's teaching about salvation, his understanding of *apokatastasis*? The rather common outline of his views says that the Alexandrian taught the pre-existence of souls. When those souls sinned, they fell into captive prisons, their human bodies. For Origen all these souls would need to return to their pristine state before their fall because the end needed to be like the beginning. Being a biblical commentator, Origen relied upon 1 Corinthians 15:24-28 as his guide for the end; God eventually would be all in all. In order for God to reach that dominance, God would need to put all enemies under God's feet, not only death but also the devil himself. Through a pedagogical process of purification, each soul will return to its original state. Whatever its hellish punishment might be, certainly internal torment more than eternal fire, that punishment would be limited. Of their own free will the devil, demons and wicked people would continually become re-embodied in other worlds until they tire of absence from God and choose to return to their origins.[9]

---

see G. Dorival, 'Origène a-t-il enseigné la transmigration des âmes dans les corps d'animaux?' *Origeniana Secunda: Second colloque international des études origéniennes (Bari, 20-23 septembre 1977)*, ed. by Henri Crouzel and Antonio Quacquarelli (Bari: Edizioni dell'ateneo, 1980), 11-32.

9   For example, see the summaries of Jaroslav Pelikan, *The Christian Tradition: A History of the Development of Doctrine, Vol. 1, The Emergence of the Catholic Tradition* (100-600) (Chicago: The University of Chicago Press, 1971), 151 and J.N.D. Kelly, *Early Christian Doctrines* 5th ed. (New York: Harper & Row, 1978), 473-474. Pelikan relies upon *On First Principles* Pref. 6, 1.6.1-2 and 3.6.3, *Traité des principes*, I, ed. Henri Crouzel & Manlio Simonetti, 'Sources chrétiennes, 252 (Paris: Les Éditions du Cerf, 1978), 84-85, 194-201 and III, SC 268, 240-243; *Against Celsus* 7.17, *Contre Celse* IV, ed. by Marcel Borret, SC 150 (1969), 50-53 and *On Prayer* 25.2., *Die Schrift vom Gebet*, ed. Paul Koetschau, GCS, 357-358. Kelly depends upon *On First Principles* 1.6.2-4, 2.10.4, 3.5.7., 3.6.3 & 6, *Traité des principes*, I, ed. Crouzel and

Those who perpetuate this outline of Origen's doctrine accept a series of grounds for it. First, from Origen's point of view this kind of speculation was evidently both permitted and beneficial. It did not destroy the simple faith of the church; it allowed the faith to be explained in the circle of intellectuals outside the church who found Christianity to be rather crude or theologians inside who worried about the vulgar literalism of some believers. In Origen's understanding the *regula fidae* contained no clear, developed eschatology and thus that doctrine could be investigated further.[10] Second, although there is no one place in which Origen offers a complete summary of this outline, each aspect can be found in some form within what we have of his writings. Each part is dependent upon specific statements that imply if they do not explicitly state these doctrines. Third, the outline has its own compelling logic; it has a kind of beauty about it, since it shows that there is a salvific purpose for suffering, even for punishment. God's love ultimately overcomes. Indeed Joseph Trigg, a sensitive interpreter of Origen, claims that on these issues Origen presents 'a vision of extraordinary moral grandeur and perhaps as satisfactory a solution, from the perspective of faith, to the problem of theodicy as has ever been suggested.' Trigg thinks that John Hick in his book *Evil and the God of Love* might have been better

---

Simonetti, SC 252, 196-207, 382-385, III, SC 268, 230-233, 240-243, 246-251; *Against Celsus* 3.79 and 6.26, *Contre Celse*, II, ed. Borret, SC 136, 178-179, III, SC 147, 242-245; the *Homilies on Jeremiah* 19.14, *Homélies sur Jérémie*, II, ed. Pierre Husson & Pierre Nautin, SC 238 (1977), 230-239 and the *Homilies on Ezekiel* 1.2, *Homélies sur Ézékiel*, ed. Marcel Borret, SC 352 (1989), 38-47.

10 *On First Principles* Pr. 7, *Traité des principes*, I, ed. Crouzel and Simonetti, SC 252, 84-85.

advised to employ Origen's scheme which so well balances love and justice in individual cases.[11]

Those three reasons appear to be persuasive, but the outline itself becomes suspicious, particularly as it portrays Origen's teachings about universal salvation and hell, when we notice that it almost duplicates the lists of charges brought forward by two of Origen's arch enemies: Jerome and the emperor Justinian.[12] Although this outline in modern histories of doctrine is usually supported only by passages from Origen, at least J.N.D.Kelly argues that these are probably Origen's positions because his opponents always raise such issues.[13] Yet few people I know would feel comfortable with having their enemies write their creeds. Henri de Lubac, a defender of Origen's reputation, warns that the Fifth Ecumenical Council condemned doctrines taught by Origenists, not views held by Origen himself. De Lubac reminds us that the *corpus* of Origen has been greatly suppressed by the victory of Justinian's forces. Volumes of letters which were known to fifth-century writers, commentaries, occasional treatises, a large number of pieces are gone.[14] What is worse is that a virtual interpolation industry marked the

---

[11]   Joseph Trigg, *Origen: The Bible and Philosophy in the Third-century Church* (Atlanta: John Knox Press, 1983), 108-115, esp. note 31.

[12]   Jerome, *Apology against the Book of Rufinus, Apologia contra Rufinum*, ed. Pierre Lardet, Corpus Christianorum, Series Latina LXXIX (Turnholt: Brepols, 1982), 42-44. Justinian, *Epistle to Menas* and the *Letter of 553*, found in Schwarz, *Acta Conciliorum Oecumenicorum* III, 189-219.

[13]   Kelly, *Early Christian Doctrines*, 5th ed., 474.

[14]   Henri de Lubac, *Histoire et Esprit, l'intelligence de l'Écriture d'après Origène* (Paris: Aubier, 1950), 13-91. William Babcock translated selected passages from these pages for the Introduction to Origen, *On First Principles*, ed. G.W. Butterworth, 'Harper Torchbook' (New York: Harper & Row, 1966), vii-xxii.

later centuries. To know exactly what Origen taught on the basis of what we now have is not possible.

We do know that Origen taught the pre-existence of souls, a speculative position I have no interest in defending. As we shall see later in this paper, both Gregory of Nyssa and Maximus the Confessor, no enemies of Origen, rejected those views. I would, however, defend him against teaching reincarnation, a favourite claim of some within the so-called New Age Movement these days.[15] My intention is to demonstrate that the doctrine of *apokatastasis*, specifically understood as universal salvation including the devil and the limited nature of hell, is not clearly and consistently taught by Origen as his only view of eschatology. Universal salvation and limited hell are not inferences demanded by his view of pre-existent souls in spite of the 553 anathema which relies on that logical connection.[16]

Henri Crouzel, perhaps the contemporary archdefender of Origen, pushes us back to what texts we have. Origen's *On First Principles* is often the treatise from which his doctrines of universal salvation and limited hell are taken. It is primarily available to us through Rufinus' translation into Latin. The Greek *Philocalia*, apparently put together by Basil of Caesarea and Gregory of Nazianzus,

---

[15]   When Origen speaks of souls moving into different states to pursue their purification for final salvation, he does not support reincarnation. In his *Against Celsus* 3.75, 5.29 & 49, 6.36 and 7.32, *Contre Celse* II, ed. Borret, SC 135, 168-173; III, SC 147, 84-89, 140-143 & 264-269 and IV, SC 150, 840-88, he had the opportunity to pick up that option in response to some of Celsus' charges, but he specifically denied reincarnation as a Christian doctrine. He calls it foolishness, mythical, and unworthy when compared to the doctrine of the resurrection.

[16]   Anathema 1 of the Council of 553, Mansi, *Sacrorum Conciliorum* IX, 395 claims that Origen's teaching about the *apokatastasis* follows from his view of pre-existent souls.

does contain some selections from *On First Principles* so that on occasion we do have Greek witnesses to the text.[17] But the important sections of *On First Principles* that deal with universalism and hell must rely on Rufinus' efforts. Yet the quality of, even the purpose of, Rufinus' translations of Origen have been the subject of debate since his own time. Rufinus insisted that Origen's enemies had often circulated copies of the Alexandrian's work with major interpolations.[18] In one of his few extant letters Origen himself says that an unnamed archheretic, whom he had debated, circulated a copy of the debate transcript which that opponent had doctored by deleting, changing and adding sections. Origen had difficulty finding his copy when friends from Palestine asked him, but he did discover it. When he later met the man, the fellow said he had only embellished and corrected his copy. For Origen that kind of correction was similar to what Marcion did for the Gospels and Paul.[19] Thus Rufinus was always alert to

---

[17] *Origène, Philocalie*, ed. Eric Junod and Marguerite Harl, SC 226 & 302 (Paris: Les Éditions du Cerf, 1976 & 1983).

[18] Rufinus, *The Adulteration of Origen's Books 6-8*, in *Tyrannii Rufini Opera*, ed. Manlio Simonetti, 'Corpus Christianorum, Series Latina, XX (Turnholt: Brepols, 1961), 10-13. Also see the new edition of *De alteratione librorum Origenis*, ed. Antonio Dell' Era, 'Collana di testi stoici, 15' (L'Aquila: L.U.Japadre, 1983). Rufinus' claims occur in Origen's *On First Principles*, Pref. 3, *Traité des princîpes*, I, ed. Crouzel and Simonetti, SC 252, 70-73 and his introduction to the translation of Pamphilus' *Apology for Origen*, ed. Simonetti, CCL XX, 231-234.

[19] The letter is condensed in different ways and translated into Latin by Jerome, *The Apology against the book of Rufinus* 2.18; *Apologia contra Rufinus*, ed. Lardet, CCL LXXIX, 50-54 and Rufinus *The Adulteration of Origen's Books* 6-8, in *Tyranni Opera*, ed. Simonetti, CCL XX, 10-13. The portion of the letter referred to here is taken from Rufinus, section 6, and was translated into English by Joseph Gauthier from the French of Henri Crouzel's 'A Letter From Origen "To Friends in Alexandria,"' *The Heritage of the Early Church: Essays in Honor of The Very Reverend Georges Vasilievich Florovsky,*

possible places in the Greek texts of Origen that had been falsified because Origen indicated such falsification had occurred.

The difficulty is that Rufinus, particularly in regard to *On First Principles*, also decided that he would not worry a Latin Western audience with some of Origen's speculations. Thus he not only removed what he considered to be interpolations but he also smoothed out positions that he thought would be upsetting to the less-sophisticated readers of the West. He claims, however, that he never made any changes without basing them on statements from other places in the *corpus* where Origen himself expressed such thoughts.[20] Since much of that *corpus* is now gone, his claim is impossible to verify independently. It is also possible, if not probable, that Rufinus used a sense of systematic theology for his translation which was not Origen's own concern.

Jerome, who already had some misgivings about Rufinus, reacted with the intensity of a junkyard dog to Rufinus' views of the translator's art. In Jerome's view translation should render the manuscript into another language with conservative care; the translator should stay as close to the literal meaning of the text as possible. Deciding what not to translate on the basis of supposed interpolations or unnecessary speculations so vitiates the text that the translator never fairly represents the views of its author. Rufinus' translations are Rufinus' opinions about Origen, not Origen's views of the subjects discussed. Jerome checked Rufinus' Latin with the Greek texts he had available to him and attacked Rufinus as

---

ed. David Neiman and Margaret Schatkin, 'Orientalia Christiana Analecta 195' (Rome: Pont. Institutum Studiorum Orientalium, 1973), 142.

20   Rufinus in Origen, *On First Principles*, Pref. 3, *Traité des principes*, I, ed. Crouzel and Simonetti, SC 252, 70-73.

unsound both as a scholar and as a believer. He translated *On First Principles* himself, a work now lost to us, collected various passages from Origen's other writings, and to his own satisfaction proved that Origen was a heretic who had been poorly translated by Rufinus.[21] Rufinus reacted with some restraint, even with the royal disdain of a Great Dane when faced with Jerome, but the dogfight was on.[22] It only ended when Rufinus withdrew from the fray.

That battle has continued in modern times particularly in terms of the critical editions and translations of *On First Principles*. Paul Koetschau, who edited the text early in this century, consistently preferred any translations he could find in Jerome's work to those of Rufinus.[23] That decision about Rufinus' efforts also led Koetschau to rely upon later Greek writings such as Justinian's *Epistle to Menas*, [24] anathemas from the Constantinopolitan synod of 543 led by Justinian and Menas, and a group of Greek fragments: most taken primarily from Origen's enemies. The possibility that Rufinus actually followed the view of the translator's work which he uttered in the preface to his translation of *On First Principles, i.e.*, that he changed

---

21   Jerome, in his *Letter 84, To Pammachius and Oceanus, Lettres*, ed. Labourt, Vol. IV, 125-139, describes his sense of translation and says he had translated *On First Principles*. Also see Jerome's *Apology against the Book of Rufinus*, I, 15; *Apologia Contra Rufinum*, ed. Lardet, CCL LXXIX, 49-50.

22   Rufinus, *Apology* 1.3, 31 & 39, 2.9 & 44; in *Tyrannii Rufini Opera*, ed. Simonetti, CCL XX, 38, 65-69, 73-74, 90-91 & 117-118.

23   *De Principiis (peri archon)*, ed. Paul Koetschau, GCS 22 (Leipzig: J.C. Heinrichs'she Buchhandlung, 1913). As well as the various decisions for individual texts, see his introduction, lxxvii-cxxxvii.

24   The letter appears in Mansi, *Sacrorum Conciliorum*, IX, 524-533. Also see Schwarz, *Acta Conciliorum Oecumenicorum* III, 189-219. The anathemas of the 553 council appear in Mansi, *Sacrorum Conciliorum* IX, 395-400.

nothing unless he had a corroborating text from Origen himself, did not persuade Koetschau that Rufinus provided a faithful rendition. G.W. Butterworth, an English translator of the work, agreed with Koetschau.[25] Both did not seriously consider that Jerome and other opponents of Origen may have translated interpolated manuscripts of Origen or may have drawn inferences from statements taken out of context.

Now, however, we have two new editions of *On First Principles*, one done by Herwig Görgemanns and Heinrich Karpp and the other by Henri Crouzel and Manlio Simonetti. Görgemanns and Karpp set a new course away from the methodological mistakes made by Koetschau although they find much of his edition worthy of acceptance without comment.[26] In Crouzel and Simonetti's five-volume work Origen's opponents are not asked to provide the true text even if they preserve what they considered to be genuine Greek fragments. Rufinus is defended as a far more accurate translator.[27] These critical editions are not

25 Butterworth, trans. *On First Principles*, xlvi-lii.

26 *Origenes, Vier Bücher von den Prinzipien*, herausgegeben, übersetz, mit kritischen und erläuternden Anmerkungen versehen von Herwig Görgemanns und Heinrich Karpp, 'Texte zur Forschung', Bd. 24 (Darmstadt: Wissenschaftliche Buchgesellschaft, 1976). They do not use all of the parallels constructed by Koetschau. See their description of their methods, 46-49.

27 *Traité des principes*, I-V, ed. Henri Crouzel & Manlio Simonetti, SC 252, 253, 268, 269 & 312 (Paris, Les Éditions du Cerf, 1978, 1980, 1984). See especially I, SC 252, 23-46. James Armantage, in a brilliant unpublished Yale dissertation of 1970, 'Will the Body be Raised?' Origen and the Origenist Controversy, 357 insists that since Rufinus had some sympathy for the positions which Origen took, and some understanding of their subtlety, he is by far the better translator. Robert Daley, 'Origen,' *Encyclopedia of Early Christianity*, ed. Everett Ferguson with Michael McHugh and Frederick Norris (New York: Garland Publishing, 1990), 667 claims that Rufinus' translations, 'formerly suspect, have been proven, by

yet reflected in the summaries of Origen's doctrine which are found in the commonly used histories of early Christian doctrine.

When we look specifically at points about universal salvation and the doctrine of hell, Crouzel calls to our attention that both Jerome and Rufinus, in translating one of Origen's letters to his Alexandrian friends (now lost to us in its Greek original) agree that Origen rejected the ultimate salvation of the devil himself. The Alexandrian did not insist that the final restoration, the *apokatastasis*, would override the free will of God's great enemy and force him to return to what he had been. Indeed Origen ridicules his opponents. According to them he teaches the salvation of the devil.

> Some of those who take pleasure in finding [occasions for] disputes ascribe to us and to our doctrine a blasphemy. On that matter let them consider the way in which they pay attention [to the scripture] 'Neither drunkards nor slanderers [or blasphemers] will possess the kingdom of God,' even though they say that the father of malice and perdition, who will be excluded from the kingdom of God, is able to be saved. Even one who has lost his mind cannot say this.[28]

Rufinus' rendering is a bit longer and redundant enough to make the point clearer, but the meaning is the same. The agreement of these two rivals on this issue is impressive for their differing approaches are also apparent. While working with this letter Jerome talks about the context of the passage in order to show that Origen was one who taught questionable doctrines and attacked orthodox

---

comparison with genuine Greek fragments, to be substantially accurate.'

[28]   Jerome *Apology against the book of Rufinus* 2.18; *Apologia Contra Rufinum*, ed. Lardet, CCL LXXIX, 54. I have adapted the English translation of Joseph Gauthier who translated Crouzel's French article, 'A Letter from Origen "To Friends in Alexandria,"' for the Florovsky Festschrift, p.140.

teachers. He raves against what he sees as Origen's
attack on bishop Demetrius of Alexandria and the proper
structure of bishops in the church. According to Rufinus'
translation, which seeks to defend Origen, Demetrius is
not named in the letter, a possible truth since Jerome only
claims that the referent for a particular sentence in the
letter is Demetrius and the bishops. Jerome seems to
have misread the nature of the opponents whom Origen
derides, but there is no doubt that both Jerome and
Rufinus agree that Origen rejected the salvation of the
devil as unbiblical, even insane.[29]

In the same *Apology Against Rufinus* in which Jerome
translates the letter to Origen's friends in Alexandria,
Jerome offers not only further evidence that Origen did not
teach the salvation of the devil, but also the context from
which the charge that Origen did teach such doctrine well
could have arisen. Jerome summarizes one of the
prominent points raised in a dialogue between Candidus, a
Valentinian Gnostic, and Origen.

Candidus asserts that the devil has a very evil nature
which can never be saved. To that Origen rightly replies
that it is not because of his substance that the devil is
destined to perish, but that he has fallen because of his
own will and that he could be saved. Because of that
Candidus slanders Origen by representing him as
saying that the devil has a nature that must be saved,
when in fact Origen refutes Candidus' false objection.[30]

This passage provides an important clue to later debate
about Origen's teaching. When the context of this

---

[29]   Crouzel, 'A Letter from Origen, "To Friends In Alexandria,"'
       136-144.
[30]   Jerome *Apology against Rufinus* 2.19; *Apologia Contra
       Rufinum*, ed. Lardet, CCL LXXIX, 55. The English
       translation is taken from the French of Crouzel, *Origen*, trans.
       A.S.Worrall, 21.

dialogue with the Gnostic Candidus was forgotten and the substantialist sense of the resurrection body provided particularly by his late third-century opponent Methodius and his fourth-century antagonist Epiphanius was put in its place,[31] Origen's opponents drew the inference that he taught the salvation of the devil and his angels.

In his *Homilies on Joshua* Origen again insisted that the devil and his angels were subject to eternal punishment, perhaps even annihilation.[32] Other homilies on Exodus, Leviticus and Jeremiah as well as comments on Matthew echo the theme of punishment for all sinners.[33] *On First Principles* insists that the 'fires of Gehenna' are found both in Scripture and in the message of Christian preaching.[34] There are other sections, particularly in Origen's *Against Celsus*, which make his teaching about the eternal punishment for sin interesting because they are asserted against a pagan critic. Celsus accuses Origen and all Christians of teaching that punishment for sin is

---

[31]   James Armantage, 'Will the Body be Raised?' unpublished 1970 Yale dissertation, repeatedly notes how Origen's fourth-, fifth- and sixth-century opponents moved Origen's sense of participation as an epistemological claim into the realm of substantialist thought. Jerome is one of those offenders, and thus is a remarkable source for this clear statement of the early context for Origen's thought on the salvation of the devil.

[32]   *Homilies on Joshua* 8.3-6; *Homélies sur Josué*, ed. Jaubert, SC 71, 222-235.

[33]   *Hom. on Jer.* 12.4-5, 19[18]. 15, 20[19].4; *Homélies sur Jérémie*, II, ed. Husson and Nautin, SC 238. *Hom. in Ex. Homélies zur l'Exode'*, ed. Borret, SC 321, 388-393. 13.4, *Hom. in Lev.* 14.4, *Homélies sue le Lévitique*, ed. Borret, SC 287, 242-249. *Homilies on Matthew* 72, ; *Matthäuserklärung X1.2*, ed. Klostermann, Benz, 2., bearbeitete Auflage, Ursula Treu, GCS, 168-172. See Brian Daley, *The Hope of the Early Church: A Handbook of Patristic Eschatology* (Cambridge: Cambridge University Press, 1991), 56.

[34]   *On First Principles*, Pref 5; 2.10.1; *Traité des principes*, I, ed. Crouzel and Simonetti, SC 252, 82-85, 374-377.

eternal. The great pagan ridicules believers who claim that
they will be saved while all others will fry; it is Celsus
who says that Christians teach that God applies fire like a
cook. Here is a golden opportunity for Origen to deny
eternal punishment. Yet he points out that even Celsus
himself thinks it is important for wickedness to be
punished. Origen insists more than once that Christian
faith demands the eternal punishment of evil and the
eternal reward of good. Without that pair of teachings the
gospel is imbalanced.[35]

The assertions of these passages become quite
important in responding to Koetschau's edition of *On First
Principles* 2.10.8. That passage is sometimes referred to
as the primary reference for Origen's doctrine of
apokatastasis. Koetschau included two fragments from
sixth-century sources as part of the text for 2.10.8. The
first came from *Concerning the Sects* 10.6 written by
Leontius of Byzantium, perhaps himself an Origenist, and
the other from the *Epistle to Menas* written by the
emperor Justinian, an opponent of Origenism. As
translated by Butterworth they read:

> there is a resurrection of the dead, and there is
> punishment, but not everlasting. For when the body is
> punished the soul is gradually purified, and so is
> restored to its ancient rank... for all wicked men, and for
> daemons, too, punishment has an end, and both wicked
> men and daemons shall be restored to their former
> rank.[36]

---

35   *Against Celsus* 5.14-17, 8.48 & 72, *Contre Celse*, III, ed.
      Borret, SC 147, 48-57, IV, SC 150, 278-271 & 340-345.

36   *On First Principles*, 2.10.8, ed. G.W. Butterworth, 146. *Traité
      des principes*, I, ed. Crouzel and Simonetti, SC 252, 392-395 do
      not think that the fragments from Justinian and Leontius
      should be used here to represent Origen's authentic thoughts.
      Interestingly Harold E. Babcock, 'Origen's Anti-Gnostic
      Polemic and the Doctrine of Universalism', *The Unitarian
      Universalist Christian* 38 (1983), 53-59 considers these

The letter translated by both Jerome and Rufinus, the passage about Candidus from Jerome's *Apology against Rufinus*, the comments in Origen's homilies, *On First Principles* and *Against Celsus* do not deny that the wicked and demons might be saved, but they deny that every soul including the devil must be saved. Both Leontius and Justinian are sixth-century figures and may be representing interpolated texts in the *corpus* of Origen. Görgemanns and Karpp print the Leontian and Justinian fragments in relation to 2.10.8, but they put them in a footnote and do not make them a part of the translation as Butterworth does in his. The new Sources Chrétiennes edition by Crouzel and Simonetti argues against the connection.[37]

There are statements, however, that teach the *apokatastasis*. In Rufinus' translation of *On First Principles* 3.5.7 Origen explains 1 Corinthians 15:24-28 with these words:

...when the Son is said to be subjected to the Father the perfect restoration of the entire creation is announced, so when his enemies are said to be subjected to the Son of God we are to understand this to involve the salvation of those subjected and the restoration of those that have been lost.[38]

---

fragments as genuine but still does not see Origen as teaching universalism.

[37] Görgemanns and Karpp, *von den Prinzipien*, 438-439 put the sections from Justinian and Leontius in a footnote. See the explanation of their method, especially p.46, n.19. Koetchau, *De Principiis*, GCS, 184 and Butterworth, *Origen: On First Principles*, 146. Crouzel and Simonetti, *Traité des principes*, I, SC 252, 392-395 and II, SC 253, 241-242, note 43, refuse Koetschau's reasons for using those fragments.

[38] Origen *On First Principles* 3.5.7; *Traité des principes*, III, ed. Crouzel and Simonetti, SC 268, 230-233.

That sentence is clear enough to support universal salvation; but you will notice that it does not specifically name the devil unless we infer that he is included under the term 'enemies'. Other passages in Origen's writings insist that evil will cease and 'all Israel will be saved': again poetic passages that connote the salvation of all.[39] Origen, however, does not always interpret 1 Corinthians 15:28 in that sense. In *On First Principles* 1.7.5. it is difficult to tell whether the claim that God will be all in all includes every creature or only the kingdom which Christ delivers to the Father, a kingdom comprised of those who have willed to follow Christ. In that passage Origen says that demons might become men or angels, but he also warns that angels might become men or demons.[40] In 3.6.1. he again focuses on the freedom of the will in the context in which he quotes 1 Corinthians 15:28. Man was made in the image of God but the likeness of God is granted to him only at the consummation and then only 'by

---

[39]   *Comm. on John* 1.16.91; *Commentaire sur saint Jean*, ed. Cecile Blanc, SC 120 (1966), 106-109. *Hom. in Joshua* 8.5; *Homélies sur Josué*, ed. Jaubert, SC 71, 230-231. *Comm. in Romans* 8.9; *PG* 14, 1184-1187. *On First Principles* 2.3.7; *Traité des principes*, I, ed. Crouzel and Simonetti, SC 268, 270-275. Both Koetschau, *De Principiis*, GCS, 286-291 and Butterworth, 250-255, include statements from Origen's later opponents in their footnotes for *On First Principles* 3.6.5-9 that insist those paragraphs teach the salvation of all, even the devil and his angels. Crouzel and Simonetti, *Traité des principes*, III, SC 268, 245-255 do not. Görgemanns and Karpp, *von den Prinzipien*, 657, n.16 warn that in 1.8.4 (their edition, 101) Origen said that the devil couldn't be saved but that in other places he seems to say the devil might be saved.

[40]   *Ibid.*, 1.7.5; *Traité des principes*, III, ed. Crouzel and Simonetti, SC 252, 216-221; Görgemanns and Karpp, *von den Prinzipien*, 240-245. In his 'Letter to Friends in Alexandria' Origen had noted that 1 Cor 6:10 said no drunkards or slanderers would inherit the kingdom, but in his *On Prayer* 25.2., GCS, 357-358, he insisted that the kingdom would not reach its fulfilment until each individual was perfected.

his own earnest efforts to imitate God.'[41] Indeed in 3.6.2. Origen insists specifically that the 'all' in the Corinthians passage should not be thought to include animals, whether cattle or wild beasts. Then he says: 'So, too, we must not suppose that any evil reaches that end, lest when it is said that "God is all in all" he should be said to dwell even in some vessel of evil.' Two inferences could be drawn from that statement: either that the devil will be saved or that he will be annihilated in the fires of Gehenna.[42]

Yet in homilies on Jeremiah and Ezekiel Origen says that God uses punishment to chasten, to improve, not to destroy, a view which may confuse the simple believers but one that must be preached in order to counter the horrid Gnostic doctrine of an evil god.[43] In *Against Celsus* Origen can say that certain Jewish doctrines are mythical and unworthy, but it is not certain that doctrine of eternal punishment is the beneficiary of those epithets. He explains that the threat of punishment is important for moral improvement even if that threat may be more apparent than real.[44] In his *Commentary on Matthew* Origen seems to imply universal salvation when he makes comparisons between the inferior and superior persons after the resurrection. Interpreting another text of

---

[41] *Ibid.*, 3.6.1; *Traité des principes*, III, ed. Crouzel and Simonetti, SC 268, 234-239; Görgemanns and Karpp, *von den Prinzipien*, 642-649.

[42] *Homilies on Joshua* 8.3-6, esp. 8.5 & 14.2 *GCS* 7, 338-342, *Homélies sur Josué*, ed. Jaubert, SC 71 (1960), 222-235. *Comm. on John* 20.21[19]; *Commentaire sur Jean*, IV, ed. Blanc, SC 290, 240-245. *Comm. on Romans* 8.9; *PG* 14, 1184-1187.

[43] *Hom. I in Ezek.* 1.3, *Homélies sur Ézékiel*, ed. Borret, SC 352, 46-59. *Hom. in Jer.* 20[19].3, ed. Klostermann, GCS, 179-182.

[44] Origen, *Against Celsus* 2.5, 4.10 & 5.14, *Contre Celse*, I, ed. Borret, SC 132, 292-293; II, SC 136, 206-209; III, SC 147, 48-51.

Matthew he talks about the purgation of sins in the last days. But in each of his comments on Matthew Origen's words are ambiguous enough that they could be read as referring only to the righteous and not to the unrighteous.[45]

Origen's specific teachings about hell and the resurrection body are also complex. They are certainly part and parcel of our concerns in this discussion. Methodius, a late third-century figure, attacked Origen's views. His *Treatise on the Resurrection of the Body* exists only in a few fragments and an Old Slavonic translation; unfortunately we do not have Origen's treatise *On the Resurrection* which Methodius attacked, a piece that would have helped us understand Origen's views. What we know is that Origen took the apostle Paul's teaching about the resurrection physical body very seriously. He thought that the body was resurrected, but that it was transformed in a way similar to what happens when the seed dies and the new plant appears. The resurrection body will not be the same fleshly body as we have now. Jesus' resurrected body was not exactly the same as our present earthly bodies. If the important aspect of humanity is the soul and the body is primarily a lesser instrument, then those who insist on a resurrected body like the one we have had in this life, whether they be simple believers or the learned theologians, are mistaken.

If our earthly body is not our exact instrument in afterlife, then punishment in hell is not designed primarily to make us suffer as we might in physical bodies. The fires of hell will consume all the false doctrines, the scandals and the logic of evil, but not the soul. Indeed, according to Origen, hell itself is probably not a place consistent with what we know is necessary for the position of the earthly

---

45   *Matthäuserklärung* X, 2-3, ed. Erich Klostermann, GCS 40, 2-
      4; *Commentaire sur l'Évangile de saint Matthieu* X-XI, ed.
      Robert Girot, SC 162, 144-153.

body, but is instead a state in which the soul remembers its past sins and suffers miserably both because of them and because of its separation from God.[46] For Origen participation in God is an epistemological process basic to salvation or damnation, not a process that demands a substantialist view of the soul or the body. The ascetic life, at least the life of disciplined morals, is a part of our salvation.

But hell is not merely what we moderns might call a psychological experience of souls that is overwhelmingly painful. The demonic powers that have warred against God will be destroyed in hell. There is the distinct possibility that the devil has been so long involved in his deception that he has become a 'liar by nature' and thus must be destroyed because of his own continuous choice to sin.[47]

Here Origen's statements about the resurrection body and hell that are known to us in what is left of the *corpus* have been taken out of his context by Methodius and put into a new context from which different inferences are drawn. Methodius had read Origen but he did not argue the meaning of his texts as Pamphilus had done in his defense of Origen. The caricatures Methodius created began to dominate the controversies. Methodius insisted that Origen denied the resurrection of the body and the existence of hell, when in fact Origen insisted on a resurrection body and hell, but not in the same substantialist terms that Methodius used. Methodius therefore claimed that Origen was a threat to the simple

---

[46]   *Matthäuserklärung* X, 2 ed. Klostermann, GCS 40, 2-3. *Commentaire sur l'Évangile de saint Matthieu X-XI*, ed. Girod, SC 162, 144-149.

[47]   *Hom. in Joshua* 8.5, 14.2; *Homélies sur Josué*, ed. Jaubert, SC 71, 230-231. *Comm. in John* 20.21[19]. 174; *Homélies sur Jean*, III, ed. Blanc, SC 290, 242-243. *Comm. in Romans* 8.9; *PG* 14, 1184-1187.

faith of the church. In fact Origen did not write exclusively
for an audience of troubled intellectuals but to make clear
to anyone what he saw as the doctrine of the apostle Paul,
a doctrine which ran counter to what a number of the
simple believers defended as the truth.[48]

To further complicate matters, Origen says the following
in *On First Principles* 1.6.3:

But whether among those orders that live under the
chieftainship of the devil and conform to his wickedness
there are some who will one day in the ages to come
succeed in turning to goodness by reason of the power
of free will which is in them, whether it be true that the
long-continued and deep-rooted wickedness turns at
last from a habit into a kind of nature, you, reader, must
judge; whether, that is, this portion of the creation shall
be utterly and entirely out of harmony even with that
final unity and concord, both in the ages that are 'seen'
and 'temporal' and in those that are 'not seen' and
'eternal'.[49]

In his *Commentary on John* Origen refuses to indicate
whether those who have been 'bound and cast into outer
darkness' must remain in that state forever or whether
they might sometime be relieved of their punishment.
According to his reading, Scripture doesn't say.[50]

This is a muddle. The problem begins with the lack of a
single treatise on universal salvation and hell from Origen
or any treatise like the *Retractions* of Augustine which
would help us know if Origen ever intended to propound a

---

48   Armantage, 'Will the Body be Raised?' especially 397-414.

49   *On First Principles* 1.6.3.; *Traité des principes*, I, ed. Crouzel
     and Simonetti, SC 252, 198-203. Again Butterworth, p.57,
     note 1, quotes a passage from Origen's enemies, this time
     Jerome's *Epistle to Pammachius and Oceanus* 7 as teaching a
     restoration in which Gabriel, Paul and the virgins will be in
     the same state as the devil, Caiaphas and prostitutes.

50   *Commentary on John* 28.8[7]; ed. Preuschen, GCS, 399-400.

systematic view of these doctrines. This lack of material is deepened by the state of Origen's *corpus*. Eusebius had included a list of Origen's work in his biography of Pamphilus, his teacher and Origen's defender, but that work is lost. Jerome, who had read that list says it included two thousand titles, but in a letter where he makes his own list he specifically mentions eight hundred. Of two hundred and ninety-one commentaries written in Greek, two hundred and seventy-five are lost. Eusebius of Caesarea had a nine-volume collection of Origen's letters, but only three letters remain, one of them extant in incomplete Latin translations.[51] As we have already noted, many of the extant works are available only in Latin translation. Surely the first conclusion then is that we will always offer educated guesses about any of Origen's views since so much is lost and so much is filtered through translators and controversy.

The educated guess, however, must do its best to allow the different views stated by Origen to stand. Hermann-Josef Vogt's study of the commentaries reminds us that on other topics Origen continued to propose alternative readings of biblical verses and made no attempt to harmonize them.[52] Anyone with strong systematic

---

[51]   Jerome, *Epistle 33, to Paula Lettres*, ed. Labourt, Vol. I, (1951), 38-44, lists 800. In his *Against the Book of Rufinus* 2.22, *Apologia Contra Rufinum*, ed. Lardet, CCL LXXIX, 58, he indicates that some say there were 6,000 titles but he speaks of the 2,000 titles. Epiphanius *Panarion*, 64.63, GCS (1980), 501, says there were 6,000. Eusebius *H.E.* 6.36.3 mentions the volumes of letters. Johannes Quasten, *Patrology*, II (Westminster, MD: The Newman Press, 1964), 51 gives the figures about the commentaries.

[52]   Hermann-Josef Vogt, 'Wie Origenes in seinem Matthäuskommentar Fragen offen lässt,' *Origeniana Secunda*, 191-198 notices that in Origen's commentaries a number of questions are left open and appear with various forms and answers in other works. As Vogt observes, Origen often calls for his readers to form their own views.

interests will either be put off by this variation or find some way to make the different claims fit. Even someone who has no interest in a tightly-structured systematic theology will suspect that there is a waffle here, an inconsistency, that no logic seems able to rectify. But to be put off or to demand a tight systematic answer is to make Origen fit our views. Unfortunately the outlines of secondary literature squeeze Origen into a somewhat consistent pattern not of his making.

In the documents we have he says that the reader must choose between whether the lost are eternally damned or whether at some time they will be released from their suffering and punishment. As he reads Scripture, he finds no answer to those alternatives. He can speak of the enemies of God being subjected and the lost restored and warn that Gnostic views of God make him unjust, even wicked. He hopes that love will conquer all. Yet also in what we have, he ridicules as blasphemers those who think the devil will be saved and suggests that the devil may even be annihilated. He can insist for both Christian and pagan audiences that Scripture and the church teach the eternal punishment of sinners, a doctrine which strikes fear in human hearts and thus restrains evil. Indeed he can argue against Celsus that the pagan knows there must be punishment of evil or there will be no justice.

What we have of Origen's *corpus* in many ways presents us with a Rorschach test: too many of our best interpreters see what they intend to see. That is not a new problem. Even those who had the fuller *corpus* were often struck by the same difficulty. Pamphilus of Caesarea, who wrote a five-volume defense of Origen in Greek and had the whole library of Caesarea at his fingertips, argued that Origen was not heretical. In the one-volume Latin translation of his work that we have from Rufinus' hand, Pamphilus does quote more of Origen's works and tries to put the quotations in larger contexts from Origen's time, but his interest in defending Origen is clear from the start; Origen was his teacher. Methodius quotes Origen less and creates a caricature that takes him out of context. But he is concerned that Origen denies the resurrection of the body and thus succumbs to Gnostic errors. Rufinus defends Origen by giving more data from Origen, particularly large translations of the Alexandrian's important works. But he imposes a coherent system on Origen by changing what is said in *On First Principles* – and perhaps other works – on the basis of what he finds elsewhere in the *corpus*. In order not to offend Western believers, he makes Origen fit what he sees as the most important views Origen held. Jerome tries to be more literal in his translations but he emphasizes Origen's theological faults while defending him as a biblical commentator and does not stress the Alexandrian's denial of the devil's salvation or the Gnostic context of the debate with Candidus. He supplies us with that information but it is not very important to him. Some of Origen's opponents make their commitments exceptionally blatant and clear. Epiphanius, the blustery old heresy-hunter, says in talking about Origen's heresies: 'Such language would be excusable in anyone else.'[53] The emperor Justinian insisted that Origen's intent was malicious; he wanted to deceive the simple.[54]

Modern interpreters known to me are not so crass. Someone might suggest that Origen only taught fiery punishment for the sake of the simple whom he found wanting and taught something else for the intellectuals whom he enjoyed. At one point in his *Against Celsus* he does say, 'It is not of advantage to go on to the truths which lie behind it [punishment] because there are people who are scarcely restrained by fear of everlasting

53   *Panarion* 67.7.4, ed. Holl, Drummond, GCS, 512.
54   Justinian, *Against Origen* in Schwartz, *Acta Conciliorum Oecumenicorum* III, 191.

punishment from the vast flood of evil and the sins that are committed in consequence of it.'[55] Yet when he felt pressed by Celsus, even when he berated the pagan for paying too much attention to what the simple believers claimed, Origen insisted on the church's teaching of eternal punishment.[56] His intention is difficult to decipher. Within the same work in which he expresses both his frustration with and his admiration of simple believers, he can insist that the letter of Scripture and the rudiments of the *regula fidae* will save.[57] An interpreter can find Origen's intention to be upright, then take Origen's most speculative positions, and systematize them without reference to his disclaimers from Scripture and tradition. That particular Origen will be the one which Joseph Trigg and others see as so compelling, one who espouses positions John Hick defends. Yet such interpreters sometimes do not even mention the texts that counter their view.

Other modern interpreters have been offended by that depiction of Origen. Crouzel argues that the systematic outlines sometimes found in secondary literature are attributed to Origen on the basis of occasional speculations and further passages taken from what may have been interpolated texts. Those outlines depend upon inferences drawn from partial statements and primarily the new contexts important to Origen's opponents from the fourth century onward.[58] Crouzel makes a strong,

---

55   *Against Celsus* 6.25-26; *Contre Celse*, III, ed. Borret, SC 147, 244-245. See the similar sentiment in *Comm. Ser. in Matt* 16; *Matthäuserklärung XI.2*, ed. Klostermann, Benz, 2. Auflage, Treu, GCS, 29-31.

56   See note 35.

57   *On First Principles*, Pref. 2-8 and 4.2. *Traité des principes*, I, ed. Crouzel and Simonetti, SC 252, 78-89 and III, SC 268, 292-342.

58   See the summary of Origen's views on the *apokatastasis* in Henri Crouzel, *Origen*, trans A.S.Worrall (San Francisco:

persuasive case, particularly over against the common outlines. There is a welcome sharpness in his arguments, but at times he leaves behind the texts that support those outlines.

There are attempts to bend over backwards in fairness. Jean Daniélou defended Origen but questioned his doctrine of *apokatastasis*.[59] An enlightened Unitarian Universalist can now stand against the claims of that group's founder and concede that Origen only insisted on God's appeal to everyone to accept salvation. The universal aspect of salvation for Origen was the call, not the result.[60]

I hope that my own attempt to represent Origen as teaching two views for his readers to choose is fair:

Harper & Row, 1989), 257-266. In another section, 153-179, Crouzel insists that Origen's views have been misrepresented because his opponents usually do not understand the necessity and the principle of doctrinal development. That is a good insight. Armantage, 'Will the Body be Raised?' shows that inferences were drawn from new contexts and that by the fifth-century caricatures of Origen's heresies had begun to replace careful study of his texts. I also think that once one works through the studies of Crouzel and Armantage, one can suggest that the stark statements about universal salvation and hell, [found in the fragments of Justinian and Leontius of Byzantium,] are probably based on interpolated texts, texts in which the inferences and caricatures have been placed in manuscripts claiming to be Origen's writings. Since Origen claimed that such meddling with the texts had already occurred during his lifetime, it certainly could have been an important part of the attacks against him later, even by people who themselves would not have been a party to interpolating texts. One has only to think of the effectiveness of the Apollinarians in placing Apollinaris' works under Athanasius' name so that even Cyril of Alexandria defended Apollinarian Christological formula as genuinely Athanasian.

59   See note 8.

60   Henry Babcock, 'Origen's Anti-Gnostic Polemic and the Doctrine of Universalism,' *The Unitarian Universalist Christian* 38 (1983), 53-59.

universal salvation and a limited hell as well as salvation
only for those who live the gospel and eternal damnation,
perhaps even annihilation, for those like the devil who
continuously refuse.[61] The sense, however, which washes
over the student of Origen with the relentless force of a
rising flood is how difficult it is for us to write good history,
how hard it is to be fair about our own presuppositions and
to the texts, and how impossible it is to be an historicist
who traces out exactly what happened or precisely what
was said.

Maximus the Confessor

Maximus the Confessor appears to be much more
circumspect in his views about universal salvation and
hell. That well may be because his *corpus* is available in
his Greek, neither subject to translators who wished to
soften what he says nor apparently to interpolators who
have scandalized his text. Yet even then there have been
some who accused him of being an Origenist. A Syriac
biography tried to make that case.[62] In this century there
has been what Brian Daley calls a 'gentle controversy'
concerning Maximus' eschatology, especially whether or
not he accepted the doctrine of *apokatastasis*.[63] Although

---

[61]   Brian Daley, *The Hope of the Early Church*, 47-64, although
       with a few different emphases, is extensive and balanced in his
       survey. He includes the two views noted here and suggests that
       Origen remained undecided, 59. I also find the 1970 Yale
       dissertation of James Armantage, 'Will the Body be Raised?' to
       be scrupulously fair in its presentation both of Origen and his
       opponents.

[62]   Sebastian Brock, 'An Early Syriac Life of Maximus the
       Confessor, *Analecta Bollandiana* 91 (1973), 299-346.

[63]   Brian Daley, 'Apokatastasis and "Honourable Silence" in the
       Eschatology of Maximus the Confessor,' *Maximus Confessor:
       Actes du Symposium sur Maxime le Confesseur, Fribourg, 2-5
       septembre 1980*, 'Paradosis 27' (Fribourg: Éditions
       universitaires Fribourg, 1982), 309.

Michaud, Grumel and Viller[64] had debated the point by 1930, it is really the work of Polycarp Sherwood and Hans Urs von Balthasar about twenty years later that put the controversy in focus.

Sherwood claims that Maximus held two poles in tension: 'the perfection and universality of God's saving work in Jesus Christ and the reality of unending punishment, that is, the seeming failure of salvation.' A number of texts from Maximus insist on the fact of unending punishment.[65] He does not always speak of hell's physical fires, but, following Gregory of Nazianzus[66] he bemoans the horrors of separation from God.

Responding to the first edition of von Balthasar's book, *Kosmische Liturgie*, Sherwood insisted that the *corpus* of Maximus did not have a large number of passages that referred to esoteric doctrines. In fact, most of the citations offered by von Balthasar only stated that Maximus was deferring comment until later, and thus in these instances honouring the biblical passage in silence only for a time. Yet even in Sherwood's view three passages within the *Questions to Thalassius* did require further interpretation.[67] Section 21 reflects on Colossians 2:14-15 but it neither supports the existence of a doctrine only for

---

[64]   E. Michaud, 'S. Maxime le confesseur et l'apocatastase,' *Revue internationale de théologie* 10 (1902), 257-272. Vénance Grumel, 'Maxime', *Dictionnaire de théologie catholique* 10.1 (Paris: Librairie Letouzey et Ané, 1926), 457. Marcel Viller, 'Aux sources de la spiritualité de S. Maxime: les oeuvres d' Évagre le Pontique,' *Revue d'ascétique et de mystique* II (1930), 259f.

[65]   *Ambigua* 20, 21, 53; *PG* 91, 1237B, 1252B, 1373B, 1376B. *Questions to Thalassius* 11; *PG* 91, 293B. *Mystagoge* 14; *PG* 91, 693B. *Letters* 4, 8, 24; *PG* 91, 416, 441D, 612BC.

[66]   Gregory Nazianzen, *Or.* 16.9; *PG* 35, 945C.

[67]   *Questions to Thalassius*, Pr., 21 & 43; *PG* 91, 260A, 316D & 412A.

the elite nor covers such a doctrine in suspicious silence. Maximus knows of 'ineffable doctrines' that 'should not be set down in writing' but he only promises Thalassius that they will later discuss the writings of Paul, not the 'ineffable doctrines.' The prologue and section 43 deal with the two trees of paradise, but they imprison the so-called 'higher' teachings in silence. There is neither a time when nor a group in which they will be discussed.

Maximus uses the word *apokatastasis* without the overtones of Origenist doctrine, either the teachings most fully developed by defenders of Origen like Evagrius of Pontus[68] and Gregory of Nyssa or those views inferred and caricatured by Origen's opponents. Indeed there are passages in which Maximus explicitly denies that the wicked will eventually be saved, that their punishment will not be eternal. In *Questions and Doubts* 13 [69] he had been asked about Gregory of Nyssa's teaching, evidently referring to the passage in Gregory's *Concerning the Maker of Man*.[70] The differences in the two positions is significant. Maximus says that the 'perverted powers of the soul' will be restored, but he does not say that the persons themselves will be restored as Gregory of Nyssa does. The condemned souls will have a knowledge, *epignosis*, of good things but not a participation, *methexis*, in them. Furthermore Maximus does not mention that the devil will be restored, a claim which Gregory of Nyssa does make in other places.[71] According to Sherwood's translation Maximus speaks of Nyssa's teaching as 'abused', *katakechretai*.

---

68   See Antoine Guillamont, *Les 'Kephalaia gnostica' d'Évagre le Pontique et l'Histoire de l'Origenisme chez les Grecs et chez les Syriens* (Paris: Éditions du Seuil, 1962), 47-170.

69   *PG* 90, 796.

70   *PG* 44, 201.

71   Gregory of Nyssa, *The Great Catechism* 26; *PG* 45, 69B-C and *Dialogue concerning the Soul and the Resurrection*; *PG* 45, 101A.

Two other passages in *Questions and Doubts* 10 and 73[72] seem to refer to 1 Corinthians 3:13-15, Paul's phrase 'saved, yet so as by fire'. But Sherwood finds that these passages which do talk about sins burned by fire refer to the wicked appearing at the final judgement, being weighed in the balance then. It is a vision similar to the New Testament image of the sheep and the goats. Also in both passages there is no mention of damnation or punishment and thus no reference to the fires of hell as curative. Maximus appears to avoid Nyssa's interpretation of 1 Corinthians 15:28 that God will be all in all only if every aspect of sin disappears.[73]

That rejection of an Origenist doctrine of *apokatastasis* is clear in *Ambigua* 42 and 65.[74] With both passages Maximus compares the different but final conditions of human beings. Those who have chosen virtue and movement in harmony with the *Logos* receive well-being; those who have chosen vice and disharmony with the *Logos* receive ill-being. The first participate in joy; the second do not. The second are fairly assigned to 'ever ill-being'.

From all the passages assembled here Sherwood claims that Maximus holds in tension the 'universality of salvation and the eternity of damnation for some'. Maximus does insist that, as Paul claimed in 1 Timothy 2:3, God desires the salvation of all. Yet that desire does not demand that there are no consequences for those who have chosen vice and disharmony with the *logos*. Their

---

72   *PG* 90, 792C and 845C.
73   Gregory of Nyssa, *In illud*: Tunc et ipse filius; *PG* 44, 1316D; *Gregorii Nysseni Opera* III.2, ed. J. Kenneth Downing. *Dialogue concerning the Soul and the Resurrection*; *PG* 46, 104B.
74   *PG* 91, 1329A-B and 1392C-D.

powers of knowledge will be restored so that they know
the truth, but their punishment will be 'eternal ill-being',
discursive knowledge of the good but no participation in
it.[75]

What is perhaps important to note here, relationships
that Sherwood does not indicate, is that Origen evidently
taught something very similar to Maximus' views as
Sherwood sees them. At least in part Origen tried to hold
in tension God's universal offer of salvation and the
eternity of punishment. The distinction between painful
knowledge of previous sins without participation in the
blissful life of God is Origen's definition of the soul's hell
in his *Commentary on Matthew*.[76] Maximus also makes
epistemological distinctions genuinely found in Origen's
understanding of participation and rejects the
substantialist views that became basic to much of the
opposition to Origen. According to Maximus the wicked in
the afterlife will know the good but will not be able to
participate in it. During the seventh century Maximus was
well enough informed of the ecclesiastical political climate
not to make the claims for similarity to Origen that we can
see today.

Although in the second edition of his study on Maximus,
the *Kosmische Liturgie*, von Balthasar praised some of the
work of Sherwood, he continued to support his own theory
that there are two strains of thought in Maximus: a
traditional statement of eternal punishment for the devil,
demons and wicked people, and a group of hints that the
Confessor accepted Origen's fallacious doctrine of the

---

75   Polycarp Sherwood, *The Earlier Ambigua of Saint Maximus
     the Confessor and His Refutation of Origenism*, 'Studia
     Anselmiana XXXVI' (Rome: Herder, 1955), 205-222.
76   *Origenes Matthäuserklärung* X, ed. Klostermann, GCS, 2-3;
     and *Commentaire sur l'Évangile de saint Matthieu X-XI*, ed.
     Girod, SC 162, 144-149.

apokatastasis. According to von Balthasar Maximus did not directly teach that all would be saved and that punishment would be limited, but in those three passages from his *Questions to Thalassius* Maximus indicated that he could provide a 'secret and higher interpretation' of the two trees in paradise and the cross of Christ. He refrained from stating that interpretation because 'one should not spread abroad in books the ineffable aspects of divine teachings.' He would 'honour' the scriptural passages 'in silence'. According to von Balthasar Maximus decided to honour these biblical passages in silence because he knew of Origen's connection of the passages with his own doctrine of salvation for all and the limitation of eternal punishment. The Confessor accepted those teachings as the truth for the elite.[77]

Brian Daley, a well-informed student of early Christian eschatology whose handbook of patristic eschatology was recently published,[78] had previously argued that Sherwood and von Balthasar's debate over the meaning of the texts in the *Questions to Thalassius* must be decided in favour of Sherwood's view. There is no indication that Maximus had Origen's famous doctrine of *apokatastasis* in view when he commented on the biblical verses about the trees in paradise and the cross of Christ. Indeed Origen in his *Homilies on Joshua*, which connect the two trees of paradise and the cross of Christ, speaks of the salvation of all humans, but he also insists that the devil and his angels are sent to the punishment of eternal fire, there to

---

77 Hans Urs von Balthasar, *Kosmische Liturgie: Das Weltbild Maximus' des Bekenners*, Zweite, völlig veränderte Auflage (Einseideln: Johannes Verlag, 1961), 355-359. He knows and compliments Sherwood's work and mentions the *Early Ambigua* specifically in the forward to this edition, but he does not respond to Sherwood's critique of his own efforts in his section on the *Wiedereinbringung*.

78 Daley, *The Hope of the Early Church*.

be annihilated along with death.[79] If Maximus had those comments of Origen in mind, they would not support the myth of the end being like the beginning, that is, a full *apokatastasis* which von Balthasar thinks he holds.

As importantly other passages in the writings of Maximus speak about 'honouring in silence', but not in the sense of keeping a systematic and esoteric set of doctrines from the simple believers. He can insist that only those whose contemplation is pure and deep can reach the heights of understanding; but that goal also may be understood in a humble fashion, one that notes how seldom anyone can attain such heights. In other contexts the Confessor refers merely to a delay. Now he cannot go into the interpretations of all the numbers in Jesus' parables. They must be honoured in silence until another time when he can more competently deal with them.[80]

Daley concedes that there are two passages from Maximus, one in his *Exposition of Psalm 59* and another in his *Mystagoge* in which the Confessor states his 'hope for a universal salvation and transformation of rational creatures with an unqualified optimism.'[81] But neither passage represents a concerted effort to outline his eschatology, indeed each is an aside, the first within the context of a pastoral exegesis of the scriptural text and the second in a discussion of how the noumenal and phenomenal are related. At the same time there is no direct attack on a sense of *apokatastasis*. Daley also suggests that Sherwood misread *katakechretai* as 'abused' in section 13 of *Questions and Doubts* when it should have been understood from the context more neutrally as only 'used'. In Daley's view Maximus is not

---

79   Origen, *Homilies on Joshua* 8.3-6; *Homélies sue Josué*, ed. Jaubert, SC 71, 222-235.

80   Daley, 'Apokatastasis', 318-321.

81   Daley, 'Apokatastasis', 321-322.

attacking Gregory of Nyssa, but neither is he accepting an Origenist rejection of eternal punishment.

What Maximus does attack is the Origenist sense of the beginning, souls that fall from their pristine state into the world of flesh. Here the most noted text is section 7 of the *Ambigua to John*.[82] In Maximus' view souls did not exist in a contemplative state from which they fell into bodies; what we know is that their fall entailed forsaking the *logos*, the divine plan or ideal of God. To quote Daley, 'only God's "conception" of a spiritual creature's potential end can be said to exist "before" the creature's life in time.'[83] Cautious talk of an *apokatastasis* concerns the restoration of that concept, that *logos*, rather than a return of pre-existent souls to their original state.

In his rejection of these views from Origen and Origenists, Maximus does not shortchange an emphasis on God's desire that all be saved and come to the knowledge of the truth. For him 1 Timothy 2:3 and other biblical passages make that clear. The point of God's love and activity both in Israel, even in Nineveh, and especially in Jesus Christ, is that the whole race of humans might continue to exist and share God's healing and grace.[84] Unlike the Origenists, however, Maximus understands

---

[82] *Ambigua to John 7*; *PG* 91, 1069A-1102C. Both Sherwood, 'Maximus and Origenism: *Arche kai telos, Berichte zum XI. internationalen Byzantinisten-Kongress* (Munich, 1958) III.1, esp. 1-5 and Endre von Ivánka, 'Der philosophische Beitrag der Auseinandersetzung Maximos' des Bekenners mit dem Origenismus,' *Jahrbuch der österreichischen byzantinischen Gesellschaft* 7 (1958), 28, n.1 find this passage important; Ivánka calls it the *locus classicus* of Maximus' objection to Origenism.

[83] Daley, 'Apokatastasis', 326.

[84] *Caritas* 1.61 & 3.29; *PG* 90, 973A & 1025C. *Ambigua to John* 10 & 31; *PG* 91, 1165D & 1280A. *Ambigua to Th.* 4; *PG* 91, 1044B. *Opusc.* 8; *PG* 91, 932C. *Questions to Thalassius* 23 & 63; *PG* 90, 328B-C, 700A-B and 712A.

that there will be individual defeats, again in Daley's words: 'salvation is for those who accept grace and cooperate with it'.[85] Divinization is the goal and the method, but any person is free enough to reject it. Isaiah 40:5 appears to claim that 'all flesh shall see the salvation of our God,' but what it means is all believing flesh. Isaiah 26:10 [LXX] insisted that the wicked man should be taken away lest he see the glory of the Lord.[86]

Humans who may share in salvation could come from odd places. Rational persons have some sense of right and wrong from their natural reason, an indication that the Holy Spirit is present in them. Even 'barbarians and nomads' show some signs of *kalokagathia*, 'moral excellence', whenever they leave previously uncivilized customs; when that happens the Holy Spirit is at work. The people of God mentioned in the Old Testament obeyed the law and expected their Messiah; once more the Spirit showed its hand. Yet only Christians gained through the Spirit the 'sonship given them by grace through faith.' But even among Christians, only some will be saved, only those who 'have understanding and who have made themselves worthy of his [the Spirit's] divine indwelling by their godly way of life.'[87]

---

85   Daley, 'Apokatastasis', 329.

86   *Questions to Thalassius* 47; *PG* 90, 428C-D. Daley, 'Apokatastasis', 330, n.1 remarks that Maximus speaks of the *Logos* '"becom[ing] all things to all, in order to save all" through the riches of his goodness' in 429C. The allusion is to 1 Cor. 9:22, but the significant change in Maximus is from Paul's 'in order to save some' to 'in order to save all'. Yet even that interesting slip does not demand that Maximus taught universal salvation. Similar views about the limited nature of salvation due to human freedom to refuse it and the giving of it only to those found worthy appears in *Ambigua* 7; *PG* 91, 1069A-1102C and *Questions to Thalassius* 2, 22 & 63; *PG* 90, 272B-C, 317B-321C & 669C.

87   *Questions to Thalassius* 15; *PG* 91, 297B-D & 300A. The translations are Daley's, 'Apokatastasis', 332-33.

Those who have opposed God suffer great turmoil. Maximus uses the terms found in both Jewish and Christian apocalyptic literature to describe hell: 'deep gloom and oppressive silence, ... eternal fire, outer darkness, the worm that never sleeps, gnashing of teeth, ceaseless tears, and limitless shame' await those 'condemned to eternal endless torture.'[88] In what Daley calls 'probably his most elaborate and moving description' of life apart from God, Maximus says:

What is more wretched and oppressive than anything else, to speak truly – and if it makes me grieve just to mention it, then how much worse to suffer it (have mercy, O Christ, and save us from this pain!) – is separation from God and his holy powers, and belonging to the devil and the evil demons, a state which lasts forever, without any prospect of our ever being liberated from this dire situation.... And more punishing, more severe than any penalty is to be joined forever with those who hate and are hated – even apart from torture, and all the more with it – and to be separated from the one who loves and is loved.[89]

This late letter to George, eparch of Africa, makes it clear that although there are statements within the *corpus* of Maximus that seem to support universal salvation and the denial of everlasting hell, those statements must be put in the context of other more frequent and terrifying claims. Perhaps like Origen Maximus hopes for the salvation of all, but unlike Origen and the Origenists that hope does not receive as much attention as the horrors of hell. Maximus is not an Origenist; his teachings do not fit the caricature of Origen which was condemned. He is

---

88   *Letter* 4; *PG* 91, 416B-417A. I have adapted Daley's translation, 'Apokatastasis', 334.
89   *Letter* 1; *PG* 91, 389A-B. Daley's translation, 'Apokatastasis', 334-335.

perhaps a worthy guide for contemporary theologians,
perhaps even a worthy guide to Origen. He rejects
Origen's speculation about pre-existent souls. More
importantly along with Origen he always remembers that
God wants everyone to be saved. He does not claim to
understand all the power and love of God. At times he
honours it in silence. But in each instance Maximus does
not see God overwhelming the will of humans, either to
save them or to condemn them. Thus in his theology he
holds humans responsible for their attitudes and actions in
this world, and thus continues Origen's concern for the
ascetic life. Maximus does not solve the problem of evil
either by resorting to the predestination found in
Augustine or the strain of universal salvation found in
some passages of Origen. He is neither overly pessimistic
nor overly optimistic.

Yet even Maximus' more straightforward *corpus*
reminds us that the questions we discuss here are thorny.
If we try to deal with them from a modern dogmatic or
systematic perspective, perhaps we will be more careful
about our sense of the philosophical and epistemological
problems that lie behind our approaches. But even in a
paper of historical theology like this one, we must take
care to confess that those difficulties do not disappear
under the guise of objectively dealing with ancient texts.

3

Descensus and Universalism: Some Historical Patterns of Interpretation

D. A. Du Toit

A study of the *descensus ad inferos* creates the impression that it can supply a foothold for the idea of universalism. This paper proposes to find whether that really happened in the early Christian church. It necessarily involves an attempt to describe the different patterns of interpretation of this doctrine during that time, which in turn needs an analysis of the nature and structure of religious expression.

Modern Universalism
It is of course a question whether the modern notion of universalism, or rather the popular and inarticulated inclination towards it, can have any relation with the *descensus* whatsoever. To much of the modern mind, the concepts of hell and *descensus* represent not only outdated mythological inventions, but also embody the unacceptable ideas of unfairness and discrimination. Through all ages religious thought had been influenced by a general view of life, man and the world. The modern mind has been thoroughly moulded by the present day concept of democracy, which precludes all discrimination and unfair, unequal or preferential treatment of some over against others. Hence the predestination, the election and the exclusiveness of Christianity and indeed of Christ himself are being questioned in contemporary ecumenical theology, but not only in ecumenical theology. The

tendency rather is towards greater recognition of non-Christian religions, accompanied by the consequent downplaying of mission and evangelism, and the forced invention of notions like 'anonymous Christians' and the like.

This kind of universalism, although differing in its material motive and origin from its classic counterpart, nonetheless leads to the same theological consequences. The choice for universalism, both old and new, involves a new and rather reduced doctrine of God. It requires a different vision of the church and its calling in the world. It also leads to an anthropology which finds it hard to maintain the dignity of man and avoid the minimising of personal responsibility.

These and other important theological issues, however, are not the subject of this paper. It will rather deal with some of the historical developments in the interpretation of hell and the *descensus Christi*, focussing on the possible relationship it had with a doctrine of universalism. At the same time such a study may reveal something of the fascinating but complex process that took place in the understanding of a specific doctrine in the early church. Unfortunately we shall have to deny ourselves the privilege and pleasure of a full and complete exposé, concentrating rather on the central issue of the interpretation of the *descensus* and whether any significant link can be traced to universalism. It is well known that some of the exponents of universalism in the nineteenth century utilized the *descensus* as a proof of universalism, referring *inter alia* to 1 Peter 3:19.

The Descensus Problem
The *descensus ad inferos* forms part of our traditional Christian confession, and therefore shares in the status of that confession. Nevertheless, it has always raised questions since medieval times and prompted attempts at

new interpretations up till the present day. Perhaps more than any other article of faith it confronted the church with the question about the authority of the confession, in the wake of which all kinds of distinctions were introduced or re-employed, *e.g.* that between fundamental and non-fundamental articles of faith, the acceptance of a hierarchy of truths, *etc*. In the background, constantly and very largely, looms the question about the real continuity of our confession of faith in unity with that of the body of Christ through the ages. This became rather critical with the advent of theologies which attempted radical new ways of interpreting the *descensus*. The theology of the death of God, for instance, saw the *descensus* as the 'descent of God into the wordless, dark silence of the Absent' (Ratzinger 243). On the other hand, it is also true that specific truths may become 'unexistentiell', even with very 'brave, orthodox Christians' (Rahner 211).

It is rather difficult to ascertain the historical and theological background of this article of faith. It does not appear in the early confessions, not even in the Nicaenum of 325, in which also the crucifixion, death and burial of Jesus were omitted. This of course was the period during which the confessions attained more than local significance and status. In the period up till 358 even less of the final period of Christ's life was mentioned beyond the mere facts of suffering and resurrection (Kelly 274).

Then, at the Council of Sirmium in 359, the *descensus* made its very sudden and almost noiseless appearance in the confession, where it stayed on in an equally unobtrusive way. Even the very carefully written commentary of Tyrannius Rufinus half a century later shed no more light on the reasons and circumstances of its inclusion (Hartvelt 6). With regard to its interpretation the meaning of *descensus* is seen simply as an emphasis and intensifying of the '*sepultus*'. What is abundantly clear is the fact that the *descensus* played no critical doctrinal role at the time and apparently had no connection with any theological dispute of the time. It is not possible to establish any connection with any specific doctrine, let alone with the issue of universalism. It simply stayed on in the confession and appeared in an increasing number of confessional statements, especially since the sixth and seventh centuries.

This, in some ways peculiar, state of affairs is also reflected in the consequent history of this doctrine and its interpretation. There seems to be a wide variety of sometimes contradictory interpretations amongst the larger confessional traditions. Particularly interesting is the position of Greek Orthodox theology: while the *descensus* appears in the Apostolicum and Athanasianum (not officially accepted by the church), it was not included in the officially accepted Nicaeno-Konstantinopolitanum, and yet it is a doctrine of great importance for them.

Historical and General Religious Background
The *descensus* appears in myths, legends and stories of all the major cultures and religions of the ancient world of the Egyptians, Persians, Greeks, Romans and Jews. Later on it is found in Hinduism and Shamanism, as well as in North America, Finland, New Zealand, Asia, West Africa, Zululand and other places (Tylor II 46-50). Usually it is the account of the visit of a person, hero, halfgod, or god to the localised realm of the dead, set in the framework of the worldview of the time, which included in most instances the three-tiered conception of the cosmos. Death is seen as the entry into some kind of continued existence, which usually represents a dull and unattractive situation. It is possible to argue that the main motive behind *descensus* stories is the fact that although death is universally accepted because of its unavoidability, the way in which it is explained and integrated in a philosophy of life points to the equally universal notion that it is unnatural,

undesirable and something to be overcome in some way or the other.

Although different specific motives for the *descensus* can be deduced from the different stories, it is not possible to find anything resembling a universalism. In the Greek-Roman stories it can be attributed to curiosity, longing for a deceased loved one, efforts to abduct such from the underworld, the obtaining of a certain object, treasure or knowledge, *etc.* Later on new motives were added, for instance in Seneca's dramas, where the descent of Heracles is linked with his role as benefactor of humanity, the bringer of peace, the *pacator inferiorum* who brings the powers of the underworld under control. In the Babylonian world visits to the underworld may or may not have a specific motive, but are usually connected with the role of a representative of the kingdom of light, the good and the life. Overall, the motive of saving a group or all of the deceased from the underworld never featured in early *descensus* stories of the ancient world. It usually deals with an object or an individual. This effort at saving was anyhow never connected with a higher or eternal salvation, but was aimed at a return to this life on this earth. One may assume that here also the most fundamental motive is the desire of man to unravel the mysteries of death in an attempt to somehow gain some control over it.

The Old Testament conceptions of death and the realm of the dead have much in common with those of the surrounding cultures and religions, though it is now employed in the service of a totally new aim, *i.e.* the proclamation of the mighty deeds of Yahweh, who has the power to protect his own even from the power of death and she'ol. As has been shown repeatedly, she'ol cannot be localized too easily in the Old Testament – it is much more an existential concept denoting the harshness and finality of death: the descent into she'ol is not a new aspect which comes *after* death – it simply is the implication of death itself (Vorgrimler 140). She'ol as indeed the deepest place known to Israel can also be manifested in illness, weakness, desperate need, being forsaken by God, as well as in death and the grave itself. Because of its basic religious concept the Old Testament in contrast to other religions shows no interest in a visit of Yahweh or anybody else to she'ol. In his might and power Yahweh also rules over the underworld, but always stays transcendent above it. One can almost say that because of his power he needs no visit. The idea of a *descensus* only occurred in the later apocryphal apocalyptic literature (the Book of Enoch, the Syrian Book of Baruch, *etc.*). The idea of the chosen people in the Old Testament presumably led to the apocalyptic description of a specific group of the deceased benefitting from the descent of the Saviour That however precludes any idea of universalism. Instead she'ol was divided in separate departments (in some cases as many as four), with a strong emphasis on hell as place of punishment (Valley of Hinnom, later Gehenna) over against She'ol (Hades) as a preliminary waiting place (divided in two) and paradise or heaven (Charles 247, 290-294).

The New Testament is a radical correction of these apocalyptic speculations and a return to the sobriety of the Old Testament. References to the underworld must not be taken as cosmological, but as theo-logical, indicating the distance between God and that underworld, as can be deduced from the words used to indicate the same reality: fiery oven, pool of life, inextinguishable fire, darkness, eternal suffering, *etc.* (Du Toit 87). The New Testament, like the Old Testament, offers no separate, independent metaphysical or dogmatic doctrine about the cosmos, death, hell or the realm of the dead. The religious pathos of the New Testament is the greatness of God and his grace in Jesus Christ, and reference to the underworld is subjected to, and in service of, the proclamation of the gospel and the invitation and challenge to accept Christ. Taking all evidence from the New Testament it is not possible to construe a doctrine of an actual descent of Christ to hell or the deceased (Du Toit 88, 205f.) while it is even more difficult to arrive at the standpoint of any universalism.

Early Christian Tradition
For the early Christian there was no clear demarcation between canonical and apocryphal sources. The influence of the last on the pious Christian mind and religious practice was remarkably strong (*cf.* the influence of the Pastor of Hermas, the Revelation of St Peter, 4 Esra and others). These stories depict the final events of the clash of Yahweh, or of the Messiah, or of angels, with the evil powers of devil, death and underworld, resulting in the victory of the good and the liberation of those that belong to God. The elaborate and spectacular breaking down of the gates of the underworld, the noise of war, the fear and defeat of the enemy, the triumphant march, *etc.* must have had considerable impact on the mind and hearts of believers.

It is therefore quite remarkable that the earliest Christian writings of, for instance, Ignatius and Polycarp contain very few references to the *descensus*. It is clear that the *descensus* stories were well-known – only short and casual references, without the need of further explanation, are to be found in these writings. The main conclusion must be that the *descensus* at this time represents no critical issue with regard to faith or doctrine, and therefore receives no systematic treatment. The first motive connected with these references seems to be the *concern for the Old Testament believers* (Brändle 59) who expected the Messiah and now have the privilege of meeting him. This forms a contrast to St Paul who simply saw them as sharing in the salvation Christ brought, and rested his case by emphasizing the eschatological event of resurrection. The concern for the Old Testament believers is then connected to the more obvious matter, *i.e.* the motive of *preaching*. Jesus' ministry was characterized by his preaching and the proclamation of the gospel, and it is therefore only logical that this activity should be continued during his projected visit to the underworld (Bieder 149f.). In the early writings this activity in fact acquires the nature of merely an announcement of the fulfilment of their faith and hope through Christ, because it is meant for the Old Testament saints (Ignatius limits it to Old Testament prophets), and certainly not for everyone.

In later writings (*e.g.* Hermas) this popular motive of preaching was expanded: *also the apostles* (*descensus apostolorum*) were seen to be preaching to the deceased after their death, and even *baptism* was introduced. Those receiving the baptism now included not only the prophets, but also the patriarchs and servants of the old covenant, *i.e.* the whole corpus of the faithful from the Old Testament (*cf.* Gospel of Peter). Nowhere whatsoever do we encounter the idea that the preaching to the deceased was aimed *at all of them*, thus also becoming a proclamation of the gospel to people who died as non-believers, calling them to repentance or offering everybody the salvation in Christ. This early line of development was followed throughout the second century (*cf. Epistula Apostolorum*). The main theme was preaching in the sense of *announcing* the freedom Christ obtained for the faithful of the Old Testament. Gradually more distinctions were made and details given of the underworld, for example in the case of Justin who stated that the souls of the martyrs do not go to Hades. Hades itself is divided in different spheres for the good and the bad. The *descensus Christi* is a visit only to the good part where the faithful of the Old Testament waited.

Irenaeus brought the *descensus* also into a polemical context, using it to demonstrate both the *vere homo* and

the *vere Deus* of Christ as well as the fact that he really
died and rose from the dead. Later on this motive was
expanded: to die is not enough – Jesus also stayed three
days in the grave to show that he took upon himself the
full consequences of death. Another motive for the
descensus evolved from this, *i.e.* the desire to explain or
fill the three days. Irenaeus took pains to show that the
work of salvation by Jesus also incorporated the faithful of
the Old Testament. This expanding of the motive of
preaching, connected very clearly with salvation, has no
parallel or analogy with the *descensus* stories from other
cultures and religions, and must be seen as consistent
with practice in the New Testament. At this stage it has
no reference to the classic liberation and struggle motive
of general folklore. And still no trace of any universalism
can be found. The central idea behind the *descensus* up till
this stage of development was not the accommodation of
any mythological and detailed, spectacular and fantastic
depictions of a mighty showdown in the underworld, but
the very sober stating of the fact that God had not
forgotten the faithful of the Old Testament. Very
interesting is the way *Marcion* turns this whole idea on its
head: Christ's *descensus* is aimed at freeing Cain, the
Sodomites, Egyptians and others who rejected the cruel
Creator God, Yahweh. Again however, no universalism.
Other traditions which developed incorporated much of the
descensus motive, but put it in totally new frameworks.
An example is the gnostic depictions, which utilized the
descensus idea for an *ascensus*: the same ideas and
motives occur, however, not in the underworld, but in the
spheres of the planets above the earth (*cf.* the Ascension
of Isaiah). But here also no notion of any universalism can
be found.

Also *Irenaeus* had no inclination to formulate the
descensus in terms of theoretical and speculative
dogmatics and rather spoke and wrote in a religious and
practical way. It is significant that *Melito* of Sardes who

gives such an elaborate and forceful description of the *descensus* does not take it up in his concluding confessional summary. To him it is an important issue as comfort for the pious mind and heart, but certainly not an important article of confession or faith-critical dogma.

The very first time that the account of the *descensus* included anything more than the position of only the Old Testament faithful was in the Christian version of the *Testaments of the Twelve Patriarchs* (200 A.D.). The deceased heathen seems to be under or in the vicinity of both the judgement and the promise of God. Mention is made of the conversion of disobedient hearts, and of the descent of the Spirit upon them. To Bieder (162) this represents a logical further development: once the circumstances of the deceased as such has entered the limelight not only the Old Testament saints but also the heathen will receive attention. It is obvious however that this state of affairs represents no universalistic thinking but only a second chance for the unbelievers, so to speak. The reference to conversion in this document however offers no material for wide-ranging conjecture or definite conclusions.

Note at this stage the role awarded to Scripture, especially to 1 Peter 3:19, 4:6. Although a number of interpreters ventured the idea that there are several allusions to the *descensus* in Scripture, the majority, while accepting a general acquaintance with the *descensus*, rejects the attempt to a direct appeal to any text of Scripture as the source or foundation of the *descensus*. The numerous appeals to 1 Peter 3:19, 4:6 in this respect in later times (especially in the 19th century from people supporting universalism) prompts the question as to its role in early centuries. It is therefore a real surprise to find that these words from 1 Peter (Bieder: 'numerous times treated and mistreated' 96) were never used as a proof for the *descensus* in the first two centuries. It was not until

Clement of Alexandria and Origen that it was awarded this role. The motive in both cases was to present to the unbelieving deceased the opportunity of conversion, which in any case is again not universalism proper. Augustine rejected this exegesis, a stance which was followed well into the Middle Ages by all with the exception of the Greek church.

The third and fourth centuries mark a definite expanding of the accounts and descriptions of the *descensus* in terms of vivid, imaginative and spectacular detail (*cf.* the Gospel of Nicodemus, the Acts of Thomas, the Acts of Andrew, the Acts of Paul, the Acts of John and the gnostic Pistis Sophia). Parallel to this development however, like in the preceding period, the other tradition was also continued, *i.e* the sober 'theological' treatment, where writers like Tertullian, Hippolytus and Cyprian limited the visit of Christ to the 'regions under the earth' to the consoling announcement of the reality of his grace and salvation to the Old Testament patriarchs and prophets (Bieder 189).

For the Alexandrian school however, the idea of salvation in connection with the *descensus* became so strong that it largely overshadowed the more sober motive of preaching or announcement. The *descensus* presented the possibility to highlight in a new way the universal consequences and application of salvation, demonstrating in what way that salvation came to all people of all generations. The motive of preaching in the underworld became much more than a mere announcement of Christ's victory over sin and death. It became indeed an offer to all the deceased to accept the salvation in Christ. For Clement this was not only a justification of God's judgement but also the logical continuation of the earthly work of Christ, who proclaimed the gospel to everybody and offered the blessings of salvation to all people.

This entails the possibility of conversion to faith in the underworld of those deceased that died as unbelievers. It should be noted that this does still not constitute a full-blown universalism. But it did have as a consequence much greater emphasis on the liberation motive. Clement believed that the souls of the faithful were freed from Hades at the *descensus*, so that no believer's soul any more need to go there at death. As a result the belief in the resurrection, so dominant in the New Testament and in the early church, faded into the background of his thinking, while in the same process the doctrine of purgatory starts to emerge (Bieder 190).

This line of thought was further developed by Origen, according to most popular sources. With the liberation of the souls of the believers and the consequent direct transport of the souls of the faithful to heaven at death, Hades became a location for the lost, *i.e.* hell. Strongly under the influence of philosophical thought, Origen developed his doctrine of *apokatastasis*, which in reality was the first real universalism. Hell has no permanence, because everybody in it will gradually be purified and saved, even the devil himself. Origen therefore was the first prominent theologian in the early church (but also the only one) to see and use the possibilities the *descensus* stories had for the foundation of universalism. In this attempt the traditional *descensus* motive of preaching in the underworld vanished almost completely in Origen's thought, while the motive of struggle, violence and victory became dominant. Recently however, Norris ventured the idea that the popular sources on Origen could contain an unfair presentation of his thought.

During this time Celsus, like Marcion, tried to turn the *descensus* tradition in its head. In his opinion the *descensus* is a pure myth, designed by the Christians to find Jesus another area to work after his complete failure on earth(!).

This brings us to the very important fourth century, *i.e.* the time of the great Christological struggle, but also the time during which the *descensus* made its first appearance in the confession. Eusebius often refers to the *descensus*, mostly in line with the historical development, but it really is Athanasius who needs our attention. It was this influential thinker who stepped forward as the most important defender of the faith against the Arian heresies. Now, if the *descensus* played any significant role in this debate one would expect Athanasius to mention it, also because of the fact that he was well aware of the *descensus* tradition. Apparently however, it played no critical role in the Christological debate. People really tried hard to find some polemical explanation for including the *descensus* in the confession, and obviously they tried to find it in the then current theological debate. It was seen by some as aimed against Apollinaris, by others as against Arian, or against docetism and gnosticism, or as an attempt to provide some basis for the idea of a purgatory. All of these attempts have been refuted and adequately been proved to be conjecture. There is no material evidence for any of these. The most likely reason could be the fact that Sirmium carried a very strong conciliatory undertone, and the inclusion of the *descensus* could be seen as a strengthening of the unity of the church. The fact that it was well known in both the East and the West and that it was a popular and well loved expression of the comprehensive work of Christ could, and probably had provided an instance of complete agreement.

It was only after its inclusion that Athanasius used it as an argument proving the deity of Christ. The same is the case with Epiphanius' use of it against Arian and Apollinaris. This type of dealing with the *descensus* was continued in the thought of Cyril of Jerusalem, Hilary, Ambrose, Jerome and others.

On the other hand the parallel line of development also continued, *i.e.* the lively, colourful, detailed and spectacular descriptions of the *descensus* in specific types or genres of literature (poems, songs, meditations, sermons, *etc. cf.* Firmicus Maternus, Carmina Nisibena, Aphraates, *etc.*).

In neither of these two traditions do we find any significant connection between *descensus* and universalism, the only exception being the case of Origen. Before we give a brief survey of the different motives put forward for the *descensus*, the form, structure and intention of *descensus* language need our attention.

Form, Structure and Intention
There is a wide variety in the form, genre, intention and nature of the articulation and expression of the content of religious beliefs. The way we phrase and act our faith in prayer and worship for example is not the same as the way we do it in witness, confession, doxology, proclamation, praise, lamentation or song. There are different elementary forms or genres of the expression of faith. It is of particular importance to take into account the distinctive structure and genre of such expressions, because it determines in a fundamental way the real and true intention, the function and also the final meaning to be conveyed. This state of affairs has important consequences for interpretation and understanding.

First it issues a stern warning against one-sided theoretical or doctrinal interpretations of all different kinds of expressions, and secondly, following from the preceding, also a caution against all attempts to simply translate such expressions in doctrinal terms. This easily results, as so often happened in the tradition of Western theology, in one-dimensional, theoretical-doctrinal and a strongly reduced and therefore impoverished rendering of the original.

The implication this has on the understanding of any historical expression of faith content is that it is necessary to take into account, not only the time, culture, general prevailing religions and theological climate, the theological issues at stake, and the general view of world and life, but also the distinct elementary form or genre of expressions. Schlink (24f.) and others explored this subject in great depth. The real problem of modern theological interpretation is that it finds it hard to deal in a proper way with the historical basis of material which now forms our doctrines. That applies also to the Apostolicum, of which the *descensus* forms a part. The Apostolicum is a concentration of doxology and doctrine, prayer and witness, and contains a richness and fulness of confession which unfortunately was lost in time. First to go was the doxological aspect with the increasing emphasis on 'true and pure' doctrine and the shift from the *act* of confession to the *doctrine about* the true confession (Du Toit 196). Schlink is of the opinion that the 'doctrinal' or 'dogmatic' statements of the early church had a definite doxological structure (Schlink 82). What really is important to take into account is the fact that transferring an expression from one elementary form or genre into another also has consequences for the content transferred.

We have seen that *descensus* stories from the ancient cultures and religions always came in the form of myths and stories which reflected the 'philosophy' about life and death, *i.e.* the deeply rooted desire to come to grips with death in one way or the other. It touched on the most central issue for every human being, and therefore the modern conception of 'myth', 'story', or 'legend' is a gross misconception of the seriousness of what lies behind it, and therefore also in many cases a serious inability to 'read' the real meaning. Now of course exactly the same will apply to the 'mythical' forms encountered in the early church.

References to she'ol in the Old Testament occur mostly in poetic, hymnal and rhetoric parts, especially in songs of thanksgiving or lamentation (Wächter 50), avoiding the elaborate and spectacular language and images of the Umwelt. This trend was again picked up by the apocryphal apocalyptic literature. The *descensus* was very much at home in esoteric, allegorical and cryptic accounts, interspersed with fantastic visions, dreams and cataclysmic events. In this respect Kelly made the observation that the *descensus* particularly developed in Eastern thought and was eventually taken up in the *credo* under the influence of the Eastern church (379). Recently also Brändle stressed the same point, referring to the fact that Sirmium was part of the Eastern church, and that the *descensus* only appeared in 404 in Western confessions (60). Mark of Arethusa, the author, came from the East, and used as his model the baptismal creed from Antioch. This church of course was strongly focused on the liturgy, and its religious expressions thoroughly moulded by the structure of song and worship. 'Doctrine' was heard as confession and doxology and not as the metaphysical, ontological statements of the Western mind.

This coincides with the observation of Kroll that the *descensus* was prominent in *liturgical texts*, especially from the end of the second century. Even at earlier stages the *descensus* featured in hymns and songs, some of them from late-Jewish, gnostic and apocryphal sources, but taken over and revised by the early Christians (Nassene psalm, Odes of Solomon). It can be demonstrated that the *descensus* in the early church found its proper *locus* in mystical, liturgical, poetical and lyrical literature and practice, accommodating the pious fantasy and poetic freedom of the believers. The aim is to assure them of the overwhelming significance of the death and resurrection of Christ, and dramatic and forceful effects are obtained through the use of traditional motives: spectacular scenes, sound, noise, clashes, colour, banners, personifying of underworld powers, topographical detail, *etc.* (*cf.* Melito of Sardes).

It is perfectly conceivable that motives, phrases and concepts from *descensus* stories from the earliest, even pre-Christian, times gradually became well-known expressions which worked their way into the very fibre of religious and other language, eventually also in Christendom. There is however definite reluctance in the Old Testament, the New Testament and the theology of the early church to also take over the mythological and fantastic decor of the *descensus* idea. In this particular line of thought the *descensus*, we could say, was thoroughly de-mythologized. This tradition continued for centuries in the church, very happily alongside the other tradition of dramatic-poetic *descensus* extravaganzas. This co-existence can very aptly be demonstrated, even in the theology and preaching of Martin Luther. I am of course referring to the well-known sermon of Luther in this regard, *i.e.* Torgau Easter sermon, in which he described the *descensus* of Christ in vivid and colourful strokes, employing the motives of the fantastic depictions known to him – the march of Christ through the gates, banners flying, the flight of the evil forces *etc*. When asked later on whether he really believed that he replied with some indignation that it was not to be understood in dogmatic terms. It was a way, using specific non-dogmatic language, to bring over a sense or awareness of the full extent of the salvific work of Christ, especially 'für Kindern und Einfältigen'. It is very easy, he said, to ask very clever questions, for example why the banner did not catch fire and the like. But, in dogmatic terms, Jesus descended nowhere!

What we have here are two different modes of religious expression.

Motives

Finally, one has to look at the different motives for using the idea of *descensus* or the *descensus* stories themselves.

The earliest motive actually was no motive at all. In many instances it was simply synonymous with dying or with *being dead*. To die meant to automatically become part of the realm of the dead, so that we should not speak of it as two separate events. It was only after and because this view was firmly established that other motives could be linked with the *descensus* of Jesus.

The main development in this regard had to do with Christ's work of *redemption and salvation*. The earliest motive for his *descensus* was to continue what he was doing on earth, *i.e. preaching*. This also provided the opportunity to accommodate another motive, namely the concern about the *faithful of the Old Testament*: prophets, patriarchs and believers who died before Christ. His preaching was mainly seen as an announcement of his victory, and therefore a confirmation and fulfilment of their faith and hope. In time this activity became associated with their *liberation* from the underworld, at first without any violence, but later on connected to an almost military operation and violent *struggle or clash*. Within this complex of motives also the appearance or *epiphany* of Christ in the underworld acquired the importance of a separate motive. If ever there was an opportunity to be seized for the propagation of *universalism*, it certainly was the *descensus*, who actually begged to be exploited for this cause. As we have seen, however, it never became part of the teaching and faith of the early church. Actually only one individual, Origen, could be found to do this. On the contrary, in time the very idea of *descensus* became a powerful aid in emphasizing the reality of hell and the eternal judgement of God.

In another sense, however, it was indeed utilized to demonstrate the *extent* and *comprehensiveness* of Christ's work of salvation – a 'universalism' of quite another kind! To the early church his work was of such a radical nature that not only the living but also the dead in the underworld were affected; not only was it important for the life in heaven and on earth, but for the whole of cosmos, *i.e.* the underworld included. His victory was so total and complete that he could break open death from the inside, so to speak.

It was to be expected that polemical motives also should get involved. *Against docetism* the *descensus* was used to prove that Jesus really died and was subjected to death in all its consequences, thus in turn proving the full and true human nature of the Saviour. At the same time it was a powerful way of demonstrating the fact that Jesus was also truly God.

In conclusion: there seems to be no connection between *descensus* and universalism in the early church, with the possible exception of Origen, despite the fact that it almost begged to be used in that way. All evidence rather suggests that it played a role in giving special form to the above-mentioned motives, not in theoretical-systematic language, but in language aimed at the minds and hearts of pious believers. As such it represents a form of religious expression which happily and without tension existed alongside the more systematic tradition of thought. To have used the *descensus* as a doctrinal or dogmatic proof for something like universalism would be an illegitimate attempt to translate one fundamental genre of religious expression into another and would result in a distortion not only of form but also of content.

Bibliography
W. Bieder, *Die Vorstellung von der Höllenfahrt Jesu Christi*, Zurich, 1949.

Von W. Brändle, Hinabgestiegen in das Reich des Todes, in *Kerygma und Dogma*, Vol. 35, 1989, p. 54-68.

R.H. Charles, *Eschatology. The doctrine of a future life in Israel, Judaism and Christianity*, New York, 1963.

D.A. Du Toit, 'neergedaal ter helle...' Uit die geskiedenis van 'n interpretasieprobleem (ThD thesis), Kampen, 1971.

G.P. Hartvelt, *Patronen van Interpretatie*, Kampen, 1966.

J.N.D. Kelly, *Early Christian Creeds*, London, 1960.

K. Rahner, Auferstehung des Fleisches, in *Schriften zur Theologie II*, Zürich & Köln, 1958.

J. Ratzinger, *Einführung in das Christentum*, München, 1968.

E. Schlink, *Der kommende Christus und die kirchliche Traditionen*, Göttingen, 1961.

E.B. Tylor, *Primitive culture. Researches into the development of mythology, philosophy, religion, language, art and custom*, 2 Vols, London, 1929.

H. Vorgsimler, 1966. Vragen over Christus' nederdaling ter helle, in *Concilium*, jr 2/1966, p. 140.

L. Wächter, *Der Tod im Alten Testament*, Stuttgart, 1967.

4

The Nineteenth and Twentieth Century Debates about Hell and Universalism

David J. Powys

Some questions have many truthful answers; others will admit only one. To contemplate the fate of the unrighteous is to confront a question which Christian theologians seem to agree can have only one answer. Yet theologians actually hold a great many positions on this question. At the extremities of this range are those which may be loosely termed 'hell' and 'universalism'. The following is not offered as an attempt to identify the correct answer. Rather, it is intended to provide an analysis which may help to identify the dynamics which have caused the present confused state of the question, and so offer pointers to a future more satisfactory resolution of this matter.

There are three parts to the following, each with its own aim. In the first, the range of positions now espoused by Christian theologians is delineated. The resultant taxonomy is comprehensive though not exhaustive. It is concerned mainly with English-speaking theologians, many of them British. This largely reflects the geography of the debate, at least in recent times. The second section is longer, falling into several parts. Its aim is to identify the roots of the diversity of viewpoint. It will be largely devoted to debates in the literature dating from around the turn of the century. Arising from consideration of the general consensus which pertained up until the late nineteenth century, and of the debates which surrounded a series of challenges to that consensus, an hypothesis will be advanced which will seek to account for the range of views that now exists.[1]

An analogy may help, though not if it is pushed too far. Finding the answer to the question of the fate of the unrighteous in our present theological predicament may be likened to searching for a key, but unfamiliar, document in a pile of other papers. The first task is to discover the extent of the pile and so establish the full range of possible locations of the vital document. The second task is to analyse the pile, sorting the papers and trying to establish the cause of the confusing proliferation. The third task is to discover means of identifying the vital document and then of ensuring that it will not again be buried. The third part of the analogy points to the aim of the third section: to briefly indicate the way forward in unravelling the pile of 'other answers', and so to facilitate the lasting resolution of the debate about the fate of the unrighteous.[2]

---

1   Whether that hypothesis can account for the *process* of the debate as well as its *outcome* remains a moot point. It is less verifiable in relation to process than outcome, not least because the books and articles written on the subject give rather more access to people's conclusions than to the means by which they arrived at them.

2   No attempt will be made to trace the earlier history of the debate. Though its roots may be found in the Patristic era, only in the last century or so, following a long hiatus, has it gained strong momentum. Rightly or wrongly, throughout most of the history of Christendom, there has been little debate about the fate of the unrighteous: one view has enjoyed a rarely challenged dominance.

The Range of Contemporary Positions on the Fate of the Unrighteous

A three-fold classification is often employed to chart the range of positions advanced by Christian theologians on the matter of the fate of the unrighteous. Under this scheme the three options are *unending punishment, conditional immortality* and *universal salvation*. But such a classification fails to accommodate all the data. To do so, a classification which includes at least twelve positions is required. Such a classification can take the following form:

Table A: A Taxonomy of Modern Positions on the Fate of the Unrighteous

1. Unrighteous will suffer everlasting physical punishment
2. Unrighteous will suffer everlasting mental punishment
3. Unrighteous will survive death but then be annihilated
4. Unrighteous will undergo discipline and correction after death
5. Unrighteous will be eternally separated from God
6. Unrighteous will have continuing freedom and potential for repentance
7. Unrighteous will be resurrected to learn their error and then suffer natural consequence – death
8. Unrighteous will be resurrected for physical punishment, then die
9. Unrighteous will be resurrected for mental punishment, then die
10. Unrighteous will neither survive nor rise from death
11. Unrighteous will survive death but not rise from death, suffering a hell of their own creation
12. Unrighteous will be raised to eternal life

The Derivation of the Diversity of Views

Through the Middle Ages the Western understanding of
human destiny came to be conformed almost entirely to the
dictates of a system of retributive justice wedded to the
conviction of universal immortality. To die was not to cease to
be but rather to pass immediately into judgment and thence to
reward or punishment, that is heaven or hell, everlastingly.
The one ameliorating factor was the expectation that many
would reach heaven by means of purgatory. The fate of the
unrighteous, however, was clear: they would be subjected to
unending punishment. Thus Queen Mary I of England
defended her persecution of her opponents with the words 'As
the souls of heretics are hereafter to be eternally burning in
hell, there can be nothing more proper than for me to imitate
the Divine vengeance by burning them on earth.'[3]

The Reformation brought many changes, but no effective
challenge to the dominance of the Augustinian doctrine of
unending punishment.[4] This survived virtually unscathed,

---

[3] W.R. Alger, *The Destiny of the Soul: A Critical History of the
Doctrine of a Future Life* (Boston: Roberts Bros, 1880, 10th ed), p.
515.

[4] L.E. Froom, *The Conditionalist Faith of Our Fathers* (2 vols,
Washington: Review and Herald, 1966, 1965) volume 2, pp. 73-79,
argues that Martin Luther rejected the Roman doctrine of the
immortality of the soul and held that those 'in Christ' sleep during
the interval before the resurrection, and that William Tyndale (see
volume 2, pp. 93-96) refuted the Roman teaching that souls pass
immediately to heaven, purgatory or hell at death. In this matter their
views seem to have had little effect.

probably because Reformation theology was as firmly grounded in retributive concepts as pre-Reformation thought.[5]

Lotz has offered the following outline of the 'classical form of Christian eschatology as this gradually attained definition in the period from A.D. 600 to 1600':

1. *temporal death,* understood as the separation of body and soul;
2. the *particular judgment* whereby God passes immediate sentence on the soul at the time of death, assigning it to heaven, purgatory, or hell;
3 . the so-called *intermediate state* which, consequent upon the particular judgment pertains to the state or condition of the disembodied souls between death and the resurrection at the Last Day;
4. the *Parousia* or second advent of Christ, when he will return in glory as the world's visible King and the agent of God's general judgment on the living and the dead;
5. the *universal resurrection* of the dead, when their souls will be reunited with their bodies;
6. the *general judgment,* or Last Day, or Great Assize, when God's ultimate sentence of acceptance or rejection will be delivered on humanity as a whole, as well as on the body and soul of each individual;

---

5   Thus S.G.F. Brandon, *The Judgement of the Dead* (New York: Charles Scribners' Sons, 1967), p. 132, writes: 'Despite their rejection of belief in Purgatory, the Reformers were as convinced and as zealous as the Catholics about the prospect of divine judgment, and the reality of Heaven and Hell. But, by abandoning the idea of Purgatory, they landed themselves in the very difficulties that Purgatory had been invented to solve.'

7.   the *end of the world,* usually understood as a cosmic conflagration;
8.   *eternal damnation,* or hell; and
9.   *eternal life,* or heaven.[6]

Lotz' systematization is instructive, particularly in the way it reveals the essential incoherence of the traditional scheme, and highlights the weak biblical warrant for certain of its aspects.[7] Its incoherence was effectively overcome by the virtual neglect of the more biblical elements. The essence of the traditional doctrine of the fate of the unrighteous is to be found in the first three and last two elements: the souls of the departed are judged at death and then proceed for ever to existence either in heaven or in hell. The remainder were retained, even if only in form, because they simply could not be dismissed.

The traditional position on the fate of the unrighteous had four elements. It held that that fate would be *immediate, unending, physical, and retributive.* It came to be directly challenged in three of these aspects. The challenges concerned the matters of *duration, quality, finality and purpose.* The way in which these challenges impinged upon the four definitive elements of the traditional position may be set out as follows.

---

6   D.W. Lotz, 'Heaven and Hell in the Christian Tradition', *Religion in Life,* 48, 1979, pp. 78,79.
7   This traditional scheme included five elements which are of dubious biblical warrant: the first three and the last two. The intervening four, that is the fourth, fifth, sixth and seventh, by contrast, are well attested in the New Testament.

Table B: The Challenge to the Traditional Position

the elements of the traditional position	the dynamics of the challenge
IMMEDIATE ————————————	little or no challenge[8]
DURATION **UNENDING**	
FINALITY	
PHYSICAL ————————————————— **QUALITY**	
RETRIBUTIVE————————————————— **PURPOSE**	

---

8   Those who denied universal immortality did not follow their logic so far as to reject consistently the notion of immediate post-mortem existence, though many participated in the challenge concerning duration. Some who denied the immortality of the soul were nevertheless strangely willing to accept the notion of an 'intermediate state' and to so allow the immediate aspect of the traditional position to go unchallenged.

Every one of the twelve positions outlined above may be regarded as the outworking of one or more of these challenges to the traditional position. These challenges are now considered in turn.[9]

Duration

The contention that divine punishment of the unrighteous would be unending proved less and less tenable in the mid to late nineteenth century on account of the dominant philosophical themes of the value of the individual and the expectation of progress, and of developments in societal views on penal practice. There arose two distinct alternatives with regard to *duration*. One of these accepted the preceding doctrine's anthropology and modified its theology. It accepted the presupposition of universal immortality, but rejected the view that God would punish everlastingly. The second rejected or at least qualified the previous anthropology and thus removed much of the tension created by the previous theology. In dismissing the presupposition of universal immortality it removed the necessity of God punishing everlastingly. The first alternative followed in the steps of Gregory of Nyssa. The second took the path travelled by Irenaeus.

Universal Immortality Assumed

In 1877 Dean Farrar of Westminster preached a series of sermons in which he challenged the traditional doctrine in several of its aspects. He objected to the contention that any

---

9 No attempt is made in what follows to treat developments in strict chronological order since the processes were both concurrent and interactive.

other than continuing impenitents would suffer everlastingly.[10] In his exposition of what he termed 'the eternal hope' he called for the substantial excision of the 'everlasting' from the doctrine of everlasting torment.[11] This challenge to the view

---

10 In prefacing the sermons for publication, which he did in the context of the strong controversy which they provoked, he went somewhat beyond the sermons in repudiating what he saw as four dark accretions to the true doctrine of Hell:

> These four elements - which make the popular view far darker than that held in the Roman Church, and far darker even than that of St. Augustine - are 1, the physical torments, the material agonies, the *'sapiens ignis'* of Eternal Punishment; 2, the supposition of its necessarily endless duration for all who incur it; 3, the opinion that it is thus incurred by the vast mass of mankind; and 4, that it is a doom passed irreversibly at the moment of death on all who die in a state of sin.

F.W. Farrar, *Eternal Hope, Five Sermons Preached in Westminster Abbey, November and December 1877* (New York: E.P. Dutton and Co., 1878) p. xvi. Farrar's views will be considered in more detail below under discussion of the issue of *finality*.

11 Farrar was not opposed to the contention that some might suffer everlastingly, but inferred that the opportunity for post-mortem repentance would make the numbers of such people very small.

> I have never denied - nay in spite of deep and yearning hope, I have expressly admitted the possibility of even *endless* misery for those who abide in the determined impenitence of final and unwilling sin.

Farrar, *Eternal Hope*, p.x.

> I have never denied, and do not now deny, the eternity of punishment ... though I understand the word eternity in a sense far higher than can be degraded into the vulgar meaning of endlessness.

Farrar, *Mercy and Judgment: A Few Last Words on Christian Eschatology with reference to Dr Pusey's 'What is of Faith'* (London: MacMillan and Co., 1881), p. 3.

that the unrighteous suffer unending torment arose not from a dismissal of the notion of universal immortality, but rather from the expectation that God would give post-mortem opportunities for the unrighteous to repent. Thus his challenge with regard to duration was at the same time also a challenge as to finality.

Farrar received opposition, not from those of differing anthropology, but from those who, while sharing his assumption of universal immortality, did not share his optimism that there would be ongoing post-mortem opportunity for repentance. E.B. Pusey was Farrar's most strident critic. Their disagreement was not about immortality, for in this they were fully agreed. Their difference had to do with the nature of God's mercy. In terms of an analysis offered by one of their contemporaries, these represented two wings of the one group.

> The array of believers in the immortality of the soul is divided into two wings; the first comprising those who maintain the eternity of sin and misery, as the necessary result of the eternity of the sinner; the second, those who maintain that the Divine Goodness will eventually recover all immortal beings from sin – and its direful consequences in hell.[12]

In time these two wings would become identifiable as the advocates of universalism on the one hand and of the

---

12 E. White *Life in Christ*, 3rd ed. (London: Elliott Stock, 1878), p. 438. White continues, p. 439:

> To each party the primary truth - that which must on no account be sacrificed, and which must give the law to the meaning of all judicial words used by prophets and apostles - is the absolute eternity of the soul of Man.

traditional doctrine of eternal punishment (albeit qualified) on the other. Farrar distanced himself from universalism,[13] but Pusey could see where the logic would lead and hence opposed Farrar as an incipient universalist.[14] Farrar and Pusey serve to point to the two basic alternatives concerning the fate of the unrighteous adopted by those convinced of the immortality of the soul: universal salvation and eternal punishment.[15]

---

13 *Eternal Hope*, p. 33: 'I cannot preach the certainty of Universalism.' He continues, referring to the omission of the forty-second article and concluding 'The omission of this Article leaves even "Universalism" an open question. But as far as I am concerned the Article would not have touched my view at all, for I am not a Universalist.'

14 See E.B. Pusey, *What is of Faith as to Everlasting Punishment* (London: James Parker and Co., 1880) pp. 25,26.

15 G.G. Stokes, *Conditional Immortality* (London: James Nisbet and Co. Ltd) p. 10 makes plain his view of the foundations of the traditional doctrine of endless torments when he writes:

> it is, as I believe, no part of the faith once delivered to the saints. It rests upon the combination of the dogma of the immortality of the soul, with what to me seems to be the clear teaching of Scripture, that the perdition of the lost is final and irreparable.

Pusey, who unlike Stokes assumes natural immortality, argues that the logic of the matter means that there are just two options for the unrighteous: restoration or endless punishment. He will not allow Farrar to deny both, because:

> If man is admitted to be immortal, and punishment is not to be endless, there is no other conclusion but that he should be restored. I am thankful that Dr. Farrar is not an universalist. There is no end of human inconsistencies. But I fear that his book will teach Universalism, since he denounces so energetically the only faith which can resist it.

Universal Immortality Denied

There was another way of tackling the question of duration,
though only for those not wedded to universal immortality.
Those who dismissed this presupposition were able to
overcome much of the theological tension involved in the
doctrine of everlasting torment. While some denied any post-
mortem existence for the unrighteous, many others held that
the unrighteous would be granted a finite post-mortem
existence, but then be destroyed. Generally such convictions
arose from the belief that none will gain life after death save
by the specific will of Christ. The denial of universal
immortality thus took various forms, but in whichever form, it
served to obviate the logical necessity of the impenitent
suffering endlessly.

This broad position was propounded with a new eloquence
beginning in the latter half of last century. But it was not
completely new; it had affinity to the view of Irenaeus. Froom
has demonstrated that throughout church history there has
been a succession of people who espoused this position (he
terms it 'Conditionalism'), or at least rejected the doctrine of

---

The 'faith' to which he refers is the faith that divine punishment is
everlasting! (Pusey, *Everlasting Punishment*, p. 27). But Pusey's
position is by no means as harsh as it may appear, because he
explicitly rejects the view in which he holds Farrar to have been
schooled: the view that the vast mass of mankind will incur eternal
punishment. Referring to that view he says that it 'has no solid
foundation whatever; it exists, probably, only in the rigid Calvinistic
school, in which Dr. Farrar was educated, and from which his present
opinions are a reaction' (Pusey, *Everlasting Punishment*, p. 6.). Thus
while Gehenna was eternal rather than temporary (Pusey, p. 102), it
would presumably be but thinly populated.

everlasting torment ('Eternal Tormentism').[16] He cites
leading Anglicans, Edmund Law (1703-1787), Bishop of

---

16 This is the chief purpose of Froom's two massive volumes. He finds
    that three competing streams of eschatology may be traced
    throughout church history: Conditionalism (Conditional
    Immortality); Eternal Tormentism (Endless Torment of Wicked);
    and Universal Restorationism (Universal Restoration of the
    Wicked). The latter two were both premissed on the assumption of
    'Universal Innate Immortality'. His work is succinctly summarised
    in two pictorial charts found in volume one pp. 524-7 and volume
    two pp. 6-9 (L.E. Froom, *The Conditionalist Faith*). His work
    suffers from lack of clarity at points. In his enthusiasm to
    demonstrate the degree of historical support for conditionalism, he
    sometimes claims the support of people who, while opposed to
    everlasting torment were by no means inclined towards conditional
    immortality. F.W. Farrar is a case in point. Froom devotes nine
    pages to Farrar (vol. 2 pp. 404-412) and quotes him as admitting 'the
    ultimate extinction of the being of sinners appears to be taught by
    the literal meaning of many passages of Scripture' (p. 412). But he
    neglects to state that Farrar rejected such literal interpretation and
    wrote of conditional immortality:

    > it seems to me to rest too entirely on the supposed invariable
    > meaning of a few words and to press that meaning too far; it
    > rejects that instinctive belief in Immortality which has been
    > found in almost every age and every race of man; and while it
    > relieves the soul from the crushing horror involved in the
    > conception of endless torment, it still - if I understand it rightly
    > - leaves us with the ghastly conclusion that God will raise the
    > wicked from the dead only that they may be tormented and at
    > last destroyed (*Eternal Hope,* p.xiv).

    A second example of this is Froom's appeal to the writings of J.A.T.
    Robinson (Froom, *Conditionalist Faith* vol. 2 pp. 849-851). Whilst
    Robinson rejects doctrines of natural immortality ('Doctrines of this
    type are the spiritual corollary of the pantheistic religions which
    supervened upon the bankruptcy of polytheism.' J.A.T. Robinson, *In*

Carlisle,[17] and Richard Whately (1787-1863), Archbishop of Dublin.[18] These were known proponents of conditionalism who nevertheless gained acceptance within Anglicanism. He also cites John Foster (1770-1843), Baptist minister and writer,[19] and Henry Dobney (died 1864), another Baptist minister,[20] both of whom wrote publicly against endless torment from a conditionalist position.

But it was Edward White (1819-1898), in Froom's judgment, who 'more than any other individual in the nineteenth century... was instrumental in bringing the principles of Conditional Immortality to prominence and respect.'[21] From the time of his ordination within the Congregational Church he advocated this position with strength and consistency in teaching and writing, publishing his convictions in his *Life in Christ* in 1846.[22] This generated a storm of indignation. 'He was immediately castigated as a heretic, and for a time it looked as though his service in the Congregational ministry was ended.'[23] But after moving to

---

the End God, (London: Collins, 1968,) p. 89), the position he finally assumes is of universal immortality.

17 Froom, *Conditionalist Faith*, vol. 2, pp. 231-234.

18 Froom, *Conditionalist Faith*, vol. 2, pp. 261-265.

19 Froom, *Conditionalist Faith*, vol. 2, pp. 318-320. Froom there anticipates and dismisses the claim that Foster was a Universalist.

20 Froom, *Conditionalist Faith*, vol. 2, p. 320-322. See also Rowell, *Hell and the Victorians*, p. 183.

21 Froom, *Conditionalist Faith*, vol. 2, p. 322.

22 E.White, *Life in Christ* 3rd ed. (London: Elliott Stock: 1878).

23 Froom, *Conditionalist Faith*, vol. 2, p. 327. Rowell, *Hell and the Victorians*, p. 188 states that the book's publication

caused a minor storm in Dissenting circles, and White himself wrote that it had not been seriously examined but the hysterical condemnation had led to his exclusion from every Nonconformist

North London and founding an independent congregation, White was able through diplomacy and reasoned argument and without compromise, to regain respect within Congregationalism and, indeed, to be appointed chairman of the London Congregational Union.[24]

White regarded the doctrine of the universal immortality of the soul as unfounded in Scripture,[25] and as the source of grave theological error:

Here, in the popular doctrine of the soul's immortality, is the *fons et origo* of a system of theological error; ...in its denial we return at once to the scientific truth and to sacred Scripture; at the same time clearing the way for the right understanding of the object of the Incarnation, of the nature and issue of redemption in the Life Eternal, and of the true doctrine of divine judgment on the unsaved.[26]

Despite this, White envisaged an intermediate state for both the righteous and the unrighteous.[27] This expectation seems

---

pulpit in the country. Although he found himself more and more at the centre of theological controversy, he was sufficiently well established at Hereford to remain there until 1851, when he moved to London.

24 Froom, *Conditionalist Faith*, vol. 2, pp. 327-329. Froom includes amongst White's circle of friends such respected figures as R.F. Weymouth, David Livingstone and William E. Gladstone (p. 328).

25 White, *Life in Christ*, pp. v-vii, 78 and p. 77:
Of the survival of souls in a Sheol, or Hades, it seems to speak often; of the actual eternal survival of the saved it also often speaks; but it never once places the eternal hope of mankind on the abstract dogma of the Immortality of the Soul, or declares that Man will live for ever because he is naturally Immortal.

26 White, *Life in Christ*, p. 70.

27 E. White, *Life in Christ*, pp. 311, 312:

to have been the product of the distinction which he drew between physical death (which the soul survives) and spiritual death (in which the soul is destroyed). His admission of the intermediate state may account for the degree of tolerance that his views came to receive.[28] It had the

---

> The eternal life begun knows no break. There is no black line in that spectrum. The light is continuous, and the spiritual inhabitant of the 'tabernacle' (2 Peter 1.), though he may 'put it off', can never die.
>
> The survival of *sinful men* in death seems also to hold an important place in the Scripture system;
>
> (1) In order that a continuity may be established between the personality of the man who sinned in time and that of the man who is to be raised for judgment at the last day ...
>
> (2) In order that in some cases the spirit may suffer in Hades for the sins of a lifetime.
>
> (3) That in other cases the ignorant rejection of God in life may be remedied by the evangelization of 'spirits in prison'.
>
> (4) That a special terror and awfulness may be assigned to the second death, in distinction from the first, - in this, that under the first death there was no 'killing of the soul,' that tremendous and final stroke being reserved as the last penalty of transgression under the gospel, in the 'damnation of Gehenna'.

28 Rowell (*Hell and the Victorians*, p. 197) quotes White in the columns of the *Christian World* in the 1870's defining two deaths,

> one in which the body is broken up, and the spirit which informed it taken away from it, while both the dust and the spirit remain in being - and another in which not only the life and individuality of the complex man is dissolved and destroyed, but also the very elements of conscious being are reduced to nothing. What we have taught is that both these modes of death are spoken of in Scripture and are called the first and second death.

White's rejection of natural immortality did not totally preclude the post-mortem survival of the soul. This possibly added to the

additional effect of allowing him to introduce the theme of post-mortem opportunity for repentance, a theme which gained much ground in the nineteenth century through the emphasis on the intermediate state,[29] and hence to challenge the traditional doctrine not only with regard to duration but also to finality.

White and Henry Constable (1816-1891) are often regarded as sharing the same views. They did both question the duration of divine punishment by challenging belief in universal immortality. But they were not agreed in all respects, as is clear in Constable's rejection of belief in the intermediate state.[30] They were agreed in anticipating a finite post-mortem

---

acceptability of his view. It is in clear contrast to Constable's position, see below.

29 Rowell finds that one of the chief results of late nineteenth century reflection on hell was that the intermediate state gained a prominence which it had never enjoyed before, *Hell and the Victorians*, pp. 215, 6.

30 H. Constable, *Hades: or the Intermediate State of Man* (London: Kellaway and Co, 1875) p.153:

> The immortality of the soul is the source of the wide-spread errors on the intermediate state, as it is the source of the errors of Origen and Augustine on the nature of future punishment. But here we must include in our condemnation very many of those who agree with us in our views on the latter question. What we *now* mean by the immortality of the soul is not the opinion that it will never die at any future time in hell, but the opinion that it does not die at the period of the first death, and survives the body throughout the intermediate or Hades state, and at the resurrection of the body rejoins its own old companion having never, up to that time, died itself. There are very many who believe that the soul will die in the scene of punishment, subsequent to resurrection, who do not believe that it dies

retribution for the unrighteous. They were not agreed, however, about when this would occur. White had located this during the intermediate state, anticipating a complete end in the second death.[31] Constable, in contrast, located this retribution after the resurrection.

Resurrection, the grandest act in God's dealings with man, is not the aimless, objectless, purposeless thing that our Platonic theology has made it. It gives life to man: to one man eternal life for his endless joy in praising God, to another man life for judgment and righteous retribution.[32]

Thus, both White and Constable held with the punishment of the unrighteous, but denied that this would be unending. Theirs and similar views sparked great controversy on account of their questioning of the deeply entrenched presupposition of universal immortality.[33] There was little real

---

> before. These we hold to be erroneous, as well as those who hold that the soul will never die in hell.

It would seem that Constable is criticising precisely the views of White outlined above.

31   See White, *Life in Christ* p. 311, his second point as quoted in footnote 30 above.

32   Constable, *Hades*, p. 171.

33   In describing the tenacity of this belief White, *Life in Christ*, pp. 435, 436, maintained

> In accounting, therefore, for the rise and establishment of the doctrine of the immortality of the soul in Christendom, with its logical consequence of the doctrine of endless misery, we have not far to seek for sufficient causes. It was not Platonism alone that operated in this direction. All the special influences of Eastern and Western thought were vigorously at work from the very beginning of the gospel to contravene the chief peculiarity of the Christian Revelation, – its declaration that immortality is the gift of God, through the incarnation, to regenerate men alone. Against this humbling 'form of doctrine' all the

interchange between those who dismissed and those who retained this presupposition. Thus writers like Alger,[34] Salmond[35] and Plumtre[36] treated the arguments of the

authority of the loftiest speculation of both Europe and Asia was arrayed with overshadowing influence. Never had such a notion been heard of, from the Pillars of Hercules to the farthest East, as the dependence of mankind for eternal life on a Jewish artisan who claimed to be 'God manifest in the flesh'! All the old religions of the world were against it – all the old philosophies. It was the last lesson which even the faithful disciples of Christ would consent to learn.

34 W.R. Alger, *The Destiny of the Soul: A Critical History of the Doctrine of a Future Life*, 10th ed. (Boston: Roberts Bros, 1880) p. 546:

Some have believed in the annihilation of the wicked after they should have undergone just punishment proportioned to their sins... All that need be said in opposition to it is that it is an arbitrary device to avoid the intolerable horror of the doctrine of endless misery, unsupported by proof, extremely unsatisfactory in many of its bearings, and really not needed to achieve the consummation desired.

35 S.D.F. Salmond, *The Christian Doctrine of Immortality*, 5th ed. (Edinburgh: T. & T. Clark, 1913) p. 488, thus dismisses the conditionalist position:

It ignores or mistakes at the same time the whole conception of an after-world that lies at the basis of the revelation recorded in Scripture. They to whom the revelation was addressed did not think of man as ceasing to be when he dies. The deeds and words which make the revelation neither presuppose nor indicate that death is an end to man. The dead man does not pass out of existence: he passes into another existence.

36 E.H. Plumtre, *The Spirits in Prison and Other Studies on the Life after Death*, 5th ed. (London: Wm. Isbister Ltd, 1886) on page 16 says this of conditional immortality:

conditionalists with sheer disdain, and White complained that his critics refused to enter into detail and did little more than make authoritative assertions 'on the immortality of the soul'.[37]

Rowell has observed of people like White and Constable that 'The adherents of systematic conditionalism were almost entirely to be found within the Augustinian-Calvinistic tradition, and placed a high value on the verbal inspiration of the Bible'. He suggests that other sections of the church had alternative ways of 'modifying the rigours of eternal punishment'.[38] Rowell is probably wrong in defining the theological orientation of the 'conditionalists' so narrowly, and in suggesting that the influence of the Augustinian-Calvinistic tradition was restricted to one grouping within the debate.

Rowell's observation is correct, however, to the extent that he suggests that the debate about everlasting torment was often conducted in separate circles. This can be seen in the two major challenges concerning the the duration of

---

> Whatever support that view may obtain from a narrow and almost slavish literalist in its interpretation of Scripture, it must be rejected as at variance with the intuitive beliefs which all God's later revelation presupposes, at variance also with the meaning of Scripture when we pass beyond the letter to the truths which it represents.

37 White, *Life in Christ*, p. iii.
38 Rowell, *Hell and the Victorians*, p. 205:
> There seem to have been no High Anglican conditionalists. The reason for this is probably to be found in the fact that they already had their own ways of modifying the rigours of eternal punishment, through the advocacy of some form of purgatory. Likewise Broad Churchmen moved towards universalism, rather than towards the elaborate theories of conditionalism.

everlasting torment. There was not a great deal of debate between those, like Farrar, who accepted the notion of universal immortality but denied that God would punish everlastingly, and those, on the other hand, who rejected the doctrine of everlasting punishment because they rejected the presupposition of universal immortality.

The Matter of Quality

In Patristic times there had been acknowledgement that the pains of hell might be spiritual as well as physical and that some of the biblical language used to depict them might be metaphorical.[39] This aspect faded during the Middle, Reformation and post-Reformation Ages. The predominant and orthodox position during that period was that the fate of the unrighteous was to suffer unending physical punishment.[40] There was then, for a long time, no doubting that the unrighteous would suffer physical torment.

In the nineteenth century the *quality* of the suffering of the unrighteous began to be questioned. This was the second of the four points at which the traditional doctrine was subjected to modification.

In some quarters this modification occurred without justification or debate. Moorhead, writing of American Protestantism, finds that 'Virtually every defender of hell, especially after the Civil War, felt compelled to disclaim overly literal interpretations of "the worm that dieth not" and "the

---

39 *City of God,* Book 20, chapter 22 and Book 21, chapter 9.
40 J.N.D. Kelly, *Early Christian Doctrines* (San Francisco: Harper and Row, 1978 (5th ed)) pp. 484, 5.

fire that is not quenched"'.[41] But he finds that the real decline in the traditional hell came as a result of a silence about, rather than explicit attack upon, that doctrine.[42] White, whose concern was more with the matter of duration than quality, and who in fact held to a physical/bodily conception of the suffering of the unrighteous,[43] argues that it was chiefly by recourse to modification of this aspect that the doctrine of 'endless misery' remained tenable for its advocates.[44]

But in addition to this quiet shift of position on the matter of the quality of the suffering of the unrighteous, there was some public discussion. The chief parties were once again Farrar and Pusey, though some of F.D. Maurice's pronouncements

41 J.H. Moorhead, 'As though nothing at all happened': Death and Afterlife in Protestant Thought, 1840-1925', *Soundings*, 67, 1984, p.455.
42 Moorhead, 'Death and Afterlife', p. 457:
    The decline of hell, however, was not primarily the result of open questioning of the doctrine. The outspoken critics probably never accounted for more than a minority of Protestants. Far more important was a growing silence on the subject. Even those who adhered to the traditional notion often gave it merely a passing nod.
43 White, *Life in Christ*, pp. 351-5.
44 White, *Life in Christ*, p. 351:
    It would be extreme folly to allow the rhetorical extravagances of some teachers of *endless* torment to blind us to the fact, - if the New Testament does really teach it as a fact, - that God's judgment will be executed by an infliction of fearful severity if of limited duration. The effect of the tenet of endless suffering has naturally been to induce its advocates to soften as much as possible the threatenings of direct infliction, until at last, in this age, the very defence of the doctrine of endless misery has come to rest on a 'figurative' interpretation of the hell threatened in the Bible.

had been broadly relevant. The following reveals how far Maurice had moved from any notion of physical punishment.

What, then, is Death Eternal, but to be without God? What is that infinite dread which rises upon my mind, which I cannot banish from me, when I think of my own godlessness and lovelessness, – that I may become wholly separated from Love; become wholly immersed in selfishness and hatred? What dread can I have – ought I to have – besides this?[45]

Farrar, in the pursuit of a humane formulation of 'Eternal Hope', repudiated and condemned four elements of the 'popular view'. The first of these was 'the physical torments, the material agonies, the *"sapiens ignis"* of Eternal Punishment'.[46] In his 'Preface to the Thirtieth Thousand' of *Eternal Hope* he maintained that Pusey himself had indicated in a letter of 30/7/1880 that while holding to a belief in 'pains of sense' as well as 'pain of loss', he (Pusey) did not consider the former to be based on indisputable authority.[47] This would seem an accurate representation of Pusey's position.[48] In what way, then, did Farrar and Pusey disagree? The dispute was about whether or not belief in 'pains of sense' could be safely or responsibly rejected. Pusey, whilst agnostic about

---

45 F.D. Maurice, *Theological Essays*, p.437.
46 Farrar, *Eternal Hope*, p. xvi. The other three elements which he rejected were:
>   2, the supposition of its necessarily endless duration for all who incur it; 3, the opinion that it is thus incurred by the vast mass of mankind; and 4, that it is a doom passed irreversibly at the moment of death on all who die in a state of sin.

He rehearses these four repudiations in *Mercy and Judgment*, p. 176, there claiming essential agreement with Pusey.
47 Farrar, *Eternal Hope*, p. vii.
48 Pusey, *Everlasting Punishment*, p. 18.

the precise nature of hell, was keen to maintain the terror of hell, since he believed that it had caused much good.[49] He desired to maintain an intermediate position, dismissing both the exclusively metaphorical and exclusively literalist interpretations as unwarranted.[50] In this he provided a lonely defence of this aspect of the traditional doctrine, albeit in a most moderate form. Had it not been for his protest, the transition in the quality aspect of the traditional doctrine, at least in non-fundamentalist circles, might have occurred without a murmur.

Dearmer sought to discount biblical passages referring to physical punishment as textual interpolations.[51] He and Alger

49 Pusey, *Everlasting Punishment*, p. 19.
50 Pusey, *Everlasting Punishment*, p. 23:

> As to 'pains of sense', the Church has nowhere laid down as a matter of faith, the material character of the worm and the fire, or that they denote more than the gnawing of remorse. Although then it would be very rash to lay down dogmatically, that the 'fire' is not to be understood literally, as it has been understood almost universally by Christians, yet no one has a right to urge those representations, from which the imagination so shrinks, as a ground for refusing to believe in hell, since he is left free not to believe them.

51 P. Dearmer, *The Legend of Hell* (Cassell's: London, 1929) p. 224, though he does not really persist with this suggestion in his treatment of specific texts in the pages which follow. Alger, *Destiny of the Soul*, p. 520, 1, while not arguing for textual interference, nevertheless finds that much of the disputed material is foreign.

> The imagery of a subterranean hell of fire, brimstone, and undying worms, as used in the Scriptures of the New Testament, is the same as that drawn from heathen sources with modifications and employed by the Pharisees before the time of Christ and his disciples; and we must therefore, since neither

both argued that belief in physical post-mortem punishment was the product of the since discredited materialistic conception of the nature of the soul.[52] But it was not such arguments that sustained the challenge.

The fundamental reason that the traditional view was overturned in regard to quality was that fewer and fewer people were able to conceive of unending, divinely imposed, physical suffering. The tension could be relieved by abandoning one or other of three features of the traditional dogma: its unending duration (and hence finality), its physical quality, or its retributive purpose. The challenge regarding quality was the first to succeed. It is arguable that it succeeded where the challenge with regard to duration had largely failed because it did not implicate other doctrines in the

---

Persians nor Pharisees were inspired, either suppose that this imagery was adopted by the apostles figuratively to convey moral truths, or else that they were left, in common with their countrymen, at least partially under the dominion of the errors of their time.

52   P. Dearmer, *The Legend of Hell* (Cassell's: London, 1929) p. 117 and Alger, *Destiny of the Soul*, pp. 520, 705:

The doctrine yet lingers by sheer force of prescription and unthinkingness, when the basis on which it originally rested has been dissipated. We know - great as our ignorance is, we know - that the soul is a pure immateriality.... What the spiritual personality becomes, how it exists, what it is susceptible of, when disembodied, no man knows. It is idle for any man, or any set of men to pretend to know. Unquestionably it is *not* capable of material confinement and penalties. The gross popular doctrine of hell as the fiery prison-house of the devil and his angels, and the condemned majority of mankind, therefore, fades into thin air and vanishes before the truth of the absolute spirituality of mind.

way in which the challenge regarding duration had implicated belief in universal immortality.

The Matter of Purpose

Once the traditional doctrine of unending physical punishment had been challenged with regard to the duration and the quality of the punishment, challenges of a more fundamental nature followed. Thus it was that even the *purpose* of the fate of the unrighteous came to be questioned.

It was inevitable that the revolution in penal theory associated with names such as Jeremy Bentham (1748-1832) should, in time, impinge upon the doctrine of post-mortem punishment. Penal practices and philosophies which had come to be regarded as unenlightened in the human arena could hardly be ascribed to God.[53] In turn even the once heralded social utility of the doctrine was brought into question,[54] a

---

53 Rowell, *Hell and the Victorians*, p.13.

By Benthamite criteria hell was not a successful punishment, for it manifestly did not prevent sin and crime; as an evil, which all punishment was held to be, it inevitably compromised the goodness of God; and an infinite punishment, which was imposed because the offence had been committed against an infinite Being, did not tally with Bentham's contention that in punishment regard should be paid to the intentions and understanding of the offender.

54 White, *Life in Christ*, pp. viii, ix, cites a statement by Rev. Rudolph Suffield, formerly a Roman Catholic priest:

My extensive experience for twenty years as confessor to thousands, whilst Apostolic Missionary in most of the large towns of England, in many portions of Ireland, in part of Scotland, and also in France, is, that excepting instances I could count on my fingers, the dogma of hell, though firmly believed in by English and Irish Roman Catholics, did no moral or

thing that not long before was inconceivable. The traditional formulation was regarded as a failure with regard to deterrence. Its objective of retribution had become discredited. Could 'eternal punishment' be said to have any utility, any justifiable purpose?

W. R. Alger and S. Cox serve as two examples of writers who challenged the traditional view that the fate of the unrighteous is merely punitive. While each was willing to retain the term 'retributive',[55] they used the term broadly, and both rejected the view that retribution was an end in itself.

Alger and Cox differed on the question of whether God actively pursues any purpose with regard to the unrighteous individual after death. Thus Alger maintained that:

> spiritual good, but rather the reverse. It never affected the right persons; it frightened nay tortured, innocent young women, and virtuous boys; it drove men and women into superstitious practices which all here would lament. It appealed to the lowest motives and the lowest characters; not however to deter from vice, but to make them the willing subjects of sad and often puerile superstitions. *It never (excepting the rarest case) deterred from the commission of sin.* It caused unceasing mental and moral difficulties, lowered the idea of God, and drove devout persons from the God of hell to Mary... we found it difficult to avoid violating the conscience, when we told them to love and revere a God compromised to the creation of a hell of eternal wretchedness, a God perpetrating what would be scorned as horrible by the most cruel, revengeful, unjust tyrant on earth.

In contrast, Pusey maintained the social utility of the 'terror of hell'.

55 Alger, *Destiny of The Soul*, pp. 521,4 and S. Cox, *Salvator Mundi or Is Christ the Saviour of all Men* (London: C. Kegan Paul and Co, 1879) pp. 205, 8, 9.

God does not arbitrarily stretch forth his arm, like an
enraged and vindictive man, and take direct vengeance on
offenders; but by his immutable laws, permeating all beings
and governing all worlds, evil is and brings, its own
punishment. The intrinsic substances and forces of character
and their organized correlations with the realities of
eternity, the ruling principles, habits, and love of the soul, as
they stand affected towards the world to which they go, –
these are the conditions on which experience depends,
herein is the hiding of retribution.[56]

Cox, on the other hand, was unwilling to dismiss notions of
divine intentionality by such appeal to intrinsic consequences
and divine passivity. He argued that the suffering of the unrighteous results from the deliberate reformative activity of
God. This led him, as a natural consequence to also question
the finality of the fate of the unrighteous, a matter noted
below.[57] He advanced one negative and three positive
arguments in favour of this reformative or disciplinary view.
On the one hand he argued that the textual evidence,
particularly with regard to the concepts of 'hell', 'damnation'
and 'everlasting', would not sustain the traditional view that

---

56   Alger, *The Destiny of The Soul*, p. 521.
57   Cox, like Farrar, in fact challenged the traditional doctrine in all
     four of its aspects. He described the dogmas which he sought to
     oppose thus:

> that there is no probation beyond the grave, that when men leave
> this world their fate is fixed beyond all hope of change; that if,
> when they die, they have not repented of their sins, so far from
> finding a place of repentance open to them in the life to come,
> they will be condemned to an eternal torment, or, at least, to a
> destructive torment which will annihilate them. (Cox, *Salvator
> Mundi*, pp.23,4.)

the fate of the unrighteous serves a merely punitive purpose.[58] His positive arguments for a reformative view were:

1. That the words of Jesus in Matthew 11:20-24 are unreasonable if they do not imply probation beyond the grave.[59]
2. That the passages which refer to universal redemption necessarily imply post-mortem discipline and reformation.[60]
3. That just as divine discipline is reformative in this life, it will continue to be same hereafter.[61]

---

58 Cox, *Salvator Mundi*, pp. 38-143.
59 Cox, *Salvator Mundi*, pp. 1-18. On p.18 he argues from Jesus' phrase 'it will be more tolerable' that

> in the future, as in the present, there will be diversities of moral condition, and a discipline nicely adapted to these diversities.... Why, then, should we always take the chastenings of the world to come to mean judgments, and the judgments to mean condemnation, and the condemnation to mean nothing short of a final and irreversible doom?

60 Cox, *Salvator Mundi*, pp. 174-191. On p. 188 he reasons thus:

> If He is to be ultimately the Saviour of *all* men, as it is very certain that a countless multitude of men are not saved in this age, they must of necessity be excluded from the presence and glory of the Lord in the age to come which the righteous will enjoy, must be exposed to a far more severe and searching discipline than any they have known here, in order that what the discipline of this age has failed to do may be done.

This argument stands or falls on the strength of the presupposition that the New Testament contains many or even any such assertions of universal redemption.

61 Cox, *Salvator Mundi*, p. 201:

> we must not hastily conclude that, in the ages to come, judgment and chastisement and punishment will change their very nature, and work to opposite effects. Analogy would rather suggest that

It is thus clear that this challenge concerning the purpose of
the fate of the unrighteous, unlike those concerning its
duration and quality, involved some argumentation. The
strength of the arguments will not be considered here. Suffice
to say that by 1938, at least within the Church of England, the
view that the divine purpose regarding the unrighteous as
merely punitive had, 'as an inference from the Christian
doctrine of God as a whole' come to be largely abandoned.

That doctrine requires us to repudiate all conceptions of the
Judgment which represent God as abandoning the appeal of
Love and falling back on the exercise of omnipotent
sovereignty to punish those who have failed to respond to
the invitation of the Gospel. God is Love; and He cannot
deny Himself.[62]

The Matter of Finality
The last challenge to be considered, that concerning *finality*,
was only in the loosest terms a challenge to an aspect of the
traditional doctrine. The other challenges had had the potential
to effect modification, but this challenge had the capacity not
merely to modify but to totally dislodge the traditional view.

An early expression of this challenge was found in the
notorious essay by H. B. Wilson, published in *Essays and
Reviews* in 1860. There he propounded the hope that

> then as now, there as here, God will still judge us in order that
> we may learn to judge ourselves, still chastise us for our good,
> still prune us that we may bring forth more fruit; and that the
> fire of his holy wrath against evil will burn up, or burn out,
> only that which has become evil in us, but liberate and
> enfranchise that which is good.

62 *Doctrine in the Church of England* (The 1938 Report with a new
Introduction by G.W.H. Lampe) (London: S.P.C.K., 1982) p. 218.

there shall be found, after the great adjudication, receptacles suitable for those who shall be infants, not as to years of terrestial life, but as to spiritual development – nurseries as it were and seed-grounds, where the undeveloped may grow up under new conditions – the stunted may become strong, and the perverted restored.[63]

Wilson was evidently too progressive. His statement evoked a legal challenge and eventually led to a written protest by 11,000 Tractarian and Evangelical clergy.[64]

Farrar was to reopen the debate about finality in the following decade and gained a far calmer hearing. While he challenged the traditional doctrine in each of its aspects, it was to this matter that the major thrust of his position was directed. This is reflected in the title under which he published his famous Westminster Sermons: 'Eternal Hope'. He explained his choice thus:

The title expresses the only seriously controverted point with which these sermons deal: the belief, which, greatly to the writer's sorrow has stirred up so much and such bitter discussion, may be summed up in the single sentence – that God's mercy may extend beyond the grave.[65]

The aspects of what he termed 'The Common View' of Eschatology which he disclaimed were

(i.) that at death there is passed upon every impenitent sinner an irreversible doom to endless tortures, either material or mental, of the most awful and unspeakable

---

63 Cited in Rowell, *Hell and the Victorians*, pp. 116, 7.

64 Rowell, *Hell and the Victorians*, p. 121.

65 Farrar, *Eternal Hope*, p. ix.

intensity; and (ii.) that this doom awaits the vast majority of mankind.[66]

He sought to do this by going back in doctrinal history and pointing to an earlier and more optimistic orthodoxy,[67] by arguing that Gehenna refers to the intermediate rather than the final state[68] and by arguing that the Church of England formularies, not least in omitting the forty-second article, had left the matter of universalism an open question.[69] In concluding his *Mercy and Judgment* Farrar outlined his beliefs, which included 'that man's destiny stops not at the grave, and that many who know not Christ here will know Him there.'[70]

The challenge assumed stronger form at the hands of Cox. He held that 'the second chance' was not just possibility. It was actuality. His arguments concerning the purpose of eternal punishment were rehearsed above. They applied equally to the matter of finality, for in concluding that the purpose of the fate of the unrighteous is reformative he had at the same time concluded that it was not final but reversible.

---

66   Farrar, *Eternal Hope*, p. xiii.
67   Farrar, *Eternal Hope*, pp. x, xi.
68   Farrar, *Eternal Hope*, p. 31.
69   Farrar, *Eternal Hope*, p. 33, though here, as elsewhere, he denies
      being a universalist (see also p. v).
70   Farrar, *Mercy and Judgment*, p. 484. He continues in the later part
      of the statement, p. 484,
          I believe that we are permitted to hope that, whether by a
          process of discipline, or enlightenment, or purification, or
          punishment, or by the special mercy of God in Christ, or in
          consequence of prayer, the state of many souls may be one of
          progress and diminishing sorrow, and of advancing happiness in
          the Intermediate State.

Alger too attacked the traditional doctrine, and set himself the task in the latter part of his massive work 'to disprove, the popular dogma which asserts that the state of the condemned departed is a state of *complete damnation absolutely eternal.*'[71] The substance of his attack is to be found chiefly in an appeal to an interpretation of the doctrine of Christ's descent to hell,[72] and in his contention that an irreversible punitive fate would be unjust, 'incompatible with any worthy idea of the character of God' and inconceivable.[73] Such a challenge was in full accord with the mood of the age. It provided an attractive marriage of belief in the immortality of the soul and belief in ongoing progress. It was this provision, Rowell suggests, that made the path to universalism the more attractive to the Victorians.[74]

---

71 Alger, *The Destiny of the Soul*, p. 525.
72 Alger, *The Destiny of the Soul*, p. 527. Elsewhere in this volume Professor D. A. du Toit questions whether the doctrine of Christ's descent into hell was used in support of an expectation of universal salvation in Patristic times.
73 Alger, *The Destiny of the Soul*. He rehearses these arguments on pages 530-539.
74 Rowell, *Hell and the Victorians*, pp. 14, 15:
    The eschatology which nineteenth-century Christianity inherited was an eschatology of the immortality of the soul, though alongside this there had also developed a secular eschatology of the progress of the world. The notion of progress had also been taken up into some of the thinking concerned with immortality, where the destiny of man was conceived as an unending progress rather than an arrival at static perfection... it was an immortality of self-realization, rather than an immortality of salvation, to which man looked forward....
    In similar vein, Rowell (p. 216) writes of the intermediate state
    It relieved, to some extent at least, the problems of the destiny of the heathen and of those who had apparently been deprived by

Bauckham has put it well:

Common to almost all versions of the 'wider hope' was the belief that death was not the decisive break which traditional orthodoxy had taught. Repentance, conversion, moral progress are still possible after death. This widespread belief was certainly influenced by the common nineteenth-century faith in evolutionary progress. Hell – or a modified version of purgatory – could be understood in this context as the pain and suffering necessary to moral growth. In this way evolutionary progress provides the new context for nineteenth-century universalism, replacing the Platonic cycle of emanation and return which influenced the universalists of earlier centuries.[75]

---

their circumstances, capabilities, and environment of all reasonable chance of appreciating the significance and importance of the Christian gospel. It fitted better with the dynamic, evolutionary picture of the universe than the conception of fixed and unalterable states into which men entered at death. (Rowell, p. 216)

75 R.J. Bauckham, 'Universalism: a historical survey', *Themelios*, 4(2), 1979, p. 51. Bauckham is probably wrong in suggesting that developments of the 'wider hope' in nineteenth-century England owed anything much to F.D.E. Schleiermacher, whose major work was only translated into English in 1928 (*The Christian Faith*: T. & T. Clark, 1928) though published in German in 1821. Interestingly, as Bauckham points out, Schleiermacher 'taught a predestination as absolute as that of Augustine and Calvin, but he rejected any form of *double* predestination. Schleiermacher, and others who followed his approach, did not arrive at their doctrine of the fate of the unrighteous as most others did. They worked *de novo*. Most others worked in reaction against the traditional doctrine. Their contributions do not form a part of the process of the devolution of the doctrine of Everlasting Physical Punishment. Another who worked *de novo*, though along yet another route was E.H. Plumtre in

Pastoral concerns were also very influential in the challenge with regard to finality.[76] E. A. Litton found in the restoration of the doctrine of the 'intermediate state' grounds for saying that

---

his *The Spirits in Prison and Other Studies on the Life after Death* (London: Wm Isbister Ltd, 1886, 5th ed). Expanding freely upon I Pet.3:19, 20 and 4:6 (pp. 3-20), and refusing to regard death as an obstacle to continuity of existence, he arrived at his own form of universalism. But he did not do so in explicit reaction against the traditional doctrine.

76 The pastoral dynamic was undoubtedly strong. Rowell finds that the nineteenth century's increasing awareness of the 'mass of the damned', brought to awareness not least through the missionary movement, gave rise to a more personal understanding of Christianity and 'sharpened the protest against an eschatology which was conceived as the end-term of a mechanical process' (Rowell, *Hell and the Victorians*, p. 16). In America, Moorhead finds that even conservative theologians were concerned to reduce to a minimum estimations of the numbers of the lost, and argued for the automatic salvation of infants (Moorhead, 'As though nothing at all had happened', p. 455). Wenham notes that even C. Hodge and B.B. Warfield taught that the numbers of the lost would be few (J.W. Wenham, *The Goodness of God* (London: IVP, 1974), pp. 31, 2). Pusey's response to Farrar's third objection to the 'popular' or 'common' view of the doctrine of hell ('the opinion that it is thus incurred by the vast mass of mankind' - Farrar, *Eternal Hope*, p. xvi, and *Mercy and Judgment*, p. 176.) was to charge that this problem was of Farrar's own making, arising from Farrar's rigid Calvinistic background (Pusey, *Everlasting Punishment*, pp. 6-11). In support of his view Pusey, pp. 7, 8, quotes 'The Rev. H.N. Oxenham in his *Catholic Eschatology* (p. 22)'... 'I am not myself acquainted with a single Universalist writer who does not argue as though the doctrine he is assailing involved the damnation of the great majority of mankind'. Pusey, it seems, was happy to defend a doctrine of everlasting punishment because he was confident that it would apply to very few (Pusey, *Everlasting Punishment*, pp. 11-18)!

'to all, we may hope, salvation will, in some way, be offered before the final judgment.'[77] White, in spite of his fundamental thesis of 'life only in Christ', was nevertheless keen to argue for post-mortem opportunities for those who had never had opportunity to respond to Christ, and in this placed heavy reliance on I Peter 3,4.[78]

It is probable that the success of the finality challenge is to be attributed to both philosophical and the pastoral factors.

Hypothesis

If one thing is notable about the foregoing account of the early challenges to the doctrine of immediate, unending, physical punishment, it is the preponderance of broad theological and philosophical arguments and the minimal reference to biblical material. The challenges and the positions which derived from them can be traced to the following issues:

---

77   E.A. Litton, *Introduction to Dogmatic Theology* (London: James Clarke and Co. Ltd, 1960 - first published 1882,1892) pp. 577, 8.

78   White, *Life in Christ*, pp. 313-328. On page 322 he writes of the Petrine passages

> By S. Peter's declaration, then, a flood of light is thrown upon the divine dealings with the heathen millions. Every soul survives. Perhaps to every human soul which has not heard it on earth, the 'gospel' will be offered in Hades. They may not accept it here; but then they will be 'without excuse', and will be condemned to death eternal as if they were 'men in the flesh' who rejected the reconciliation.

He is perhaps less rational in his response to teaching that excluded infants from salvation:

> A more fiendish dogma than this in inconceivable, - the consummation of theological hardness of heart, and a fitting revenge on the people of Europe for ever permitting the sin of enforced clerical celibacy. (p. 326)

whether or not humanity is universally immortal;

how human free will and divine sovereignty may both be preserved;

whether or not there is scope for post-mortem conversion (a question closely related to the issue whether or not humanity is universally immortal); and

the nature of divine response to the refusal of divine initiatives.

Thus, some of those described above presupposed universal immortality; others denied it. Some assumed the subjection of all human will to that of God; some refused that notion in the name of human freedom. Some readily embraced the notion of post-mortem growth and change as being necessary and obvious; others could not countenance this possibility. Some maintained the necessity of divine retribution in order to uphold the principle of divine justice; others dismissed this as impossible of the God of love.

What can account for these divisions of opinion? In small part this divergence is attributable to the ambiguity of the biblical data. In larger part it may be attributed to the diversity of opinion generated through strong recourse to human reason. For the most part, however, the divergence is rooted in divergent presuppositions with regard to the four issues set out above. The relationship between such presuppositions, the dynamics of the challenge (whether admitted or dismissed) and the elements of the traditional position (whether dislodged or retained), may be set out as follows.

Table C: The Possible Role of Presuppositions in the Challenges to Traditional Orthodoxy on the Fate of the Unrighteous.

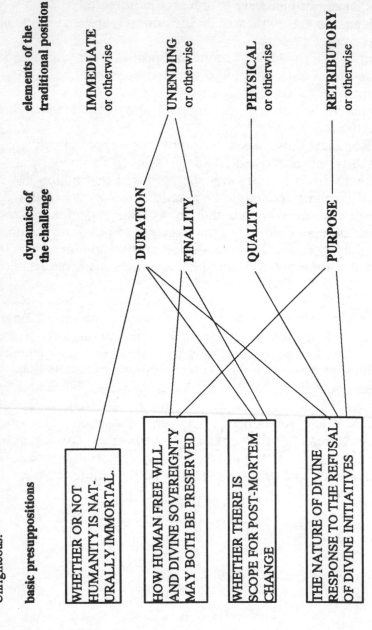

This analysis indicates the abiding relevance of presuppositions in relation to the matter of the fate of the unrighteous. This is indicated through the left column of the above table. Presuppositions had the capacity to determine whether and how the traditional doctrine was challenged and hence the way in which it was subjected to modification. Presuppositions have probably had a determinative influence on participants in the modern debate.[79]

This observation leads to an hypothesis. This hypothesis will probably commend itself intuitively to all who have read amongst the diverse literature in this field, or to return to the analogy, all who have sought to rummage through the plethora of paper to find the one definitive document. It arises out of a recognition of the significance of presuppositions and also the continuing significance of the 'traditional position' for most participants in the debate. The hypothesis is that the *great majority of modern positions on the fate of the unrighteous may be classified and largely explicated in terms of presuppositionally-determined reactions against 'traditional orthodoxy'*. This may be tested diagrammatically.[80]

In the chart which follows (see end of chapter) the traditional doctrine is set out at the top and is also found intact at position one. The other eleven positions are each

---

79 A similar case may be made with regard to the Patristic debate about the fate of the unrighteous.

80 The chart is not exhaustive. Works notable for their eclecticism, of which there have been several recent examples (*e.g.* H. Küng, *Eternal Life* London: Collins, 1984, tr. E. Quinn, J. Hick, *Death and Eternal Life* London: McMillan, 1985, and M. Kelsey, *Afterlife: The Other Side of Dying* New York: Crossroad, 1986) have been deliberately not included.

shown to be explicable in terms of presuppositionally-determined reactions to successive challenges to the traditional doctrine with regard to the duration, the quality, the purpose and the finality of the 'punishment' of the unrighteous.[81]

---

81 The following are the details of the works representative of the twelve positions.
Position one:
E.B. Pusey *What is the Faith as to Everlasting Punishment* (Oxford: Devenport Society of the Holy Trinity, 1880); W.G.T. Shedd, *The Doctrine of Endless Punishment* (London: James Nisbet and Co., 1886); L. Berkhof, *Systematic Theology* (London: Banner of Truth, 1939); W. Hendriksen, *The Bible on the Life Hereafter* (Grand Rapids: Baker, 1959); J.H. Bratt, *The Final Curtain. Studies in Eschatology* (Grand Rapids: Baker, 1978); R.A. Morey, *Death and the Afterlife* (Minneapolis: Bethany House, 1984); J.H. Gerstner, *Repent or Perish* (Ligonier: Soli Deo Gloria Publications, 1990).
Position two:
S.D.F. Salmond, *The Christian Doctrine of Immortality* (Edinburgh: T. & T. Clark, 1903, 5th ed.); R. Anderson, *Human Destiny: After Death - What?* (London: Pickering and Inglis, 1913); H. Buis, *The Doctrine of Eternal Punishment* (Philadelphia: Presbyterian and Reformed Pub. Co., 1957); A.A. Hoekema, *The Bible and The Future* (Exeter: Paternoster Press, 1979); M.J. Harris, *Raised Immortal* (London: Marshall, Morgan and Scott, 1983); P. Toon, *Longing for the Heavenly Realm. The Missing Element in Modern Western Spirituality* (London: Hodder and Stoughton, 1986).
Position three:
no consistent advocates.
Position four:
F.W. Farrar, *Eternal Hope. Five Sermons Preached in Westminster Abbey, November and December, 1877* (New York: E.P. Dutton and Co., 1878); S.Cox, *Salvator Mundi* (London: C. Kegan Paul and Co, 1879, 6th ed.); J. Peterson Smyth, *The Gospel of the Hereafter* (London: Hodder and Stoughton, n.d.); J.A.T. Robinson, *In the End,*

God (London: Collins, 1968, first published 1950); G.C. Studer, *After Death, What?* (Scotdale, Penn.: Herald Press, 1976).
Position five:
J.A. Motyer, *After Death, A Sure and Certain Hope* (London: Hodder and Stoughton, 1965); E.J. Fortman, *Everlasting Life After Death* (New York: Alba House, 1977); S.H. Travis, *Christ and the Judgment of God._Divine Retribution in the New Testament* (Basingstoke: Marshall, Morgan and Scott, 1986); H. Blamires, *Heaven and Hell* (Ann Arbor: Servant Books, 1988).
Position six:
W.R. Alger, *The Destiny of the Soul: A Critical History of the Doctrine of a Future Life* (Boston: Roberts Bros., 1880, 10th ed.); E.A. Litton, *Introduction to Theology* (London: James Clarke & Co. Ltd., 1960, ed P.E. Hughes); S. Baring Gould, *The Restitution of All Things or 'The Hope That is Set Before Us'* (London: Skeffington and Son, 1907); A.H. McNeile, *The Problem of the Future Life* (Cambridge: W. Heffer and Sons Ltd., 1925); H.E. Fosdick, *The Assurance of Immortality* (London: SCM, 1934); C.S. Lewis, *The Great Divorce. A Dream* (Glasgow: William Collins, Sons and Co.,1946); T.F. Torrance, *His Appearing and His Kingdom* (London: The Epworth Press, 1953); E. Brunner, *Eternal Hope* (London: Lutterworth, 1954, tr.H. Knight).
Position seven:
H. Constable, *Hades; or the Intermediate State of Man* (London: Kellaway and Co., 1875, 2 ed.); R. Aldwinckle, *Death in the Secular City: Life After Death In Contemporary Theology and Philosophy* (Grand Rapids: W.B. Eerdmans, 1974); D. Edwards and J. Stott, *Essentials. A liberal-evangelical dialogue* (London: Hodder and Stoughton, 1988); P.E. Hughes, *The True Image: The Origin and Destiny of Man in Christ* (Grand Rapids: W.B. Eerdmans, 1989).
Position eight:
L.E. Froom, *The Conditionalist Faith of Our Fathers* (Washington: Herald and Review Publishing Association, 1965, 1966, 2 vols.) [Froom might also be assigned to position nine]; E. Fudge, *The Fire that Consumes: A Biblical and Historical Study of Final Punishment* (Houston: Providential Press, 1982); E. White, *Life in Christ: A*

Pointers to the Resolution of the Debate

While it will never be possible to establish with complete confidence how anyone in the past arrived at their views, the fact that the presuppositional analysis offered by means of the chart is able to embrace so much of the data does, in the nature of the case, constitute relatively strong verification of the hypothesis. It suggests the strong, if not dominant, role of presuppositions, and further, that the debate has been largely constrained by a perceived need to take traditional orthodoxy

Study of the Scripture Doctrine of the Nature of Man, the Object of the Divine Incarnation, and the Conditions of Human Immortality (London: Elliott Stock, 1878, 3rd ed. rev.); H.E. Guillebaud, *The Righteous Judge. A Study of the Biblical Doctrine of Everlasting Punishment* (published privately, 1964).

Position nine:

B.F.C. Atkinson, *Life and Immortality: An Examination of the Nature and Meaning of Life and Death as they are revealed in the Scriptures* (published privately, n.d.); L.E. Froom, *The Conditionalist Faith of Our Fathers* (Washington: Herald and Review Publishing Association, 1965, 1966, 2 vols.) [Froom might also be assigned to position eight]; R. Whately, *A View of the Scripture Revelations Concerning a Future State* (Philadelphia: Lindsay and Blakiston, 1877, 10th ed.).

Position ten:

W. Temple, 'The Idea of Immortality in Relation to Religion and Ethics', *The Congregational Quarterly*, X, 1932, 11-21.

Position eleven:

The works by White, Stott and Buis which contain suggestion of this position are cited above.

Position twelve:

P. Tillich, *Systematic Theology* (Welwyn, Hert: James Nisbet & Co., 1968); M. Paternoster, *Thou Art There Also* (London: SPCK., 1967); J. Macquarrie, *Christian Hope* (Oxford: A.R. Mowbray & Co. Ltd., 1978).

as the point of departure. Each challenge to the traditional position would seem to have had presuppositional roots, whether it be the challenge with regard to *duration, quality, purpose* or *finality*.

If this general assessment of the causes of confusion in the debate concerning the fate of the unrighteous is correct, the way forward is clear. It will involve the following.
1. the elimination of all unjustified presuppositions,
2. a new openness to the biblical data,
3. a willingness to embrace and apply biblical convictions and presuppositions to the question,[82]
4. if necessary a willingness to move freely of the traditional orthodoxy.

It would seem that much of the energy that has gone into the nineteenth and twentieth century debates about hell and universalism may have been wasted on account of the undue influence of unjustified presuppositions. The waste has arguably been compounded by the way in which the debate has been constrained by a pervasive though perverse allegiance to a questionable 'orthodoxy': the doctrine of immediate, unending, physical punishment.

If what has been propounded has any soundness it suggests that future constructive contributions to the debate will be made by those deeply committed to fresh, radical and unbridled examination of the biblical data. To this end human reason will need be employed to the full, but to elucidate rather than evaluate that data. This process is now urgent.

---

82 Notably biblical convictions and presuppositions concerning the nature of God, the work of Christ, and the nature of humanity, life and death.

The church and the world have already suffered too long confused as to what consequences, if any, flow from being righteous before the Righteous One.

The Fate of the Unrighteous' - devolution of the

UNENDING PHYSICAL
|
(DURATION)
|

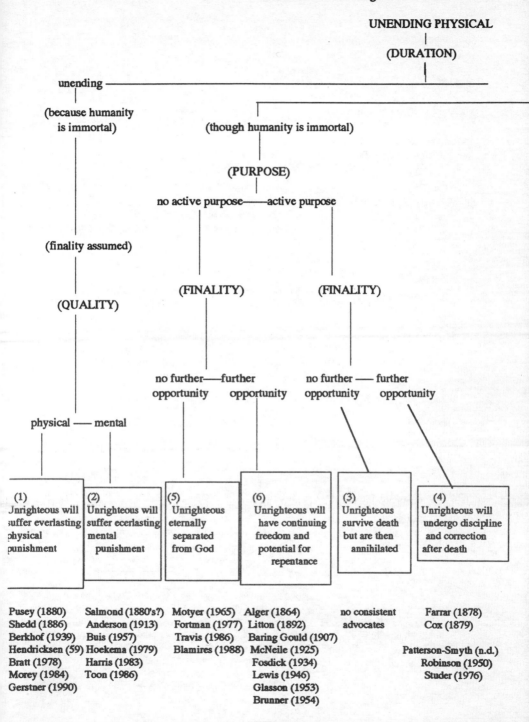

unending ——

(because humanity
is immortal)

(though humanity is immortal)

(PURPOSE)
|
no active purpose————active purpose

(finality assumed)

(QUALITY)

(FINALITY)   (FINALITY)

no further——further   no further —— further
opportunity   opportunity   opportunity   opportunity

physical —— mental

| (1) Unrighteous will suffer everlasting physical punishment | (2) Unrighteous will suffer everlasting mental punishment | (5) Unrighteous eternally separated from God | (6) Unrighteous will have continuing freedom and potential for repentance | (3) Unrighteous survive death but are then annihilated | (4) Unrighteous will undergo discipline and correction after death |

Pusey (1880)	Salmond (1880's?)	Motyer (1965)	Alger (1864)	no consistent	Farrar (1878)
Shedd (1886)	Anderson (1913)	Fortman (1977)	Litton (1892)	advocates	Cox (1879)
Berkhof (1939)	Buis (1957)	Travis (1986)	Baring Gould (1907)		
Hendricksen (59)	Hoekema (1979)	Blamires (1988)	McNeile (1925)		Patterson-Smyth (n.d.)
Bratt (1978)	Harris (1983)		Fosdick (1934)		Robinson (1950)
Morey (1984)	Toon (1986)		Lewis (1946)		Studer (1976)
Gerstner (1990)			Glasson (1953)		
			Brunner (1954)		

eighteenth century doctrine

PUNISHMENT (1)

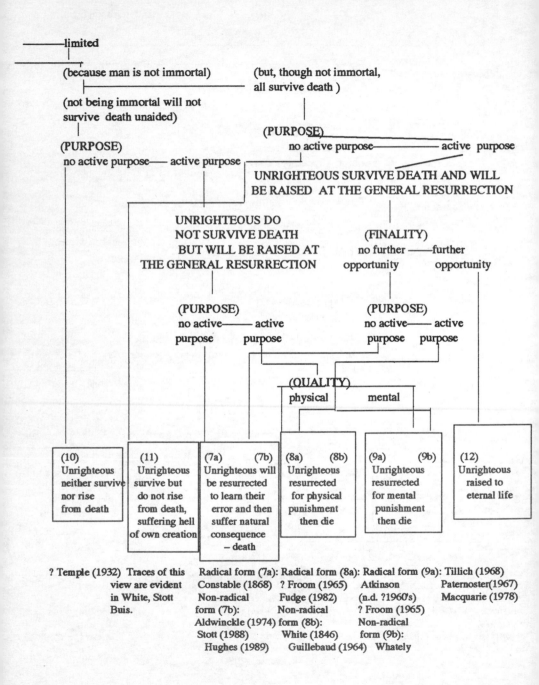

——limited

(because man is not immortal)   (but, though not immortal,
                                        all survive death)

(not being immortal will not
survive death unaided)

(PURPOSE)   (PURPOSE)
no active purpose— active purpose   no active purpose————— active purpose

                                        UNRIGHTEOUS SURVIVE DEATH AND WILL
                                        BE RAISED AT THE GENERAL RESURRECTION

                    UNRIGHTEOUS DO
                    NOT SURVIVE DEATH   (FINALITY)
                    BUT WILL BE RAISED AT   no further ——further
                    THE GENERAL RESURRECTION opportunity opportunity

                    (PURPOSE)   (PURPOSE)
                    no active—— active   no active—— active
                    purpose   purpose   purpose   purpose

                                        (QUALITY)
                                        physical   mental

| (10) Unrighteous neither survive nor rise from death | (11) Unrighteous survive but do not rise from death, suffering hell of own creation | (7a)   (7b) Unrighteous will be resurrected to learn their error and then suffer natural consequence – death | (8a)   (8b) Unrighteous resurrected for physical punishment then die | (9a)   (9b) Unrighteous resurrected for mental punishment then die | (12) Unrighteous raised to eternal life |

? Temple (1932) Traces of this   Radical form (7a): Radical form (8a): Radical form (9a): Tillich (1968)
                view are evident   Constable (1868)   ? Froom (1965)   Atkinson   Paternoster(1967)
                in White, Stott   Non-radical   Fudge (1982)   (n.d. ?1960's)   Macquarie (1978)
                Buis.   form (7b):   Non-radical   ? Froom (1965)
                                   Aldwinckle (1974)   form (8b):   Non-radical
                                   Stott (1988)   White (1846)   form (9b):
                                   Hughes (1989)   Guillebaud (1964)   Whately

5

The Contemporaneity of the Divine Decision: Reflections on Barth's Denial of 'Universalism'

John Colwell

My intention is to review certain key elements in Barth's theology rather than merely to rehearse a defence of Barth against the charge of universalism. He has already been ably and effectively defended. In any case, it really should suffice Barth's critics that Barth himself both continually rejected the charge in relation to his own teaching and criticized universalism as taught by others. Whatever else one may think of Barth he was no liar, nor is it likely that he would have been unaware of the direct implications of his own theological scheme. Indeed it is this observation that I find intriguing. On the one hand we are faced with Barth's repeated denials of the charge of universalism. On the other hand we have to reckon with the persistent criticisms of his detractors that the salvation of all men and women must be the logical consequence of Barth's idiosyncratic conception of the doctrine of election. The choice is simple. Either Barth remained blissfully oblivious to the most obvious implication of a fundamental tenet of his theology; or there must be some factor in his doctrine of election that has been overlooked by his critics.

Given the comparison between the apparent perception of at least some of Barth's critics and the apparent perception and ability of Barth himself I am inevitably drawn to the latter possibility: that there is in Barth's

conception of the doctrine of election some crucial factor
that is either overlooked or misunderstood by his critics.
Moreover, I want to suggest that this factor, once
recognized, represents at least a different perspective on
the *impasse* so often felt by Western theology concerning
the relatedness of divine sovereignty and human
accountability – an impasse which, all the more since the
Enlightenment, has tended to be resolved in a humanistic
fashion.

Perhaps it is necessary to clarify from the beginning that
while Barth consistently rejects universalism as a
doctrine, he certainly does not reject the possibility that all
men and women may ultimately be saved. If it is
presumptuous for those who advocate universalism to
suggest that God is in some way obliged to save all men
and women, then it is equally presumptuous to suggest
that he is obliged not to do so. We may not be permitted
to cheapen God's grace by counting upon universal
salvation as an obligatory right, but neither are we
permitted to limit God's grace by excluding universal
salvation as at least a possibility for God.[1] Without
wishing in any way to weaken the warnings implicit in the
Scriptural references to perdition, such references need not
preclude the possibility that, at the very least, the final
circle of God's people may prove to be 'greater than was
previously visible'. We certainly ought not to assume that
the present visible circles of belief and unbelief coincide
with the eternal identities of the elect and the non-elect.[2]

But to admit the possibility of the ultimate salvation of
all men and women, to hope for it and even to pray for it,
falls well short of the opinion that the salvation of all men

---

[1]   *C.D.* II 2, p. 418.
[2]   *Ibid., cf.* Karl Barth, *The Humanity of God*, trans. by John
        Newton Thomas and Thomas Wieser (London and Glasgow,
        1961), pp. 59f.

and women is both necessary and guaranteed. Universalism in this sense is first rejected by Barth during the course of his exposition of the doctrine of election in *C.D.* II 2 and is repeated and reinforced in *C.D.* IV 3 in the context of the doctrine of reconciliation.[3] According to Barth, the presumptuous expectation of a universal salvation arises whenever God's love for all men and women is perceived as the necessary consequence of the nature of God as loving in himself. According to this scheme, if God is to be recognized as loving in himself then it must be necessary for God to love all men and women and for that love to be concluded in the ultimate salvation of all men and women. In this manner Universalism constrains God by an *a priori* and external necessity: a definition of God's inner nature as loving is seen to be dependent upon his external work in loving and saving all men and women. For Barth it is wholly unacceptable that the freedom of God should be limited in this manner by effectively tying God to humankind by an external necessity. If God were to love in this necessitated manner then his love would not be grace; it would not be love in freedom. Love which can be presumed upon is not grace:

> If we are to respect the freedom of divine grace, we cannot venture the statement that it must and will finally be coincident with the world of man as such.... No such right or necessity can legitimately be deduced. Just as the gracious God does not need to elect or call any single man, so He does not need to elect or call all mankind.[4]

The definition of God as 'the One who loves in freedom' carries a similar weight in volume two of the *Church Dogmatics* as was carried in volume one by the phrase

---

3   *C.D.* II 2, pp. 417ff; *C.D.*IV 3, pp. 461ff.
4   *C.D.* II 2, p. 417.

'God reveals himself as Lord'.[5] The recognition that the living God has defined himself in this way is fundamental to Barth's understanding of the doctrine of God. There can be no external or *a priori* necessity determining the being of God as love. That God exists in himself as love, in the perfect communion of Father, Son and Spirit, is the outcome not of some abstract external necessity but of the internal and *a posteriori* necessity of God's will so to exist.[6] Neither ought his relatedness to that which is other than himself be perceived as a necessary consequence of this relatedness of love within himself. That God is loving to the creature is similarly the outcome of God's free decision to love that which is other than himself. It is a love which is not subject to any form of external necessity. It is love in freedom. It is grace.[7]

However, the form of freedom referred to here ought not to be misconstrued as arbitrariness. God's love to the creature is free in the sense that it is not determined by any external or *a priori* necessity but it is not arbitrary; it is a freely willed reiteration of God's own inner relatedness as Father, Son and Spirit; it is determined by the constancy of his free decision to be God in this way. In this sense, while remaining free from all external necessity, the decision of God to love the creature can be perceived as the outcome of the internal and *a posteriori* necessity of God's unnecessitated will:

> What takes place is the divine fulfilment of a divine decree. It takes place in the freedom of God, but in the inner necessity of the freedom of God and not in the play of a sovereign *liberum arbitrium*. There is no possibility of something quite different happening.[8]

---

5   *C.D.* II 1, pp. 272ff.
6   *C.D.* II 1, pp. 268ff.
7   *C.D.* II 1, pp. 351ff; *cf. C.D.*IV 2, p. 345.
8   *C.D.*IV 1, p. 195.

If we can speak of a necessity of any kind here, it can only be the necessity of the decision which God did in fact make and execute, the necessity of the fact that the being of God, the omnipotence of His free love, has this concrete determination and no other, that God wills to magnify and does in fact magnify His own glory in this way and not in any other, and therefore to the inclusion of the redemption and salvation of the world. This fact we have to recognise to be divinely necessary because it derives from and is posited by God.[9]

But this is precisely where some of Barth's critics stumble. How can it be valid for Barth to appeal to the freedom of God as a means of evading universalism when he has previously limited this freedom of God by the *a posteriori* necessity for him to be self-consistent? The point made by critics such as G.C.Berkouwer is not that Barth's God is bound by some external necessity to save all men and women but that he is bound by this internal necessity of his self-consistent grace. From Berkouwer's perspective it is Barth's definition of God's freedom as the positive freedom to elect as distinct from the freedom to elect or not to elect which orientates his doctrine of Election towards universalism.[10] Now I have argued elsewhere (as have others) that the alternative offered by Berkouwer is defective not only in its reaffirmation of Calvin's concept of a 'double decree' but also in that Berkouwer himself appears to fall into the trap of defining

---

9   *C.D.* IV 1, p. 213. For a fuller description of the distinction between these two forms of necessity see John McIntyre, *St Anselm and his Critics: a Re-interpretation of the Cur Deus Homo* (Edinburgh and London, 1954), pp. 117ff. & 162ff. Also John E. Colwell, *Actuality and Provisionality: Eternity and Election in the Theology of Karl Barth* (Edinburgh, 1989), pp. 221ff.

10   G.C. Berkouwer, *The Triumph of Grace in the Theology of Karl Barth*, translated by Harry R. Boer (Grand Rapids, 1956), pp. 290ff.

God's love in terms of his love for the creature.[11] But this
of itself by no means diminishes the weight of
Berkouwer's criticisms of Barth, it merely questions his
suggested alternative.

Perhaps the best known defence of Barth against such
criticisms occurs in an essay by J.D. Bettis in which he
observes that the fundamental difference between
Berkouwer and Barth is that for the former, reprobation is
an outworking of God's justice, whereas for Barth it is
itself an outworking of God's love. For Barth, the
possibility of reprobation is not excluded by the constancy
of God's love for men and women but is itself a
manifestation of that love, the love in which God allows
human disobedience to be real albeit in the form of an
impossible possibility. For Berkouwer the possibility of
reprobation is not a manifestation of the love of God at all
but of the freedom of God's justice.

Bettis concludes his defence of Barth with the
observation that the error of universalism stems from the
substituting of Jesus Christ for the *decretum absolutum* of
the Reformed tradition: the work of Christ being perceived
as an ontological reorganization of the universe which men
and women, through the proclamation of the gospel, are
called to acknowledge. But in refuting universalism in this
manner Bettis is also rejecting this *schema* as the
common caricature of Barth's theology. That is to say: for
Bettis firstly Barth's location of the ontological definition
of man and woman in Jesus Christ does not imply a
reorganization of the universe, and, secondly, men and
women are saved by faith rather than merely called to
acknowledge an already existing state of affairs.[12] In

---

11   John E. Colwell, *op. cit.* p. 271; *cf.* J.D. Bettis, 'Is Karl Barth
      a Universalist?' *Scottish Journal of Theology*, 20 (1967), pp.
      423-436 (pp. 428f.).
12   J.D. Bettis, *op. cit.*, pp. 434ff.

stating the matter in this way Bettis highlights the problem. In essence the common criticism of Barth, reiterated by so many of his detractors, is precisely that he does conceive of the work of Christ as an ontic (rather than ontological) reorganization of the universe and that he does define faith in exclusively noetic terms. It is in these two areas that either Barth is in error or his critics have seriously misunderstood him.

Certainly, for Barth, the doctrine of election is that which determines the theological definition of all men and women. Human existence is not some autonomous state determined by a man or a woman's own being and actions, it is rather determined by God's gracious decision of election. Jesus Christ himself is both the electing God and the elected man. He himself has borne God's rejection on behalf of all men and women and he himself is the elect of God: all who are elect are so exclusively in him and, since all men and women are defined ontologically as elect in him, there can be no other authentic definition of humanity.[13] Barth criticizes the traditional doctrine of predestination for its failure clearly to attest Jesus Christ as the true subject and object of election. Both by its reference to a hidden decree of God beyond his revelation of himself in Jesus Christ, and also by its conceiving of election as an independent relationship between this hidden God and certain individuals, the traditional conception of this doctrine displaced Christ.[14] For Barth, the true object of the doctrine of election is not some abstract concept of humanity in general, nor the totality of the human race, nor particular individuals; the true and sole object of election is Jesus Christ himself:[15]

---

13   *C.D.* II 2, pp. 94ff.
14   *C.D.* II 2, pp. 306ff.
15   *C.D.* II 2, p. 55.

Those whom God elects He elects 'in Him,' not merely 'like Him,' but in His person, by His will, and by His election.[16]

No one outside or alongside Him is elected. All who are elected are elected in Him. And similarly – since no one outside or alongside Him is elected as the bearer of divine rejection – no one outside or alongside Him is rejected.[17]

The man or the woman who chooses to reject this decision of election and to live under the rejection of God does so by choosing that possibility which God, by choosing it for himself in Christ, has determined to be impossible. Such a choice cannot be dignified by according to it any validity; it is a choice that is null and void; it can only be made under the 'non-willing' of God.[18] The Christian community has been brought by the Holy Spirit to know this truth of election in Jesus Christ, both for themselves and for all men and women.[19] The content of their proclamation therefore is that this decision has been made:

> In Jesus Christ thou, too, art not rejected – for He has borne thy rejection – but elected. A decision has been made, in Jesus Christ, concerning the futility of thy desire and attempt to live that life; and it has been decided that thou canst live only this other life.[20]

But if the choice to live other than by this divine definition is null and void, an impossible possibility, an ontological contradiction, then, despite all Barth's protests, how can universalism be avoided? How can this be interpreted other than as implying an ontological reorganization of the universe? How can Barth's readers

---

16   *C.D.* II 2, p. 121.
17   *C.D.* II 2, p. 421.
18   *C.D.* II 2, pp. 237, 315ff., 349 & 458.
19   *C.D.* II 2, pp. 318ff.
20   *C.D.* II 2, p. 322.

not infer that temporal history in its entirety is enclosed and completed either in the event of the Incarnation, death and resurrection of Christ or in some decision of Father, Son and Holy Spirit before the foundation of the world? It is at this point that Barth is most seriously misunderstood.

To begin with, we must recognize that it is not Barth's intention in these passages to speculate concerning the ultimate destiny of each individual but rather to emphasize and define the inclusive nature of the church's witness to each individual. In this sense, Barth's insistence that all men and women are defined ontologically by the death and resurrection of Jesus Christ serves within his dogmatics as an affirmation of the universality of the atonement. If it is possible to affirm a universal atonement while avoiding the implications of a universal salvation, then it must also be possible to affirm with Barth that there can be no valid manner of understanding the being of men and women other than as that being is defined by the death and resurrection of Jesus Christ. The gospel which the church is commissioned to proclaim is unequivocally good news. Since the being of all men and women is defined in Jesus Christ, this determines the manner in which they must be addressed by the church in its proclamation of the gospel:

> It is, therefore, impossible... to regard any of them as if they were not elect, as if God's love for men did not apply to them too, as if His covenant of grace had not been sealed for them, as if the godlessness in which they deny their real status were to be seriously taken as conclusive, as if it were therefore senseless and futile to witness to them too of the divine election of grace that has taken place in Jesus Christ.[21]

It is clear throughout that Barth's concern is with a definition of being rather than with any assumption

---

[21] *C.D.* II 2, p. 416.

regarding the actual being of particular individuals, a concern for the ontological rather than for the ontic. His reference is to an ontological definition as distinct from any realization of an ontic actuality. Since there is no other valid definition of the being of men and women the church's proclamation must be inclusive and unequivocal but the church does not possess the power to make any individual man or woman one of the elect nor even to make it plain to them that they are one of the elect. This remains the prerogative of God alone.[22] Though the church in its proclamation of the gospel is forbidden to reverse the ordained relationship between election and rejection, promise and threat, it certainly knows the reality of a threatened rejection and can exercise no control whatsoever over the outcome of its proclamation.[23] Whoever rejects this gracious election falls under the threat that they will be taken seriously in this their rejection. Such a man or woman stands under the real threat of condemnation; the threat which is the unwillingness of God for everything which he does not positively will; the threat of the wrath of God which is the form his love takes when it is ignored and rejected.[24]

Barth prohibits too simplistic a relationship between the ontological definition of all men and women as elect in Jesus Christ and the actual election of individual men and women. The church must proclaim the election of Jesus Christ that has occurred on behalf of all men and women; but this does not imply the ultimate salvation of all men and women as its necessary consequence.[25] The actual election of any individual man or woman only occurs

---

[22]   *C.D.* II 2, p. 320; *cf.* pp. 410ff.
[23]   *C.D.* II 2, p. 320.
[24]   *C.D.* IV 3, pp. 462ff.; *cf. C.D.* IV 1, pp. 482ff.; *cf.* J.D. Bettis, *op.cit.*, p. 432.
[25]   *C.D.* II 2, p. 423.

through the continuing (though self-consistent) activity of
God:

> It is always the concern of God to decide what is the
> world and the human totality for which the man Jesus
> Christ is elected, and which is itself elected in and with
> Him. It is enough for us to know and remember that at
> all events it is the omnipotent loving-kindness of God
> which continually decides this. For the fact that Jesus
> Christ is the reality and revelation of the omnipotent
> loving-kindness of God towards the whole world and
> every man is an enduring event which is continually
> fulfilled in new encounters and transactions, in which
> God the Father lives and works through the Son, in
> which the Son of God Himself, and the Holy Spirit of the
> Father and the Son, lives and works at this or that place
> or time, in which He rouses and finds faith in this or that
> man, in which He is recognized and apprehended by this
> and that man in the promise and in their election – by
> one here and one there, and therefore by many men.[26]

Statements such as this express a dynamic which is
wholly ignored by those who would dismiss Barth's
exposition of the doctrine of election as implying some
completed and static decision of the past on the basis of
which all continuing decisions and actions of men and
women, their belief and their unbelief, are determined. To
dismiss Barth in this manner is to fail totally to
comprehend the most elementary aspects of his
theological thought. There is nothing static about Barth's
conception of the being of God, his eternity, his decisions,
his actions. He is the living God. He is not to be defined in
the terms of a supposed static otherness to the world and
the history of men and women. He exists as dynamic
being, as event, as this event of electing love, as being in
this becoming.

---

[26]   *C.D.* II 2, p. 422.

In defining God's eternity as a perfection of his freedom, Barth is careful to distinguish this eternity both from concepts of timelessness and from concepts of everlastingness.[27] On the one hand God's eternity must not be misconstrued as his absolute otherness to time. Barth distances himself from the traditional identification of eternity with timelessness. Conceptions of God's eternity ought to inform us positively of that which God is rather than negatively of that which he is not. God's eternity is his freedom to have the time which he himself has freely chosen. It is not his timelessness but his authentic temporality. It is his freely chosen time for us and therefore the possibility of our time for him. If we are rightly to understand the eternity of God we must begin in that place where God has defined himself; we must begin with the actuality of the Incarnation:

> In Jesus Christ it comes about that God takes time to Himself, that He Himself, the eternal One, becomes temporal, that He is present for us in the form of our own existence and our own world, not simply embracing our time and ruling it, but submitting Himself to it, and permitting created time to become and be the form of His eternity.[28]

But neither ought God's eternity to be misconstrued simplistically in terms of everlastingness. Such an identification would fail to distinguish eternity as God's time from the fallen time known to us. Indeed it is Barth's perception that concepts of timelessness arose as negative projections of this fallen time of our experience: a theological method which begins in the wrong place in its attempts to define God by defining man negatively. God's eternity is authentically temporal but it is *authentically* temporal: it is our experience of time that is *unauthentic*. We only experience time in its lostness; in the succession

---

[27]   *C.D.* II 1, pp. 608ff.
[28]   *C.D.* II 1, p. 616.

of past, present and future in which we are unfree; in that succession in which we never possess time but it rules over us. God's eternity as a perfection of his freedom cannot possibly be this unfree experience of time as it is known to us. If God's eternity were merely to be his everlastingness then he would be as unfree in the succession of past, present and future as we are. He would not be the Lord of time. Barth therefore defines God's eternity as that 'pure simultaneity' in which beginning, succession and end, past, present and future are simultaneously present to God without those distinctions between them being forfeited in some timeless abstraction.

While accepting an undeniable relationship between God's eternity and his omnipresence Barth expresses an unease in viewing these two perfections of the divine freedom as parallels.[29] Nonetheless, because omnipresence is a spatial concept it is perhaps easier for us to comprehend even if we cannot ultimately understand it. God knows that we are now meeting in Edinburgh. He is fully present here and we are fully present to him. He knows that this isn't Eastbourne. He knows the difference botwoon Edinburgh and Eaotbourno. Ho io fully prooont both in Edinburgh and Eastbourne and both are fully present to him yet the distinction between them is neither a limitation upon him nor is it obscured by his simultaneous presence. Barth seems to be suggesting that, in a similar fashion, past, present and future are simultaneously present to God without their temporal distinctions collapsing into some abstract eternal moment. God's eternity is no more a negation of time than is his omnipresence a negation of space but in both he remains free as the living Lord he is.

---

[29]   *C.D.* II 1, p. 465; *cf.* John E. Colwell, *op.cit.*, pp. 31ff.

Now if Barth is generally on the right track in his conception of God's eternity, if eternity is his living history, the pure simultaneity of his past, present and future, then the implications for a doctrine of election should be immediately apparent. An eternal decision of election could not then be relegated to the infinite past of an unfree everlastingness nor could it be abstracted from human history in timeless otherness. In the authentic temporality of God's eternity his decision of election would be simultaneously absolutely previous, absolutely contemporary and absolutely future. It would not be an eternal decision if it ceased as an event at the beginning of time; if it were left behind by the progress of time. God's eternal decision of election is therefore to be conceived in a manner which does not preclude the reality of human history and decisions:

The fundamental significance of the character of predestination as act ought to be clear without further discussion. If it is unchanged and unchangeably the history, encounter and decision between God and man, there is in time an electing by God and an election of man, as there is also a rejecting by God and a rejection of man, but not in the sense that God Himself is bound and imprisoned by it, not as though God's decree, the first step which He took, committed Him to take a corresponding second step, and the second a third. If it is true that the predestinating God not only is free but remains free, that He does not cease to make use of His freedom but continues to decide, then in the course of God's eternal deciding we have constantly to reckon with new decisions in time. As the Bible itself presents the matter, there is no election which cannot be followed by rejection, no rejection which cannot be followed by election. God continues always the Lord of all His works and ways. He is consistent with Himself. He is also consistent with the prearranged order of election and rejection. But He is always the living God.[30]

It is at this point (I hope) that the significance of this paper's title becomes apparent: when Barth's doctrine of election is considered in the context of this understanding of eternity the divine decision to elect is seen to be contemporaneous with the human history of those elected. But this in turn raises a further issue which needs to be clarified. Does this authentically temporal divine decision remain genuinely a *divine* decision or, in its contemporaneity with the acts and decisions of individual men and women, is it reduced to a merely human decision? Is it the human decision for belief or unbelief that finally determines the inclusion or exclusion of individual men and women with respect to their election in Jesus Christ? In the matter of election do men and women effectively have the last word (though not necessarily the last laugh)?

The criticism that Barth understands faith in merely noetic terms has already been noted. Certainly when he is speaking of faith as that human act by which a man or a woman can be identified as a Christian this is an accurate assessment of his view. Christians are those who have recognized the fact of their inclusion in the election of Jesus Christ. Non-Christians are those who have not yet, or no longer, recognize this fact. Barth describes the call to faith by coining terms which are constructs of the German word meaning 'to know' (*kennen*): it is a call 'to acknowledge' (*anerkennen*), 'to recognize' (*erkennen*), and 'to confess' (*bekennen*).[31] The man or the woman addressed by the church in its proclamation is one who 'lacks the knowledge of the Gospel';[32] one who 'suffers by

---

[30]   *C.D.* II 2, pp. 186f.
[31]   *C.D.* IV 1, pp. 740ff.
[32]   *C.D.* IV 3, p. 806.

reason of ignorance'.[33] Knowledge and obedience are that which make a man or a woman a Christian but they are not that which make a man or a woman elect or reconciled:[34]

As this human act it has no creative but only a cognitive character. It does not alter anything. As a human act it is simply the confirmation of a change which has already taken place, the change in the whole human situation which took place in the death of Jesus Christ and was revealed in His resurrection and attested by the Christian community.[35]

In these respects the distinction between the Christian and the non-Christian is noetic rather than ontic. The being of both the Christian and the non-Christian is defined in the life, death and resurrection of Jesus Christ. In this sense election is that which has happened 'to' rather than 'in' the human nature and history of individual men and women.[36]

But Barth is seriously misrepresented by those who claim that he describes the distinction between the Christian and the non-Christian in merely noetic terms. For Barth as for the Bible 'knowledge', in this sense, cannot mean merely the 'acquisition of neutral information' but itself implies the process whereby that which is known confronts and totally transforms the knower. The event in which salvation is known is itself an event of salvation:

---

33   *Ibid.*, p. 809.
34   *C.D.* IV 1, pp. 90ff.
35   *C.D.* IV 1, p. 751.
36   *C.D.* II 2, p. 321; *cf.* John E. Colwell, *op. cit.*, pp. 259ff.; also John E. Colwell, 'Proclamation as Event: Barth's supposed "universalism" in the context of his view of mission' in *Mission to the World: Essays to celebrate the 50th anniversary of the ordination of George Raymond Beasley-Murray to the Christian ministry*, ed. Paul Beasley-Murray (Baptist Historical Society, 1991), pp. 42-46.

the 'total alteration of the one whom it befalls'.[37] Although
the act of faith as a human act can only have a cognitive
and not a creative character this act of faith can only
actually occur in the power of the Holy Spirit and, as such,
it is also a creative event: the positing of a new being, a
new creation, a new birth, a total change in a man or a
woman's whole situation.[38] As an event in the power of
the Holy Spirit it creates a 'distinction and alteration' of
the Christian's being and is thereby both noetic and ontic
in character.[39]

For this reason Barth can refer to the work of the Holy
Spirit in the 'calling' of the elect as the 'objective
difference' (die objektive Unterscheidung) which
'corresponds objectively' (entspricht objektiv) to the
distinction which is peculiar to the elect.[40] It is the means
by which 'their election is accomplished in their life' (zur
Vollstreckung ihrer Erwählung in ihrem Leben).[41] In the
power of the Holy Spirit the reconciliation of a man or a
woman to God is an event not only de iure but also de
facto.[42] Only by the awakening power of the Holy Spirit is
the Christian called to believe in that justification which
has been made actual in Jesus Christ.[43] Only by the
quickening power of the Holy Spirit is the Christian given
the freedom to correspond to the sanctification which has
been made actual in Jesus Christ.[44] Only by the
enlightening power of the Holy Spirit is the Christian
thrust into the service of the prophetic work of Jesus

---

[37]   C.D. IV 3, p. 510; cf. pp. 183ff. & 218ff.
[38]   C.D. IV 1, pp. 751ff.
[39]   C.D. IV 3, pp. 650ff.
[40]   C.D. II 2, p. 345; cf. Die Kirchliche Dogmatik, II 2 (Zurich,
       1942), p. 380.
[41]   C.D. II 2, p. 348; cf. Die Kirchliche Dogmatik, II 2, p. 383.
[42]   C.D. IV 2, p. 511.
[43]   C.D. IV 1, p. 740.
[44]   C.D. IV 2, pp. 727ff.

Christ.[45] The divine nature of this event is most clearly
stated in the 'fragment' of the fourth part of Barth's
doctrine of reconciliation in the course of his exposition of
Baptism with the Spirit:

> Baptism with the Spirit is effective, causative, even
> creative action on man and in man. It is, indeed, divinely
> effective, divinely causative, divinely creative. Here, if
> anywhere, one might speak of a sacramental happening
> in the current sense of the term. It cleanses, renews and
> changes man truly and totally. Whatever may be his
> attitude to it, whatever he himself may make of it, it is
> ... his being clothed upon with a new garment which is
> Jesus Christ Himself, his endowment with a new heart
> controlled by Jesus Christ, his new generation and birth
> in brotherhood with Jesus Christ, his saving death in the
> presence of the death which Jesus Christ suffered for
> him. All this is to be taken realistically, not just
> significantly and figuratively. As this divine change
> takes place in his life, as he is baptised with the Holy
> Ghost, he is to be claimed in all seriousness for this
> change which has come upon him. In the light of it, he is
> in truth a man who has been changed by God's act on
> him and in him.[46]

But this of course is not to imply that the one who
apparently lacks the Holy Spirit, who is apparently
'uncalled', who does not seem to respond to the gospel in
faith, love and hope, is thereby necessarily not also elect
in Jesus Christ. Such a man or woman may be described
as 'apparently rejected' but their rejection remains an
ontologically impossible possibility. They continue to exist
under a real threat of condemnation but we may no more
presume upon the ultimate finality of their rejection

---

45   *C.D.* IV 3, p. 902.
46   *C.D.* IV 4, p. 34.

(limiting God's grace) than we are permitted to presume upon their ultimate salvation (limiting God's freedom).[47]

In his outline of Barth's doctrine of the Holy Spirit Philip Rosato comments that, for Barth, the Spirit is the 'divine Noetic which has all the force of a divine Ontic':[48] he actualizes in man 'what was already an actuality both in the historical existence and in the eternal election of Jesus Christ';[49] he 'makes real in man what was and still is real in Jesus Christ';[50] he is the subjective reality of the objective revelation in Jesus Christ;[51] he is the means by which that which is already *extra nos* is made effective *in nobis*.[52] Rosato accepts that all this implies an alteration of man's being;[53] an 'ontic renewing'[54] by means of which the ontological connection between Jesus Christ and all men and women is made 'an existential reality'.[55]

It is therefore quite surprising that Rosato later concludes that for Barth the Spirit 'is purposely conceptualized as possessing from eternity a purely noetic function'.[56] It is as if his own assessment of Barth's thinking, painstakingly worked out earlier in his study, is belittled in favour of a predetermined conclusion. Now it may be that within Barth's *Dogmatics* the person and work of the Holy Spirit is not granted the prominence which some of us might have wished. It may be that, despite the clear import and consistency of the passages

---

[47]   *C.D.* II 2, pp. 345ff. & 449ff.
[48]   Philip J. Rosato, S.J., *The Spirit as Lord: The Pneumatology of Karl Barth* (Edinburgh, 1981), p. 126.
[49]   *Ibid.*, p. 67.
[50]   *Ibid.*, p. 69.
[51]   *Ibid.*, p. 70.
[52]   *Ibid.*, p. 86.
[53]   *Ibid.*, p. 112.
[54]   *Ibid.*, p. 123.
[55]   *Ibid.*, p. 126.
[56]   *Ibid.*, p. 161.

mentioned, Barth retains an observable reticence concerning the Spirit. It may even be valid for us to speculate concerning the possible reasons for such reticence. It may also be true that there remains in Barth a persistent orientation towards pastness and completion together with a consequent weakness with reference to the present and the future. But it would be a great disservice to Barth to exaggerate any apparent imbalance in this respect. Rather than acknowledge that which Barth actually says there appears to be a strange tendency among several of Barth's critics either to consider one strand of his teaching in isolation or to resolve the complementary aspects of his thought in a monistic manner: to resolve the ontic into the noetic; the dynamic into the static; the authentically temporal into the mists of an abstract timelessness which Barth himself would disown.[57]

When both aspects of Barth's thought are seriously heard then election can be perceived as a living and thoroughly Trinitarian event. The primal decision of the Father does not preclude but includes the actualization of that decision in the life, death and resurrection of the Son. Similarly the decision of the Father as it is actualized in the Son does not preclude but includes the real event of the participation of men and women in that decision through the power of the Holy Spirit. In the authentic temporality which is God's eternity the faith, hope and love of individual men and women are genuinely comprehended within the event of election.[58] Through the work of the Holy Spirit the relationship between Jesus Christ and individual men and women is dynamic as well as ontological. This work of the Holy Spirit is no more an addendum to the completed work of the Son than the work

---

57   John E. Colwell, *op. cit.*, pp. 66, 71ff. & 298ff.
58   *C.D.* II 2, pp. 183ff.

of the Son is an addendum to the eternal decision of the Father.

Barth can avoid the charge of universalism without logical contradiction because he understands the decision of election in dynamic rather than static terms; as a truly Trinitarian event rather than as a binitarian or unitarian event; as an event of God's eternity which includes human history rather than as a timeless abstraction or an event of the infinite past which would invalidate the authentic futurity of God's eternity. Within this dynamic God is self-consistent with his self-determination to be this electing God in Jesus Christ; he is unchangeable but not static, immutable but not immobile, constant but not to be presumed upon, faithful but never unfree.[59] His primal decision never becomes his prison because it is not a decision of the infinite past, binding him in the present and the future, but a decision which is authentically temporal in which past, present and future are simultaneously comprehended and included.[60]

In his *Introduction* to Barth's *Dogmatics* and towards the conclusion of his exposition of Barth's doctrine of election Geoffrey Bromiley notes an 'ambivalence at this decisive point -- will all be saved or not, and if not, why not?-', an ambivalance which Barth only overcomes by a final 'appeal to the divine freedom'. Bromiley regrets that Barth did not 'bring this out much earlier' which is a surprising comment when few if any could have read the text of the *Church Dogmatics* more diligently than this amazingly avid translator.[61] That God 'reveals himself as the Lord', that he is the 'One who loves in freedom' is

---

59   *C.D.* II 2, p. 185; *cf. C.D.* II 1, pp. 491ff.
60   John E. Colwell, *op. cit.*, p. 284.
61   Geoffrey W. Bromiley, *Introduction to the Theology of Karl Barth* (T. & T. Clark, Edinburgh, 1979), pp. 97f.

arguably the most fundamental element of Barth's theological thought.

If some of Barth's critics refuse to take this divine freedom seriously with respect (especially) to Barth's doctrine of election and consequently suspect him of implicit universalism then that is their problem rather than his and probably says more about them than it says about him. This is not at all to underestimate the seriousness of the error that is universalism, but it is to take Barth seriously in his consistent refutation of that error. The more interesting and serious questions concerning Barth's theological contribution relate to the implications of his dynamic interpretation of the divine will and being, the implications of the manner in which Barth speaks of Father, Son and Spirit, particularly in the later volumes of the *Church Dogmatics*, the implications of his conception of God's eternity as his authentic temporality and the consequences of this view for our understanding of the contingency of the created order and human history. Barth's understanding of election as a continuing dynamic certainly does not resolve the paradox of divine sovereignty and human responsibility but at least it sets it in different and perhaps more helpful parameters. It would be encouraging to suppose that we might eventually turn our back on insinuations of universalism and give our attention to these more substantive issues.

6

The Case for Conditional Immortality

John W. Wenham

This paper is deliberately restricted in scope.[1] The *presupposition* on which it is based is an acceptance of the canonical books of the Old and New Testaments as divinely inspired and harmonious in their teaching when interpreted in the natural and intended sense. There is therefore no discussion of critical questions which see one part of Scripture in conflict with another. By way of

---

[1] It should be seen as part of a larger argument on the Christian view of the Bible which I am conducting in a series of books: *Christ and the Bible* (Leicester: IVP, 1984; Guildford: Eagle, 3rd ed. 1992), which deals with inspiration, canon and text; *The Enigma of Evil* (Leicester: IVP, 2nd ed. 1985), which deals with the moral difficulties of the Bible. The present paper is an expansion of the chapter on 'Hell' in that book. By the time I wrote that book I had come to the conclusion that all the learned and earnest attempts at deriving universalism from the Bible had failed (*e.g.* J.H. Leckie, *The World to Come and Final Destiny*, 1918; John Baillie, *And the Life Everlasting*, 1934; John Hick, *Evil and the God of Love*, 1936; J.A.T. Robinson, *In the End God*, 1950) and that it was really not an option for those who believed in the doctrine of the Bible expounded in *Christ and the Bible*. So I shall not address this point of view again here. *Easter Enigma* (Exeter: Paternoster, 1984) and *Redating Matthew, Mark and Luke* (London: Hodder and Stoughton, 1991) deal with critical questions, showing that it is not necessary to regard biblical divergences as evidence of disharmony. The temptation to pit one Scripture against another must be resisted if the straightforward teaching of the Bible is to be accepted as the Word of God.

definition: belief in conditional immortality is the belief that God created Man only potentially immortal. Immortality is a state gained by grace through faith when the believer receives eternal life and becomes a partaker of the divine nature, immortality being inherent in God alone. It is a doctrine totally different from universalism, which I have long believed quite irreconcilable with Scripture. It shares the doctrine of judgment held by the upholders of everlasting torment in almost every particular – except for one tremendous thing: it sees no continuing place in God's world for human beings living on in unending pain, not reconciled to God. The wrath of God will put an end to sin and evil.

An Answer Awaited

I am grateful for the opportunity of expounding this case, for it is seventeen years since I tentatively committed myself to it in print. This was in my book *The Goodness of God*,[2] where I dealt with the subject of 'Hell' in one short chapter. I could do little more than outline the main points of the case for unending conscious torment and for conditional immortality (the latter in seven pages) as convincingly as I could and leave the reader to make his choice. I said, however, that I felt under no obligation to defend any doctrine more shocking than conditionalism until the arguments of L.E. Froom, Basil Atkinson and Harold Guillebaud[3] had been effectively answered.

---

2   First edition, IVP, Leicester; second edition, under the title *The Enigma of Evil*, 1985.

3   L.E. Froom, *The Conditionalist Faith of Our Fathers* (Washington, D.C.: Review and Herald Publishing Ass., 1966); B.F.C. Atkinson, *Life and Immortality* (privately printed, no date, still obtainable from the Revd B.L. Bateson, 26 Summershard, S. Petherton, Somerset TA13 5DP for £1 post free); H.E. Guillebaud, *The Righteous Judge* (privately printed, 1964; photocopies obtainable also from Bateson for £2 post free). (Basil Atkinson, an eccentric bachelor academic, was the main adviser of the Cambridge Inter-Collegiate Christian

I had learnt the doctrine from Basil Atkinson in (I suppose) about 1934. Hitherto I had held the doctrine of unending torment, which had been particularly impressed on me by R.A. Torrey in *What the Bible Teaches*.[4] The torments of the lost had occupied a considerable place in my prayers and I felt deflated when I first heard their everlastingness questioned. But I was fairly certain that Basil Atkinson was right.

In spite of his censures he and I remained good friends and in 1940 we had a considerable correspondence in which I put many questions to him. When I left Cambridge in 1938 I had to teach doctrine at St John's Hall, Highbury. There till 1941 I taught conditionalism with much reserve and restraint. After that I had twelve years out of direct academic work, before joining the staff of Tyndale Hall, Bristol. Here I taught with rather less reserve, particularly after a Tyndale House Study Group in 1954 which was devoted to The Intermediate State and the Final Condition of the Lost. Here some of the best brains in IVF studied the subject for (I think) three days. Though bringing home to me the great difficulty of coming to assured conclusions about the intermediate state, I was more than ever persuaded that the final end of the lost was destruction in the fires of hell.

Matters reached crisis point in 1973, when I presented Inter-Varsity Press with the MS of *The Goodness of God*. IVP had already published my *Christ and the Bible*, which

---

Union during the years when the Inter-Varsity Fellowship was being built up and conservative Evangelicals were trying to extricate themselves from liberalism. He was the great pillar of orthodoxy and was not slow to oppose any deviation from Evangelical tradition, as I knew to my cost when during the war I questioned current 'worldliness' taboos. At no other time has anyone been so rude to me in print!)

4   London, Nisbet, n.d., pp. 303-314.

I had let them have on condition that they would publish
its sequel, concerning the moral difficulties of the Bible. I
thought that hell was too big a subject to treat in this book
and decided simply to content myself with presenting the
biblical images without comment. IVP sent the MS to a
discerning reader who then asked for help on this topic. So
I wrote half-a-dozen pages advocating conditional
immortality. At this IVP were up in arms and a long
correspondence ensued which ended with a conference
with some of their senior people. I was astonished at how
little they had thought about the subject. But at least we
were agreed that the biblical research which we were
promoting should be more concerned about fundamental
doctrines than archaeological minutiae and they allowed
me to try to state both doctrines as fairly as I could. This
was a great step forward for neither Atkinson nor
Guillebaud had been able to find a publisher. So I have
been waiting since 1973 for a reply to the massive work of
Froom (2,476 pages), to Atkinson's closely argued 112
pages, to Guillebaud's 67 and (more important) to the one
additional book which has appeared on the conditionalist
side: Edward Fudge's *The Fire That Consumes*.[5]

An Answer Attempted

To my knowledge there have been four serious attempts
at reply. In 1986 The Banner of Truth Trust republished
the work of the Reformed theologian W.G.T. Shedd, *The
Doctrine of Endless Punishment*, first published in 1885,
which faithfully reasserts the doctrine of the Westminster
Confession, chapter 32 of which says: 'The bodies of men
after death return to dust, and see corruption; but their
souls, (which neither die nor sleep) having an immortal
subsistence, immediately return to God who gave them.
The souls of the righteous, being then made perfect in
holiness, are received into the highest heavens, where

---

5   Published in 1982 by Providential Press, POB 218026,
       Houston, Texas 77218, a book of 500 pages.

they behold the face of God in light and glory, waiting for the full redemption of their bodies; and the souls of the wicked are cast into hell, where they remain in torments and utter darkness, reserved to the judgment of the great day. Besides these two places for souls separated from their bodies, the scripture acknowledgeth none.' In 1989 the same Trust published Paul Helm's *The Last Things: Death, Judgment, Heaven and Hell.* In 1990 J.H. Gerstner's *Repent or Perish*[6] was published, which has four chapters directed specifically against Fudge. In the same year J.I. Packer published his Leon Morris Lecture, 'The Problem of Eternal Punishment', which he declares to be 'a dissuasive... particularly from conditionalism.'[7]

The extraordinary thing about these replies is that none of them actually addresses the arguments used by the conditionalists. Shedd, it is true, refers to the eighteenth century Anglican Bishop Warburton, who 'denied that the immortality of the soul is taught in the Old Testament'. Shedd's reply is that it 'is nowhere formally demonstrated, because it is everywhere assumed' (pp. 50f). He then proceeds to demolish views which as far as I know no conditionalist holds. Similarly I did not recognise the conditionalism to which Helm refers – he gives no references. He says annihilationists hold that 'when the impenitent die they do not go on to await the judgment, but they go literally out of existence' (p. 117). He does, however, acknowledge that 'Scripture does not teach the immortality of the soul in so many words' (p. 118).

When we come to Gerstner and Packer an important new factor has arisen: J.R.W. Stott and P.E. Hughes, two leading conservative Evangelicals, have written

---

6   Soli Deo Gloria Publications, 213 W. Vincent St., Ligonier, PA 15658.
7   *Crux* 26.3 (Sept 1990), p. 25.

sympathetically of conditionalism.[8] In *Essentials*, his
dialogue with David Edwards, Stott writes that he holds
his belief in the ultimate annihilation of the wicked
'tentatively'. He also expresses his hesitation in writing
this (although he has told me that he has spoken about it
for thirty or forty years) 'partly because I have great
respect for longstanding tradition which claims to be a true
interpretation of Scripture, and do not lightly set it aside,
and partly because the unity of the worldwide evangelical
constituency has always meant much to me' (p. 319). He
says he prefers to describe himself as 'agnostic' which, he
tells me, is how the late F.F. Bruce also described his
position. Since in his view Scripture does not come down
unequivocally on either side, he pleads 'that the ultimate
annihilation of the wicked should at least be accepted as a
legitimate, biblically founded alternative to their eternal
conscious torment' (p. 320). Hughes, who lectured at
Westminster Theological Seminary, Philadelphia, and was
one of the editors of *Westminster Theological Journal*, has
no such hesitations. He says, 'It would be hard to imagine
a concept more confusing than that of death which means
existing endlessly without the power of dying. This,
however, is the corner into which Augustine (in company
with many others) argued himself' (p. 403). He wrote me
that he had 'long been of this judgment and common
Christian candour compelled me to state my position.'
Gerstner pitches into Hughes, Stott and Fudge for their
revolt against hell. It is a wonderful example of circular
argument. He assumes that the Bible teaches what he
believes about hell and then proceeds to show that they
believe otherwise. He just does not seriously address
their arguments. Not sharing his beliefs about hell is

---

8   See D.L. Edwards and J.R.W. Stott, *Essentials* (London:
     Hodder and Stoughton, 1988), pp. 312-329. Incidentally I find
     Stott's way of distinguishing annihilationism and conditional
     immortality on p. 316 somewhat confusing. P.E. Hughes, *The
     True Image* (Grand Rapids, Eerdman and Leicester: Inter-
     Varsity Press, 1989) chap. 37.

equated with a rejection of hell itself, which it is absurd to attribute to such as Stott, Hughes and Fudge.

Packer is in some ways even more disappointing. With all his capacity for reading and digesting material and with his gift of lucid exposition, one hoped to see the conditionalist arguments carefully considered. He had certainly read the slight treatments of Stott and Hughes and was aware of Fudge's work, but he shows no signs of having read Fudge, Froom or Atkinson and provides no answers to their arguments, but gives instead answers to arguments which they do not use.[9]

While not answering the conditionalist arguments with any seriousness, these writers do of course state their own case. They set out certain well-known texts and claim that their meaning is 'obvious'.[10] Of conditionalist

---

9   Since writing the above I have read Ajith Fernando's *Crucial Questions About Hell* published in 1991 by Kingsway with a foreword by Packer. Fernando is a Methodist, a Youth for Christ worker in Sri Lanka, who in the mid-seventies wrote a thesis on universalism for his Master of Theology degree at Fuller Theological Seminary. His book is an updated, popular version of his thesis, written in an admirable spirit, with most of which I thoroughly agree. He pays some attention to conditionalism, referring to Stott, Travis and Pinnock, but to no major conditionalist work. From the other side, Michael Green also committed to print his belief in conditional immortality last year: E.M.B. Green, *Evangelism through the Local Church* (London: Hodder and Stoughton, 1990), pp. 69f.

10   *E.g.* Packer, p. 24. I was reminded by a theologian for whose learning and acuteness I have profound respect of another old book, not republished: E.M. Goulburn, *Everlasting Punishment* (London: Rivingtons, 1880). He takes the same line: 'Most certain it is that the objectors do not *found* their views on Holy Scripture... probably none of them would maintain that Scripture on the surface favours them.' Similarly W. Hendriksen, *The Bible on the Life Hereafter* (Grand Rapids: Baker, 1959), p. 197 says: 'The passages... are so numerous that one actually stands aghast that in spite of all this there are

interpretations Packer says: 'I will say as emphatically as I can, that none of them is natural.... Conditionalists' attempts to evade the natural meaning of some dozens of relevant passages impress me as a prime case of avalanche-dodging' (p. 24).

people today who affirm that they accept Scripture and who, nevertheless, reject the idea of never-ending torment.'

The Biblical Data

I would claim that the natural meaning of the vast majority of relevant texts is quite otherwise. Of course what seems natural and obvious to a person with one set of presuppositions may not seem so to someone with a different set. What we must try to do is to think the way the biblical writers thought and clear our minds of ideas from other cultures. This makes the Old Testament very important, but demands of space make it necessary to pass over the Old Testament, though earlier writers and Fudge quite properly pay it considerable attention. But this is not central to the debate and we will simply quote one sentence of Fudge: 'The Old Testament utilizes some fifty Hebrew words and seventy-five figures of speech to describe the ultimate end of the wicked – and every one sounds... like total extinction.'[11] He also shows that in

---

[11]   *Resurrection* 93 (Fall, 1990) p. 4.
This is the summary of his chapter 'The End of the Wicked in the OT': 'The Old Testament has very much to say about the end of the wicked. Its poetic books of Job, Psalms and Proverbs repeatedly affirm the principle of divine government. The wicked may thrive now and the righteous suffer, these books tell us, but that picture will not be the final one. These books reassure the godly again and again that those who trust will be vindicated, they will endure forever, they will inherit the earth. The wicked, however proud their boasts today, will one day not be found. Their place will be empty. They will vanish like a slug as it moves along (Ps. 58:8, Kidner 1.210: 'like a miscarriage'). They will disappear like smoke. Men will search for them and they will not be found. Even their memory will perish. On these pillars of divine justice the world stands, and by these principles the Lord God governs His eternal kingdom.
The historical books of the Old Testament take us another step. Not only does God declare what He will do to the wicked; on many occasions He has shown us. When the first world became too wicked to exist, God destroyed it completely, wiping every living creature outside the ark from the face of the earth. This is a model of the fiery judgment awaiting the present heavens and earth. When Sodom became

the Apocrypha and pseudepigrapha the Old Testament
view predominates, although the notion of endless torment
is beginning to appear in Jewish literature.

When we come to the New Testament, the words used
in their natural connotation are words of destruction rather
than words suggesting continuance in torment or misery.
When preparing this paper I found in my files thirty pages
of foolscap (dating, I think, from the '40s) on which I had
attempted to jot down from the RV all passages referring

---

too sinful to continue, God rained fire and brimstone from
heaven, obliterating the entire population in a moment so
terrible it is memorialized throughout Scripture as an example
of divine judgment. From this terrible conflagration emerged
not a survivor – even the ground was left scorched and barren.
Only the lingering smoke remained, a grim reminder of the fate
awaiting any man who attempts to quarrel with his Maker.

Cities and nations also tasted God's wrath. Edom and Judah,
Babylon and Nineveh turn by turn came under his temporal
judgments. Some were spared a remnant. Others were not. God
described these divine visitations in terms of fire and darkness,
anguish and trouble. Unquenchable fire consumed entirely until
nothing was left. Again smoke ascended, the prophetic cipher
for a ruin accomplished.

The inspired declarations of the prophets combine moral
principle with historical fate. The details of actual destruction
wrought on earth become symbols for another divine visitation.
The prophets speak to their own times, but they also stand on
tiptoe and view the distant future. A day is coming, they tell
us, when God will bring to an end all he has begun. That
judgment will be the last. Good and evil will be gathered alike
to see the righteousness of the Lord they have served or
spurned. Again there will be fire and storm, tempest and
darkness. The slain of God will be many – corpses will lie in
the street. Amidst this scene of utter contempt worms and fire
will take their final toll. Nothing will remain of the wicked
but ashes – the righteous will tread over them with their feet.
God's kingdom will endure forever. The righteous and their
children will inherit Mount Zion. Joy and singing will fill the
air. All the earth will praise the Lord.' (*The Fire that
Consumes*, 116f. The evidence on which this summary is based
is set out on pp. 87-116).

to life after death. This is certainly not a complete list, but I have worked through it again and this interesting statistic results. I found 264 references to the fate of the lost.

Ten (that is 4%) call it Gehenna, which conjures up at once the imagery of the rubbish tip in the Valley of Hinnom outside Jerusalem, where the maggots and the fire destroy the garbage (Mt. 5:22, 29, 30; 10:28; 18:9; 23:33; Mk. 9:43, 45, 47; Luke 12:5). Two of these call it the Gehenna of fire.

There are twenty-six other references (that is 10%) to burning up, three of which concern the lake of fire of the Apocalypse.[12] Fire naturally suggests destruction and is much used for the destruction of what is worthless or evil. It is only by a pedantic use of the modern concept of the conservation of mass and energy that it is possible to say that fire destroys nothing. It has a secondary use as a cause of pain, as in the case of Dives.

Fifty-nine (22%) speak of destruction, perdition, utter loss or ruin.[13] Our Lord himself in the Sermon on the Mount uses destruction, which he contrasts with life, as the destination of those who choose the broad road (Mt. 7:13). Paul uses it of 'the objects of his wrath – prepared for destruction' (Rom. 9:22); of 'those who oppose you' who 'will be destroyed' (Phil. 1:28); of the enemies of the cross of Christ whose 'destiny is destruction' (Phil. 3:19).

---

12   Mt. 3:7, 12; 7:19; 13:40, 42, 50; 18:8f; 25:41. Mk 9:43, 48f. Luke 3:7, 17. 1 Cor. 3:13. 2 Thes. 1:7. Heb. 6:8; 10:27; 12:29. 2 Pet. 3:7,10. Jude 7,23. Rev. 20:14f.; 21:8.

13   Mt. 7:13,27; 10:6,28,39; 15:13; 16:25f; 21:41, 44; 22:7. Mk 8:35f; 12:9. Lk. 6:49; 9:25; 13:3,7; 17:29,33; 19:10,27; 20:18. Jn. 3:16, 36; 6:39; 12:25. Acts 2:25,31; 13:41. Rom. 2:12; 9:22, 29; 14:15. 1 Cor. 1:18; 10:10; 15:18. 2 Cor. 2:15; 4:3. Phil. 1:28; 3:19. 1 Thes. 5:3. 2 Thes. 1:9; 2:8,10. 1 Tim. 6:9. Heb. 10:39. Jas 4:12. 2 Pet. 2:1,3,12; 3:7,9,16. 1 Jn. 2:17. Jude 5,10f.

'The man of lawlessness is ... doomed to destruction' (2 Thes. 2:3); harmful desires 'plunge men into ruin and destruction' (1 Tim. 6:9). Hebrews 10:39 says 'we are not of those who shrink back to destruction, but of those who believe and are saved.' 2 Peter speaks of 'destructive heresies ... bringing swift destruction... their destruction has not been sleeping' (2:1-3); 'The present heavens and earth are reserved for fire, being kept for the day of judgment and destruction of ungodly men'(3:7). The old order will disappear and 'the elements will be destroyed by fire' (3:10-12). The beast will 'go to his destruction' (Rev. 17:8,11). The very common word *apollumi* is frequently used of eternal ruin, destruction and loss, as in John 3:16 'should not perish', but it is also used of the lost sheep, the lost coin and the lost son, who though metaphorically dead and whose life was in total ruin was restored (Lk. 15).

Twenty cases (8%) speak of separation from God,[14] which carries no connotation of endlessness unless one presupposes immortality: 'depart from me' (Mt. 8:23); 'cast him into the outer darkness' (Mt. 22:13); he 'shall not enter' the kingdom (Mk 10:15); 'one will be taken and the other left' (Lk. 17:34); 'he is cast forth as a branch' (Jn 15:6); 'outside are the dogs, *etc.*' (Rev. 22:15). This concept of banishment from God is a terrifying one. It does not mean escaping from God, since God is everywhere in his creation, every particle of which owes its continuing existence to his sustaining. It means, surely, being utterly cut off from the source and sustainer of life. It is another way of describing destruction.

---

14   Mt. 7:21; 8:11; 10:32; 22:13; 25:30,41,46. Mk 8:38; 10:15. Lk. 12:9; 13:27f; 14:21,34; 16:26; 17:34. Jn 15:6. Eph. 5:5. 2 Thes. 1:9. Rev. 22:15.

Twenty-five cases (10%) refer to death in its finality, sometimes called 'the second death'.[15] Without resurrection even 'those who have fallen asleep in Christ have perished' (1 Cor. 15:18). This has been brought out with great force by a number of modern theologians like Oscar Cullmann, Helmut Thielicke and Murray Harris.[16] They show that the teaching of the New Testament is to be sharply contrasted with the Greek notion of the immortality of the soul, which sees death as the release of the soul from the prison of the body. What the Christian looks forward to is not a bodiless entrance 'into the highest heavens' at death, but a glorious transformation at the *parousia* when he is raised from death. Life is contrasted with death, which is a cessation of life, rather than with a continuance of life in misery.

One hundred and eight cases (41%) refer to what I have called unforgiven sin:[17] adverse judgment, in which the

---

[15] Lk. 20:36. Jn 8:51; 11:26. Rom 1:32; 4:17; 5:12; 6:13; 11:15. I Cor. 15:22,54. 2 Cor. 2:15; 5:4; 7:10. Eph. 2:5. 2 Tim. 1:10. Heb 5:7. Jas 5:20. 1 Jn 3:14; 5:16. Jude 12. Rev. 2:7,10; 20:6, 14; 21:8.

[16] O. Cullmann, *Immortality of the Soul or Resurrection of the Dead?* (London: Epworth, 1958); *Immortality and Resurrection* (New York: Macmillan, 1965). H. Thielicke, *Death and Life* (Philadelphia: Fortress, 1970); M.J. Harris, *Raised Immortal* (London: Marshall, 1983). See also the recent work of the Oxford Dominican, S. Tugwell: *Human Immortality and the Redemption of Death* (London: Darton, Longman and Todd, 1990).

[17] Mt. 12:36,41; 18:18; 23:35f. Mk 3:29; 12:40; 16:16. Lk. 3:9; 11:31,50; 12:10,20; 20:35f; 20:47; 21:19. Jn. 3:17; 5:28; 8:21,24; 12:48. Acts 2:40; 4:12; 8:22; 10:42; 13:26, 38f, 47; 15:1,11; 16:17,30; 24:25; 26:18. Rom. 1:16, 18; 2:3, 5, 16; 3:6; 4:7; 5:9; 8:24; 9:27; 10:9f; 11:26, 32; 14:10. 1 Cor. 1:21; 3:13; 9:22; 10:33; 11:32; 15:2, 17; 16:22. 2 Cor. 6:2. Eph. 5:6. Phil. 4:3. Col. 3:6,25. 1 Thes. 1:10; 2:16; 4:6; 5:9. 2 Thes. 1:8; 2:10. 1 Tim. 2:4; 4:10. 2 Tim. 1:9, 18; 2:10; 4:1,14,16. Tit. 2:11,13; 3:5. Heb. 2:10; 5:9; 6:1; 9:27f; 10:27. Jas 1:21; 2:13; 5:12. 1

penalty is not specified (*e.g.* 'they will receive greater condemnation', Mk 12:40); life forfeited, with the wrath of God resting on the unbeliever (Jn 3:36); being unsaved, without specifying what the saved are delivered from (Mt. 24:13). Other passages show salvation contrasted with lostness (Mt. 16:25), perishing (1 Cor. 1:18), destruction (Jas 4:12), condemnation (Mk 16:16), judgment (Jn 3:17), death (2 Cor. 17:10), never with everlasting misery or pain.

Fifteen cases (6%) refer to anguish[18] – this includes tribulation and distress (Rom. 2:9), deliverance to tormentors (Mt. 18:34), outer darkness (Mt. 22:13), wailing and grinding of teeth (Mt. 25:30), the undying worm (Mk 9:48), beaten with many stripes (Lk. 12:47), the birth-pains of death (Acts 2:24), sorer punishment (Heb. 10:29).

There is one verse (Rev. 14:11) – this represents less than a half per cent – which refers to human beings who have no rest, day or night, the smoke of whose torment goes up for ever and ever, which we shall come back to in a moment.

It is a terrible catalogue, giving most solemn warning, but in all but one of the 264 references there is not a word about unending torment and very many of them in their natural sense clearly refer to destruction.

Immortality of the Soul
There is thus a great weight of material which *prima facie* suggests destruction as the final end of the lost. The

---

Pet. 1:5,9; 4:5f, 17. 2 Pet. 2:9. 1 Jn. 2:28; 4:17. Jude 15,21. Rev. 3:5; 6:10, 17; 7:10; 11:18; 20:18f; 22:12.

18   Mt. 18:34; 22:13; 24:51. Mk. 9:48. Lk. 12:46; 13:28; 16:23f, 28. Acts 2:24. Rom. 2:9. 2 Thes. 1:6. Heb. 10:29. 2 Pet. 2:17. Jude 13.

traditional view gains most of its plausibility from a belief that our Lord's teaching about Gehenna has to be wedded to a belief in the immortality of the soul. A fierce fire will destroy any living creature, unless that creature happens to be immortal. If man *is* made immortal, all our exegesis must change. But is he? From Genesis 3 onwards man looks mortal indeed; we are clearly told that God alone has immortality (1 Tim. 6:16); immortality is something that well-doers *seek* (Rom. 2:7); immortality for the believer has been brought to light by the gospel (2 Tim. 1:10) – he gains immortality (it would appear) when he gains eternal life and becomes partaker of the divine nature; immortality is finally put on at the last trump (1 Cor.15:53). No, say the traditionalists, God in making man made him immortal, so that he must live on, not only beyond death, but also beyond the second death, for ever and ever. The fires of hell will continue to inflict pain on persons they cannot consume.

Now the curious thing is that when asked for biblical proof of the immortality of the soul, the answer usually given is that it is nowhere explicitly taught, but that (as we have already quoted from Shedd) 'it is everywhere assumed'. Goulburn similarly says that the doctrine of man's immortality 'seems to be graven on man's heart almost as indelibly as the doctrine of God's existence' (p. 68). The great Hermann Bavinck defends it as a biblical doctrine, but says that it is better demonstrated by reason than by revelation.[19] That life-beyond-death is repeatedly taught in Scripture and is instinctively believed by everyone I readily agree, but of its nature and endurance we know nothing except by revelation. If anything has become pellucidly clear to me over the years it is this: philosophisings about the after-life are worthless, we must stick to Scripture and Scripture alone. Certainly

---

[19]   Quoted in Fudge, p. 53 n. 11.

something as important as the immortality of the soul and
the endless pain of the lost cannot be *assumed*!

Passages Relied on For Endlessness of Punishment

What are these 'dozens of relevant passages' which we
conditionalists attempt to evade by 'various exegetical
expedients' (Packer p. 24)? They seem in fact to be
fourteen in number.

There are seven passages which speak of everlasting
punishment (Mt. 25:46), everlasting fire (Mt. 18:8; 25:41),
an eternal sin (Mk 3:29), everlasting destruction (2 Thes.
1:9), everlasting judgment (Heb. 6:2), the punishment of
everlasting fire (Jude 7). Fudge rightly devotes a chapter
early in his book to the meaning of *aionios* and shows (as
is well known) that it has two aspects. It has a qualitative
sense, indicating 'a relationship to the kingdom of God, to
the Age to Come, to the eschatological realities which in
Jesus have begun already to manifest themselves in the
Present Age.'[20] This aspect is perhaps best translated
'eternal'. When I analyse my own thoughts, I find that
(rightly or wrongly) everlastingness has virtually no place
in my concept of eternal life. Everlasting harp-playing or
hymn-singing or even contemplation is not attractive.
What the heart yearns for is deliverance from sin and the
bliss of being with God in heaven, knowing that the
inexorable march of death has been abolished for ever.
Aionios also has an aspect of temporal limitlessness
which can be rightly translated 'everlasting'. It is common

---

[20]   P. 49. *cf.* D.A. Carson, *The Gospel according to John*
(Leicester: IVP and Grand Rapids: Eerdmanns, 1991, p. 202);
'*zoe aionios* here makes its first appearance in the Fourth
Gospel. Properly it means 'life of the age to come', and
therefore resurrection life. But in John's Gospel that life may
in some measure be experienced before the end .... The eternal
life begun by the new birth is nothing less than the eternal life
of the eternal Word.'

to argue that since everlasting punishment is set against everlasting life in Matthew 25:46, and since the life lasts as long as God, so must the punishment. This was the position of Augustine, of which Hughes writes: 'Augustine insisted... to say that "life eternal shall be endless, punishment eternal shall come to an end, is the height of absurdity" (*City of God* 21.23)... But, as we have seen, the ultimate contrast is between everlasting *life* and everlasting *death* and this clearly shows that it is not simply synonyms but also antonyms with which we have to reckon. There is no more radical antithesis than that between life and death, for life is the absence of death and death is the absence of life. Confronted with this antithesis, the position of Augustine cannot avoid involvement in the use of contradictory concepts.'[21] To this we might add three further considerations: (1) It would be proper to translate 'punishment of the age to come' and 'life of the age to come' which would leave open the question of duration. The Matthean parallel to the *aionios* of Mark 3:29 is indeed 'age to come' (Mt 12:32). (2) We have a number of examples of once-for-all acts which have unending consequences: eternal redemption (Heb 9:12), Sodom's punishment of eternal fire (Jude 7). (3) Just as it is wrong to treat God and Satan as equal and opposite, so it is wrong to assume that heaven and hell, eternal life and eternal punishment, are equal and opposite. Both are real, but who is to say that one is as enduring as the other?[22]

---

21 Hughes, p. 403. The rest of his discussion in this chapter is excellent, meriting careful study.

22 There is the further question as to whether the life of the age to come should be thought of as in time at all. Post-Einsteinians naturally think of space and time as so related that creation would be the creation of space-time, the two being inseparable. This is a philosophical question which the Bible does not address, but it does use time-language concerning heaven. However, this may well be because this is the only category in which we can think.

There are three passages which speak of unquenchable fire, two in the teaching of the Baptist (Mt. 3:12 = Lk. 3:17) and one from our Lord who speaks of going away 'into Gehenna into the unquenchable fire' (Mk 9:43). The chaff of course is burnt up by the irresistible fire – there is nothing to suggest that the fire goes on burning after it has destroyed the rubbish. The same Markan passage (9:48) gives us the one reference to the undying worm, which (as we have seen) is a quotation from Isaiah 66:24 which depicts corpses being consumed by maggots, which fits precisely the imagery of the rubbish of Jerusalem.

There is nothing in any of these ten texts which even suggests (let alone requires) an interpretation contrary to the natural interpretation of the great mass of texts which tell of death, destruction, perishing and consumption by fire. Nor has the imagery of outer darkness and grinding of teeth any bearing on the question of endlessness.

This leaves us with one passage in Jude and three passages in the Book of Revelation. Jude has spoken of the people saved from Egypt and the destruction of those who did not believe; and of angels kept in eternal chains in the nether gloom awaiting the day of judgment, when they will suffer as Sodom suffered; he then goes on to speak of those who defile the Christian love feasts 'for whom the nether gloom of darkness has been reserved for ever'(v. 13). These immoral Christians will suffer the same fate as the fallen angels: nether gloom till the day of judgment, then destruction.

In the Book of Revelation two passages speak of the smoke of torment rising for ever and ever. 14:11 says of those with the mark of the beast, tormented with burning sulphur, 'the smoke of their torment goes up for ever and ever; and they have no rest, day or night, these worshippers of the beast'. 19:3 says of the great whore, 'the smoke from her goes up for ever and ever'. Finally, 20:10 speaks of the devil 'thrown into the lake of fire and brimstone where the beast and the false prophet were, and they will be tormented day and night for ever and ever.'

Of these three passages two are concerned with non-human or symbolic figures: the devil, the beast, the false prophet and the great whore, and only one refers to men. But the imagery is the same and they need to be examined together. The mind of John of the Apocalypse is steeped in Holy Scripture and it is to the Old Testament that we must go for enlightenment. After Noah's flood, the second great demonstration of divine judgment is the raining down of burning sulphur on the cities of Sodom and Gomorrah. What is left is total irreversible desolation and dense smoke rising from the land (Gen. 19:24-28). This fearful example is recalled by Moses (Deut. 29:23), Isaiah (13:19), Jeremiah (50:40), Lamentations (4:6), Amos (4:11), Zephaniah (2:9), Peter (2 Pet 2:6), Jude (7) and Jesus himself (Lk. 17:28-32). It seems best to interpret the lake of fire and brimstone, the smoke and the torment of the Apocalypse in the light of this great archetypal example. The concept of second death is one of great finality; the fire consumes utterly, all that is left is smoke, a reminder of God's complete and just triumph over evil.

The third passage (Rev. 14:11) is the most difficult passage that the conditionalist has to deal with. I freely confess that I have come to no firm conclusions about the proper interpretation of the Book of Revelation. While I would not want to be guilty of undervaluing its symbolism, I am nonetheless chary about basing fundamental doctrine upon its symbolism. Certainly, on the face of it, having no rest day or night with smoke of torment going up for ever and ever, sounds like everlasting torment. But, as Stott points out, the torment 'experienced "in the presence of the holy angels and ... the Lamb," seems to refer to the

moment of judgment, not to the eternal state.'[23] This is the
time of which Jesus gave warning (Lk. 12:8) when the
unbeliever is denied before the angels of God. Final
judgment is an experience of unceasing and inescapable
pain, and as at Sodom all that is left is the smoke of their
torment going up for ever. It is a reminder to all eternity of
the marvellous justice and mercy of God. The proof texts
of the Westminster Confession add the passage
concerning the rich man and Lazarus (Lk. 16:19-31),
which is indeed one of great exegetical difficulty.[24] But the
scene with Lazarus in Hades can hardly represent the
final state of the lost seeing Hades itself is to be cast into
the lake of fire (Rev. 20:14), and in any case there is no
reference to the everlastingness of that place of torment.
So this 'avalanche', these 'dozens', these fourteen
passages whose natural meaning we are attempting to
evade reduces to perhaps one, and that is far from
insuperable, representing less than a half of one per cent
of the New Testament passages on the doom of the lost.
So both Old and New Testaments taken in their natural

---

23 *Essentials*, p. 318.

24 Useful points are made about this passage in Froom Vol. 1 pp.
234-51, Atkinson pp. 49f., Fudge pp. 203-8. It is clear that it
is not intended as a literal description of the world of the life-
to-come. Hades is the Sheol of the Old Testament, the
immediate destination of all who die, bad and good, normally
and rightly translated in NIV as 'the grave'. Here they sleep
the sleep of death awaiting the resurrection. Luke's story is a
highly figurative fable-parable, which, if taken literally, does
not agree with the Old Testament. From the context its
primary aim is seen to be the necessity of living according to
the way God has revealed now, there being no room for
repentance after death. The motif of roles reversed after death
was common in contemporary folk-lore. What is difficult to
understand is that Jesus should use such material knowing that
it did not correspond to the literal reality. Possibly it is
something like modern stories about St Peter at the pearly
gates and how he treats his suppliants. The preacher can use
such stories to make his points effectively without danger of
his hearers taking him literally.

sense seem to be almost entirely, if not entirely, on the conditionalist side.

The nub of the whole debate is the question of the natural meaning of the texts, but there are other objections to the conditionalist position which should be briefly looked at.

Other Objections to Conditionalism

1. *Belief in endless torment is said to have been the view of Jesus and the Jews of his day, of the New Testament writers and Fathers of the Church, of the Reformers and all Bible-believers, and never seriously questioned till the twentieth century.*[25] I myself, resting largely on the authority of Charles Hodge,[26] at one time believed this to be true. But it is quite untrue. It was certainly an almost unchallenged view during the Middle Ages, but it was not so either in first-century Judaism or in the early Fathers or at the Reformation and most certainly not in the nineteenth century, which was the heyday of conditionalism among Evangelicals.[27] This is all

---

[25]   Packer. 'directly from Jesus, and the apostolic teaching' (p. 19); belief in 'everlasting conscious distress... belonged to the Christian consensus from the first. Fathers, medievals, and moderns up to the time of the Enlightenment were unanimous about it; Protestants, Catholics and Orthodox were divided on many things, but not on this. The consensus existed ... because Bible-believers of all schools of thought found it inescapable' (p. 22).

[26]   C. Hodge, *Systematic Theology*, Vol. 3 (London: Nelson, 1873) p. 870.

[27]   Packer says 'it was never queried with any seriousness (by Evangelicals) until the twentieth century' (p. 23). B.L. Bateson in a private communication writes: '(that statement) is absolute nonsense. The subject was much discussed by evangelicals in the nineteenth century, not only in Britain, but also in the United States and at least fifty books and pamphlets appeared and many items of correspondence appeared on both sides in Christian magazines. Here are some of the best works: Edward White,

meticulously documented in Froom's great volumes, and
Fudge devoted three chapters to the inter-testamental
period and four to the period from post-apostolic times to
the present day – something over a quarter of his book.

2. *Belief in annihilation is said to miss out on the
awesome dignity of our having been made to last for
eternity* (Packer p. 24). But how a long period of hopeless,
ceaseless pain, 'learning' (in Packer's words) 'the
bitterness of the choice' the unbeliever has made, can be
said to enhance the dignity of man, I fail to see. Long-term
imprisonment is one of the horrors of our supposedly
civilised society and long-term prisoners normally gain a
hang-dog look. What would be the effect of such unending
'learning' which yields no reformation? Certainly not
awesome dignity. Or is it the believer who has this

Congregationalist, *Life in Christ*, 1878, 3rd ed., 541pp. E.
Petavel, D.D., Swiss pastor, *The Problem of Immortality*,
1878, 600pp. Richard Whately, Protestant Archbishop of
Dublin, *A View of the Scripture Revelation concerning a
Future State*. There were nine editions from 1829 of which the
later ones were conditionalist. Canon Henry Constable, *The
Duration and Nature of Future Punishment*. Six editions
between 1868 and 1886. W.R. Huntingdon, D.D., Rector of
All Saints, Worcester, U.S.A., *Conditional Immortality*,
1878, 202pp. J.H. Pettingell, Congregational minister, *The
Life Everlasting*, 1882, 761pp. Reginald Courtenay, Bishop in
Jamaica, *The Future States*, 1843. H.H. Dobney, Baptist
minister, *The Scripture Doctrine of Future Punishment*, 1846.
J.M. Denniston, Scottish Presbyterian missionary to Jamaica,
The Perishing Soul, 2nd ed. 1874. Dr Cameron Mann,
Protestant Episcopal Bishop of N. Dakota, *Five Discourses on
Future Punishment*, 1888. Dr Joseph Parker, Congregational
minister of the City Temple, London from 1874 for 28 years
proclaimed conditionalism in the 25 volumes of *The People's
Bible*.' Bateson then goes on to mention R.W. Dale, whose
book on the atonement was the most recommended book on the
subject in my student days and W.H.A. Hay Aitken, who was a
well known mission preacher and Canon of Norwich Cathedral.
More about these men and many others can be found in Froom,
Vol. 2; see also Fudge pp. 395-402.

dignity? Surely he gains his dignity by grace, rather than by creation?

3. *Believing in annihilation the Christian 'will miss out on telling the unconverted that their prospects without Christ are as bad as they possibly could be…. Conditionalism cannot but impoverish a Christian and limit our usefulness'* (p. 24). It seems to me to be a complete fallacy to think that the worse you paint the picture of hell the more effective your evangelism will be.[28] I felt a growing distaste as I read through Shedd and a worse distaste as I read through Gerstner. This is not the God that I am trying to present to unbelievers. Shedd quotes Jonathan Edwards: 'Wrath will be executed in the day of judgment without any *merciful* circumstances… in hell there will be no more exercises of divine patience.' Faber likewise says

O fearful thought! one act of sin
Within itself contains
The power of *endless* hate of God
And *everlasting* pains.[29]

Packer says, 'every moment of the unbeliever's …bitterness… furthers the glory of God' (p.24). But the God whom I know had compassion on the crowds 'because they were harassed and helpless, like sheep without a shepherd' (Mt. 9:36). He teaches us to think of him as like a good earthly father who won't give a snake to the son who asks for a fish (Lk. 11:11). 'He knows how we are formed, he remembers that we are dust' (Ps. 103:14). Faber said rightly, there is no place where

---

[28]   Fernando can be completely exonerated from this fault. He stresses the degrees of punishment in hell and makes clear that those with little light will suffer less than those with much. But 'more tolerable', hopeless, unceasing, unreforming pain still remains a hideous prospect, hardly reconcilable with the glory of God.

[29]   Edwards, Sermon 12; Faber's Hymn on Predestination; both quoted by Shedd, p. 196.

kindlier judgment is given than in heaven.[30] I think that the ordinary decent person who is groping his way through life, ignorant of God, battered and perplexed by the sinful world around him, is helped best by introducing him or her to the Jesus of the gospels in his gentleness, truthfulness and power. As we talk, while not hiding the seriousness of sin, we must see that the *love* of God gets through. To present God as the one whose 'divinely executed retributive process' (Packer p. 24) will bring him into everlasting torment unless he believes, is hardly likely to help. To any normal way of thinking (and Jesus has told us when we think about God to think how a human father acts) this depicts God as a terrible sadist, not as a loving Father.

Whether in practice the adoption of conditionalism makes our evangelism less effective, it is impossible to say. Many preachers of endless torment have been greatly used by God, but it is doubtful whether that part of the message effected the conviction. Equally I have no reason to think that the adoption of conditionalism impairs a man's evangelism. Basil Atkinson was always on the look-out to put in a word for Jesus. I was very touched when one day I heard that he, a man whose mind lived in academia and Christian theology, had gone up to a group of lads lounging around in the Cambridge market-place and told them that Jesus loved them. I haven't noticed that John Stott's or Michael Green's conditionalism has made them any less of evangelists. In personal talks I often find myself explaining the self-destructive power of sin and of its ultimate power to destroy absolutely. I explain that that is how God has made the world. Judgment expresses his wrath against the abominable thing which he hates.

---

[30]   The hymn: There is a wideness in God's mercy.

The Glory of Divine Justice

4. *We are said to miss out on the glory of divine justice, and, in our worship, on praise for God's judgments* (Packer p.21). We should have 'a passionate gladness' that God's 'adorable justice' should be done for the glory of our Creator (p. 21). I cannot see that this is true. In my book *The Enigma of Evil* I try to grapple with all the moral difficulties of the Bible and many of the difficulties of Providence. My main theme is to show how God's judgments reflect the goodness of the God we adore. The one point at which I am so seriously perplexed that I have to devote a whole chapter to it is the subject of hell. My problem is, not that God punishes, but that the punishment traditionally ascribed to God seems neither to square with Scripture nor to be *just*. Many stress that on the cross Jesus suffered the pains which we deserve. But, though he suffered physical torture, the utter dereliction of separation from the Father, and death, he did not suffer endless pain. I know that no sinner is competent to judge the heinousness of sin, but I cannot see that endless punishment is either loving or just.

C.S. Lewis was brought up in Northern Ireland where that extraordinary hell-fire preacher W.P. Nicholson had exerted so great an influence. In one of his early books *The Pilgrim's Regress* he tells of his spiritual pilgrimage in allegory. Chapter one starts in Puritania, where he dreams of a boy who is frustrated by the prohibitions of his elders. He is told that they are the rules of the Steward, who has been appointed by the Landlord who owns the land. One day his parents take him to see the Steward: 'when John came into the room, there was an old man with a red, round face, who was very kind and full of jokes, so that John quite got over his fears, and they had a good talk about fishing tackle and bicycles. But just when the talk was at its best, the Steward got up and cleared his throat. He then took down a mask from the wall with a long white beard attached to it and suddenly clapped it on his face, so that his appearance was awful. And he said,

'Now I am going to talk to you about the Landlord.

The Landlord owns all the country, and it is *very very* kind of him to allow us to live on it at all – very, very kind.' He went on repeating 'very kind' in a queer sing-song voice so long that John would have laughed, but that now he was beginning to become frightened again. The Steward then took down from a peg a big card with small print all over it, and said, 'Here is a list of all the things the Landlord says you must not do. You'd better look at it.' So John took the card: but half the rules seemed to forbid things he had never heard of, and the other half forbade things he was doing every day and could not imagine not doing: and the number of rules was so enormous that he felt he could never remember them all.

'I hope,' said the Steward, 'that you have not already broken any of the rules?' John's heart began to thump, and his eyes bulged more and more, and he was at his wit's end when the Steward took off the mask and looked at John with his real face and said, 'Better tell a lie, old chap, better tell a lie. Easiest for all concerned,' and popped the mask on his face all in a flash. John gulped and said quickly, 'Oh, no, sir.' 'That is just as well,' said the Steward through the mask. 'Because, you know, if you did break any of them and the Landlord got to know of it, do you know what he'd do to you?'

'No, sir,' said John: and the Steward's eyes seemed to be twinkling dreadfully through the holes of the mask. 'He'd take you and shut you up for ever and ever in a black hole full of snakes and scorpions as large as lobsters – for ever and ever. And besides that; he is such a kind, good man, so very, very kind, that I am sure you would never *want* to displease him.' 'No, sir,' said John. 'But, please, sir...' 'Well,' said the Steward.

'Please, sir, supposing I did break one, one little one, just by accident, you know. Could nothing stop the snakes and lobsters?' 'Ah!...' said the Steward; and then he sat down and talked for a long time, but John could not understand a single syllable.

However, it all ended with pointing out that the Landlord was quite extraordinarily kind and good to his tenants, and would certainly torture most of them to death the moment he had the slightest pretext. 'And you can't blame him,' said the Steward. 'For after all it *is* his land, and it is so very good of him to let us live here at all − people like us, you know.' Then the Steward took off the mask and had a nice, sensible chat with John again, and gave him a cake and brought him out to his father and mother. But just as they were going he bent down and whispered in John's ear, 'I shouldn't bother about it all too much if I were you.' At the same time he slipped the card of the rules into John's hand and told him he could keep it for his own use.[31]

Unending torment speaks to me of sadism, not justice. It is a doctrine which I do not know how to preach without negating the loveliness and glory of God. From the days of Tertullian it has frequently been the emphasis of fanatics. It is a doctrine which makes the Inquisition look

---

[31] *The Pilgrim's Regress*, first published 1933. Reissued in Collins Fount Paperbacks 1977, pp. 29-31. The Roman Catholic Gerard Hughes in *God of Surprises* (London: Darton, Longman and Todd, 1985, p. 34), like C.S. Lewis, indulges in a fantasy. God is seen as a relative (Uncle George) who has a fiery torture-chamber in his basement. The child knows that he has got to say that he loves him, when in reality he loathes him. I simply do not know how to avoid this honest and common-sensical impression in preaching everlasting torment.

reasonable. It all seems a flight from reality and common sense.[32]

---

[32]   I have a suspicion (though I may well be wrong) that many of the sincere Christians who hold this doctrine don't *quite* believe it themselves. They are tempted to whittle down some of the Bible's teaching. Jesus speaks of the many on the broad road to destruction in contrast to the few on the road to life, but Charles Hodge says, 'We have reason to believe ... that the number of the finally lost in comparison with the whole number of the saved will be very inconsiderable' (Shocking adjective!) (*Systematic Theology*, Vol. 3, London: Nelson, 1973, p. 870). B.B. Warfield speaks of them as 'a relatively insignificant body'. (Art. 'Predestination,' *Hastings Dictionary of the Bible*, Vol. 4, p. 63). Goulburn says (p. 164), 'no one to whom the offer of grace and salvation is fully and fairly made, can possibly perish except by the wilful, deliberate open-eyed rejection of the offer.' But what of the multitudes who have heard the offer imperfectly presented and what of the multitudes who have simply neglected their great salvation? Goulburn seems to suggest that there are few on the road to destruction. Salmond (p. 674) sets great hope on deathbed repentances, however faint and feeble, as does Pusey (*What is Of Faith as to Everlasting Punishment?* Oxford: Parker, 3rd ed. 1881, pp. 11-17).

  Packer says that hell is 'unimaginably dreadful' (p. 20), 'far, far worse than the symbols' (p. 25) and he recommends that we 'do not attempt to imagine what it is like.' But is it not the preacher's *duty* to exercise his imagination in a disciplined way to bring home to his hearers the dread truth, whatever it is? It seems to me that Fudge is a most unwavering preacher of hell, not tempted to whittle down what the Bible actually says. Its solemn teaching appears to be that our destiny is sealed at death, and this gives great urgency to our preaching. (See Heb. 9:27, 'It is appointed for men to die once, and after that comes judgment.' 2 Cor. 5:10, 'We must all appear before the judgment seat of Christ so that each one may receive good or bad, according to what he has done in the body.' Rom. 2:5-8, 'On the day of wrath... he will render to every man according to his works: to those who by patience and well doing seek glory and honour and immortality, he will give eternal life; but for those who are factious and do not obey the truth, but obey wickedness, there will be wrath and fury.' John 3:36, 'He who does not obey the Son shall not see life, but the wrath of

Some argue that destruction is no punishment, since many an unbeliever wants to die, so mere death would be a denial of justice. This assumes that the first death is the end and that there is no Day of Judgment and that we are not judged according to our works. This is plainly unscriptural and not the view of any conditionalist that I know. The very wicked who have suffered little in this life will clearly get what they deserve. Perhaps a major part of the punishment will be a realisation of the true awfulness of their sin, in its crucifixion of the Son of God and in its effects on others. The horror (particularly of the latter) would be greater for some than for others.

5. *Conditionalists, we are told, 'appear to back into' their doctrine 'in horrified recoil from the thought of millions in endless distress, rather than move into it because the obvious meaning of Scripture beckons them'* (Packer p. 24). As I have already shown, I was drawn to conditionalism by Scripture rather than by a horrified recoil from the other doctrine. But I do plead guilty to a growing horror at the thought of millions in endless distress, which I find exceedingly difficult to reconcile not only with the goodness of God, but also with the final supremacy of Christ. If there are human beings alive suffering endless punishment, it would seem to mean that they are in endless opposition to God, that is to say, we have a doctrine of endless sinning as well as of suffering. How can this be if Christ is all in all? I plead guilty also to failing to see how God and the saints could be in perfect bliss with human beings hopelessly sinning and suffering.[33] Packer (p. 24) tells us that God's joy will not

---

God rests upon him.' John 8:24, 'I told you that you would die in your sins, for you will die in your sins unless you believe that I am he.')

[33] Hughes (p. 406) says concerning this: 'It leaves a part of creation which, unrenewed, everlastingly exists in alienation from the new heaven and the new earth. It means that suffering

be marred by the continuance in being of the damned, so that the Christian's joy will not be either.

These speculations don't look to me like the beckonings of Scripture's obvious meaning. I have thought about this subject for more than fifty years and for more than fifty years I have believed the Bible to teach the ultimate destruction of the lost, but I have hesitated to declare myself in print. I regard with utmost horror the possibility of being wrong. We are all to be judged by our words (Mt. 12:37) and teachers with greater strictness (Jas 3:1). *Whichever side you are on, it is a dreadful thing to be on the wrong side in this issue.* Now I feel that the time has come when I must declare my mind honestly. I believe that endless torment is a hideous and unscriptural doctrine which has been a terrible burden on the mind of the church for many centuries and a terrible blot on her presentation of the gospel. I should indeed be happy if, before I die, I could help in sweeping it away. Most of all I should rejoice

---

and death will never be totally abolished from the scene. The inescapable logic of this position was accepted, with shocking candor, by Augustine, who affirmed that "after the resurrection, when the final, universal judgment has been completed, there will be two kingdoms, each with its own distinct boundaries, the one Christ's, the other the devil's, the one consisting of good, the other of bad." (*Enchiridion* 111). To this it must be objected that with the restoration of all things in the new heaven and new earth, which involves God's reconciliation to himself of *all things*, whether on earth or in heaven (Acts 3:21; Col. 1:20), there will be no place for a second kingdom of darkness and death. When all is light there can be no darkness; for "the night shall be no more" (Rev. 22:5). When Christ fills all in all and God is everything to everyone (Eph. 1:23; 1 Cor. 15:28), how is it conceivable that there can be a section or realm of creation that does not belong to this fulness and by its very presence contradicts it? The establishment of God's everlasting kingdom of peace and righteousness will see the setting free of the whole created order from its bondage to decay as it participates in the glorious liberty of the children of God (Rom. 8:21).'

to see a number of theologians (including some of the very first water) joining Fudge in researching this great topic in all its ramifications.

7

The Case Against Conditionalism: A response to Edward William Fudge

Kendall S. Harmon

The seeds of evangelical confusion about the final state of those who reject Christ have been widely sown in our generation. An overwhelming reluctance to address any eschatological subjects, and especially the topic of hell, characterises most pulpits and books.[1] Among those few who are willing to reflect on this ominous doctrine, the disagreements have become increasingly sharp in recent times.

Consider three examples. In 1990 a group of evangelicals in North America gathered to formulate a statement of faith. One of the few major areas in which they could not find common ground was on the doctrine of hell.[2] Three years earlier the American periodical

---

[1] James Montgomery Boice, whose popular four-volume theology *Foundations of the Christian Faith* (Downers Grove, Illinois: InterVarsity Press, recent reissue in a single volume in 1986) is widely circulated in evangelical circles, includes only two references to hell (pp. 173, 518). Even more surprising is the fact that in the final volume, 'God and History,' which is devoted to eschatology, there are *no* references to hell (though there are to judgment).

[2] In reporting on the gathering of 350 Christian leaders to formulate a statement of faith, *Christianity Today* noted that 'strong disagreements did surface over the position of annihilationism, a view that holds that unsaved souls will

Christianity Today published a study by its institute on the subject of universalism. In it, Dr Clark Pinnock, a leading contemporary evangelical thinker, argued that the wicked are resurrected, judged, and then extinguished. Pinnock also maintained that the traditional view of everlasting punishment for unbelievers was based on an unbiblical 'Greek view of the immortality of the soul', and that those who were propounding the traditional view were accelerating the move of many people toward universalism. Dr David Wells of Gordon Conwell Theological Seminary, another influential evangelical thinker, responded to Pinnock by rearticulating the traditional position, insisting that it had Scripture and morality on its side.[3]

A third example comes from an interaction between two of today's best known Anglican evangelicals, John Stott and J.I. Packer. In a 1988 work entitled *Essentials* in which he engaged in a dialogue with David Edwards, John Stott went into print with his understanding of hell for the first time. Dr Stott insisted that the impenitent will finally be destroyed, although claiming to hold his position 'tentatively'.[4] The same year, another highly regarded evangelical, Dr Philip Hughes, promulgated a similar position in his book *The True Image*.[5] The prominence of John Stott and Philip Hughes led J.I. Packer to re-examine

---

cease to exist after death. Debate arose in the final plenary session over whether such a view should even be denounced in the affirmations.... A show of hands revealed the conference was almost evenly divided as to how to deal with the issue in the affirmations statement, and no renunciation of the position was included in the draft document' (*Christianity Today*, June 16, 1989, pp. 60, 63).

3   *Christianity Today*, March 20, 1987, pp. 40-42.
4   David L. Edwards and John Stott, *Essentials* (London: Hodder and Stoughton, 1988), pp. 313-320.
5   Philip Hughes, *The True Image: The Origin and Destiny of Man in Christ* (Grand Rapids: Eerdmans, 1989), pp. 398-407.

his own position,[6] after which Dr Packer argued in the 1990 work *Evangelical Affirmations* that the biblical arguments which Stott, Hughes, and others used were 'special pleading' which reflected 'not superior spiritual sensitivity, but secular sentimentalism.'[7]

These are only three among many examples which reveal a growing trend. When mainstream evangelical theologians such as those mentioned disagree on an important doctrine like hell, clearly a re-examination of the evidence involved is in order. I propose in this paper to interact with one of the recent proponents of final destruction, Mr Edward William Fudge, a member of the (North American) Evangelical Theological Society whose 1982 book, *The Fire That Consumes*,[8] was an alternative selection of the (American) Evangelical Book Club. There are two reasons for choosing the work of Mr Fudge. First, although not as prominent as John Stott or Philip Hughes, Mr Fudge's work is much more substantial than theirs (500 pages) and is devoted exclusively to the doctrine of

---

6   Dr Packer addressed a conference in 1989 in Charleston, South Carolina, at which I asked him about hell and he spoke of the recently published views of Stott and Hughes and said that as a result of their writings he 'would reconsider' his own position. Such scholarly admiration for others and a willingness to reexamine the evidence is a fine precedent for all of us. As Packer's subsequent writing makes clear, he decided to reaffirm the traditionalist case.

7   J.I. Packer, 'Evangelicals and the Way of Salvation: New Challenges to the Gospel: Universalism and Justification by Faith,' in Kenneth Kantzer and Carl Henry (eds.) *Evangelical Affirmations*, (Grand Rapids: Zondervan, 1990), p. 126. Much of the same material may be found in Dr Packer's Leon Morris Lecture which he read in Australia in September, 1990: J.I. Packer, 'The Problem of Eternal Punishment,' *Crux* XXVI, No. 3 (September, 1990), pp. 18-25.

8   Edward Fudge, *The Fire that Consumes* (Houston: Providential Press, 1982).

hell.[9] Secondly, Mr Fudge's book has been praised for its tone and its thoroughness. Dr John Gerstner, an evangelical Presbyterian who taught at Pittsburgh Theological Seminary for many years, recently called Fudge's book 'the ablest critique of [the traditional understanding of] hell by a believer in the inspiration of the Bible... there hasn't been anything comparable to it in this century.'[10]

There are two problems with which we should wrestle before interacting with Mr Fudge's arguments, the first of which is *the problem of definition*. Many people tend to think that in the debate about hell there is on the one side universalism, the view that ultimately all will be saved, and on the other the traditional view that those who refuse God's offer of salvation in Christ will be consciously punished forever. In between these two understandings is often placed that of Roman Catholicism, which is usually described as saying that the really wicked go directly to hell after death, and the truly good gain an immediate vision of God, but the bulk of humanity goes to purgatory, there to experience disciplinary cleansing before ultimately gaining access to heaven.

Other positions also exist, however, and need to be carefully distinguished. The problem arises because this discussion involves not only eschatology but also anthropology and one has to be discerning enough to consider *both* aspects of a teacher's doctrine and not to assume, based on what a person's view is on one of these doctrinal areas, that you can deduce the other. Conditional immortality, strictly speaking, refers only to the view that

---

9   John Stott's section on the nature of hell in *Essentials* is really
     only 8 pages (2 of which are partial pages, *cf.* Stott, *op. cit.*,
     pp. 313-320) and Philip Hughes' slim chapter covers some 10
     pages (*cf.* Hughes, *op. cit.*, pp. 398-407.).
10   *Christian Observer*, July 6, 1990, p. 11.

all men and women are created mortal but that for those who respond to the gospel the gift of eternal life is given. There are two different understandings of individual eschatology which have been attached to this conditionalist label, the first of which I call *conditionalist uniresurrectionism*. In this view man is naturally mortal and immortality is given through the gospel only to the righteous in the next life; the wicked who do not respond to Christ are not resurrected since death is their judgment. This doctrine was held by some sixteenth century Anabaptists and seventeenth century Socinians; today it is believed by the Jehovah's Witnesses. The second approach, which is the far more dominant type in terms of its influence and the number of its adherents, I call *conditionalist eventual extinctionism*. This group argues that both the wicked and the good are resurrected, and that the wicked suffer God's judgment until they are finally extinguished, the punishment being proportionate to their sin. The most well-known denomination among this school are the Seventh Day Adventists. Both these conditionalist views are to be distinguished from *immortalist eventual extinctionism*, a perspective which says that men and women were created immortal but that after the resurrection of both the good and the unrighteous, the latter are annihilated after a period of suffering.[11]

---

[11]   These distinctions are admittedly artificial but are nevertheless very necessary in order to keep this discussion as conceptually clear as possible. In addition to *even these* distinctions there are others. For example, some people in the literature seem to believe that after the resurrection the wicked are *immediately* destroyed, whereas others suggest there is a period of suffering until such destruction. In my schema this would lead to terms such as *conditionalist immediate extinctionism*, or *immortalist immediate extinctionism*. I have also ignored the whole question of the intermediate state in this debate. Immortalists must believe in the post-mortem existence of the soul, but some nevertheless deny that there is an intermediate state. Many conditionalists believe in 'soul sleep' between death and the final resurrection, but not all.

These conceptual distinctions should be emphasised since the terminology has recently become very confused. On the one hand both J.I. Packer[12] and Donald Bloesch[13] lump Jehovah's Witnesses and Seventh Day Adventists together, in spite of the fact that the first believes only the righteous will be resurrected, and the second that both the good and the wicked will be. On the other hand, traditionalist writer Jon Braun[14] seems to believe that all who are not traditionalists hold the Jehovah's Witness position, thereby eliminating conditionalist extinctionism and immortalist extinctionism from the debate. Perhaps most confusing of all, Edward Fudge does not want to be described as an annihilationist but a conditionalist[15], whereas John Stott makes clear that he is an annihilationist not a conditionalist[16] – yet in terms of the

---

[12] J.I. Packer, *Evangelical Affirmations, op. cit.*, p. 135 footnote 13.

[13] Donald Bloesch, *Essentials of Evangelical Theology* (San Francisco: Harper and Row, 1978), Volume II, p. 219.

[14] Jon Braun, *Whatever Happened to Hell?* (Nashville: Thomas Nelson, 1979), p. 49.

[15] Fudge, *op. cit.*, p. 38 footnote 2. It is very important to note the historical background to Fudge's disavowal at this point. In the 19th century when conditionalism was at its peak of influence conditionalists avoided the word 'annihilationism' to describe their position because many materialists who did not believe in *any* life after death seemed to have a view which could be termed annihilationism (*cf.* Geoffrey Rowell, *Hell and the Victorians: A Study of the Nineteenth-Century Theological Controversies concerning Eternal Punishment and the Future Life* (Oxford: Clarendon Press, 1974), p. 197).

[16] '"Annihilation" is not quite the same as "conditional immortality",' writes John Stott. 'According to the latter, nobody survives death except those to whom God gives life (they are therefore immortal by grace, not by nature), whereas according to the former, everybody survives death and will even be resurrected, but the impenitent will finally be destroyed' (*Essentials, op. cit.*, p. 316). Stott here makes the error of failing to distinguish between conditionalist

ultimate end of the wicked Fudge and Stott are both arguing for the same view![17] Amidst this confusion, let me be quite clear: Fudge argues for 'penal suffering culminating in total extinction.'[18] It is this doctrine of eventual extinctionism, whether in its conditionalist or immortalist form, which has been steadily gaining evangelical adherents in recent years, which I am seeking to critique.

This brings us to a second preliminary issue which I term the *problem of perspective*. What should be our attitude as we approach the evidence in the present debate? I suggest it should be one of reverent scepticism about the validity of eventual annihilationism for two reasons. First, it ought to give us pause that many unbelievers have come to the conclusion that Jesus taught eternal punishment. The Unitarian Theodore Parker, for example, said: 'I believe that Jesus Christ taught eternal punishment... I do not accept it on his authority.'[19] Bertrand Russell, in his 1927 address entitled *Why I am not a Christian*, argued that Jesus' belief in hell was the one 'serious defect' in his character. 'I do not myself feel that any person who is really profoundly humane can believe in everlasting punishment. Christ certainly as depicted in the gospels did believe in everlasting punishment' and therefore we may not consider him a great moral teacher. After citing a number of biblical

---

uniresurrectionists and conditional eventual extinctionists, thereby identifying all conditionalists with the Jehovah's Witness' position.

17   Fudge and Stott do differ on anthropology, however, Fudge being a conditionalist and Stott an immortalist. Stott clearly believes in a conscious intermediate state between death and resurrection; Fudge's book avoids discussion of the intermediate state.

18   Fudge, *op. cit.*, p. 364.

19   As cited in Harry Buis, *The Doctrine of Eternal Punishment* (Philadelphia: Presbyterian and Reformed, 1957), p. 34.

passages, Russell asserted that Jesus' teaching on hell was repeated 'again and again. I must say that I think all this doctrine, that hell fire is a punishment for sin, is a doctrine of cruelty. It is a doctrine that put cruelty into the world and gave the world generations of cruel torture; and the Christ of the gospels, if you could take him as his chroniclers represent him, would certainly be considered partly responsible for that.'[20]

A second and more important reason for our scepticism about Mr Fudge's view is the role of Christian history, a role which is unfortunately neglected in much recent evangelical thinking. The great majority of the finest theologians in the church for the last twenty centuries have held to the traditional view.[21] This, in itself, is not definitive – the Scriptures are always the final court of appeal. But it does mean that if we are going to disagree with Augustine and Aquinas and Luther and Calvin and Jonathan Edwards (to name only a few among so many) we need to have extremely strong grounds for doing so, and the burden of proof is on those who wish to change the traditional dogma. When John Wenham, who shares Fudge's position, claims that 'we shall consider ourselves under no obligation to defend the notion of unending torment until the arguments of the conditionalists have

---

[20]   Bertrand Russell, *Why I Am Not a Christian* (London: National   Secular Society, reprint, 1970), pp. 7-8.

[21]   A careful evaluation of the evidence from the Christian tradition is a very challenging undertaking. Philip Schaff's statement that 'everlasting punishment of the wicked always was, and always will be the orthodox theory' (*History of the Christian Church*, (New York: Charles Scribner and Sons, 1916, Vol. II, pp. 506-507), for example, would be disputed both by conditionalists and universalists. A fair generalisation might be that this theory found an overwhelming majority among the early church witnesses, though there was certainly not unanimity (*cf.* the evidence as it is set out in E.B. Pusey, *What Is Of Faith as to Everlasting Punishment?* (Oxford: James Parker and Company, 1880), pp. 173-289.

been refuted',[22] I respectfully suggest he shows an inadequate appreciation for the role of tradition in Christian thinking. It may be that the traditional doctrine of hell is wrong ('errors creep in and they die hard',[23] as Wenham puts it) but the relatively recent emergence (really since the nineteenth century if it is to be considered a significant school of thought) of eventual extinctionism means that *its* adherents need to show both the inadequacy of Augustine's position and the evidence for their own before they should be taken seriously as having presented a Christian option.

With this crucial groundwork laid, we now turn to the arguments of Mr Fudge himself. His substantial book covers the biblical material, the intertestamental literature and the witness of Christian history; for our purposes his main propositions will be broken down under four headings. First, Fudge insists that the classical doctrine of hell does not inevitably flow from an examination of biblical anthropology. He notes how various writers from the traditionalist school have used the idea of man's immortality as a foundation on which to build their understanding. 'If every soul lives forever, the traditional view of hell as unending *conscious torment* seems to follow.'[24] The key word here is 'seems,' for even those who advocate man's immortality understand this immortality to be derived from the creator – it is a gift which can therefore be withdrawn. Fudge himself prefers

---

22 John Wenham, *The Enigma of Evil* (Leicester: InterVarsity Press, 2nd edition with a new title in 1985), p. 41. John Wenham's plea stems from an important motivation, however, which is that the arguments for conditionalism have not been heard by many traditionalists. In my combing of the literature of the last hundred years I would say that very often this has been the case, particularly because conditionalists have not been able to find mainstream publishers for their work.

23 *Ibid.*, p. 39.

24 Fudge, *op. cit.*, p. 56.

to be aligned with the school called Christian mortalism[25] which understands our nature to be mortal from creation. Even Christian mortalists, however, say that 'the eternal preservation of the wicked is possible – if God so wishes.'[26] The key question therefore becomes: 'Since God is *able* to preserve or to destroy His human creature, what does Scripture *indicate* that He *will* do to those He finally expels to hell?'[27]

To answer this query Fudge then examines the Old Testament evidence. What do the passages indicate? 'They tell us in many ways that the godless will come to nothing. They will perish, will disappear, will not be found. Their place will be empty and they will be no more.'[28]

---

[25]   Fudge frequently cites the work of Norman T. Burns, *Christian Mortalism from Tyndale to Milton* (Cambridge, Mass.: Harvard University Press, 1972), calling Burns' anthropology 'the sparkling pure water of pristine Christianity' (Fudge, *op. cit.*, p. 76). But the idea that the New Testament contains only a Hebrew view of man as a psychosomatic unity which was later corrupted by Hellenistic influence so that it developed into an unbiblical dualism of body and soul is open to question. There was clearly a significant Hellenistic influence on some intertestamental Judaism which forms part of the background to the New Testament ('Palestinian Judaism must be regarded as Hellenistic Judaism' asserts Martin Hengel (John Bowden, trans., *Judaism and Hellenism* (Philadelphia: Fortress, 1974), p.252)). Also there is no getting around the powerful impact of Hellenistic ideas on the New Testament itself. As Carol Zaleski notes: 'Some modern interpreters of the Christian message have tried to separate the Christian (or Hebrew) position on death from distorting Platonic influences but the result never seems to do justice to this complex religious heritage, in which Athens and Jerusalem have been mingled from the very beginning' (*Otherworld Journeys: Accounts of Near Death Experience in Medieval and Modern Times* (Oxford: Oxford University Press, 1987), p. 50). Zaleski's point about death is also valid for anthropology.

[26]   Fudge, *op. cit.*, p. 57.

[27]   *Ibid.*, p. 57.

[28]   *Ibid.*, p. 96.

God's judgment on Sodom and Gomorrah in Genesis 19 serves as a paradigm in that it completely destroys the sinners involved. When later prophets spoke of Babylon's punishment being everlasting ruin (Isaiah 13:19-22; Jeremiah 50:40), they used Sodom as an example. Throughout the Old Testament, the fire of God's judgment consumes (hence the title of Fudge's book).

A third area of inquiry is the intertestamental evidence, which Fudge admits is quite diverse. In the period between Malachi and Matthew 'the imagery of fire begins to change significance.... Instead of the Old Testament fire which cannot be quenched until it totally consumes, the literature begins to speak of a fire which torments its victims but does not destroy them.'[29] A notable example of the change in the use of fire is Judith 16:17: 'The Lord Almighty will take vengeance on them in the day of judgment, to put fire and worms in their flesh; and they shall weep and feel their pain forever.' Fudge maintains, however, that this verse 'contains the single explicit reference to conscious everlasting pain'[30] in the Apocryphal literature, and regards the vast majority of that material to reflect the teaching of the Old Testament that the wicked will be destroyed.

When it comes to the Pseudepigraphal literature, Fudge finds the material even more diverse in its views, and so he breaks it up into three categories: those documents which unambiguously assert final destruction, those which seem to teach both final destruction and final conscious suffering, and those which speak of conscious pain being experienced forever. In concluding his chapter Fudge insists:

Because of this unquestionable range of opinions, which can be so thoroughly documented, we cannot presume a

---

[29]   *Ibid.*, p. 127.
[30]   *Ibid.*, p. 132.

single attitude among Jews of the time of Christ on this subject. We cannot read Jesus' words or those of the New Testament writers with any presupposition supposedly based on a uniform intertestamental opinion.[31]

How then should an interpreter approach the New Testament? With the clear conviction that while 'much of the New Testament *language*' shares the background of the apocalyptic writings, 'its crucial *ideas* regarding final punishment come from the biblical books of the Old Testament, not from these imaginative writings between the Testaments'.[32]

Building on the Old Testament teaching that the wicked are ultimately destroyed and believing that the key ideas in the New Testament flow from this source, Fudge proceeds to examine the New Testament data. He concentrates on Matthew's gospel, arguing that the vast bulk of the references speak of ultimate extinction. In commenting on Jesus' statement in Matthew 5:29, 30, that 'it is better for you to lose one part of your body than for your whole body to go into hell (Gehenna)', for example, Fudge says:

> Jesus makes Gehenna the place of final punishment. Here he gives no graphic description of its destruction or even its duration; only this, that those who enter it go from another place, having been discarded and expelled by God. The picture is one of total loss, and it is entirely in keeping with the Old Testament to see that loss as ultimately consummated in destruction by fire.[33]

Similar comments follow on the figure of the devouring worm and the unquenchable fire (Mark 9:43-48): each refers to a process which destroys the wicked utterly. What about the phrase 'weeping and gnashing of teeth'

---

[31]   *Ibid.*, p. 154.
[32]   *Ibid.*, p. 122.
[33]   *Ibid.*, p. 166.

which occurs six times in Matthew and once in Luke? Fudge claims that it points to two aspects of the ungodly's fate. First, it describes 'the terror of the doomed as they begin to truly realize that God has thrown them out as worthless' and second it 'seems to express the bitter rage and acrimony they feel toward God, who sentenced them, and toward the redeemed, who will forever be blessed.'[34] These comments emphasize an important aspect of Fudge's position. He does not deny conscious suffering of the wicked in the next life, a punishment that will involve their whole resurrected being: nor does he deny degrees of punishment which are hinted at in a few New Testament passages (*i.e.* Luke 12:47, 48), but he insists that this agony precedes ultimate extinction.[35]

Fudge devotes considerable space to the parable of the sheep and the goats at the end of the gospel of Matthew, a pericope which is arguably the most important in terms of its influence on the doctrine of hell in church history. The crucial adjective *aionios* is understood both qualitatively and quantitatively:

Neither the fire nor the punishment are of this age – in origin or in quality. When the wicked have perished, it will be forever – their destruction and punishment is unending as well as qualitatively different from anything we now know. The fire is also 'eternal' in this sense – just as Sodom was destroyed by 'eternal fire' since its results were to last forever (Jude 7). The life is also 'eternal' in quality as well as quantity.[36]

Fudge emphasizes here that the *result* of the punishment is eternal, not the punishment itself. Matthew speaks of eternal punishment, but not eternal punishing. Other New Testament usages of *aionios* support this interpretation

---

34   *Ibid.*, p. 172.
35   *Ibid.*, p. 190.
36   *Ibid.*, p. 195.

according to Fudge. Hebrews 9:12, for example, describes Christ as having obtained 'eternal redemption'; since Christ's sacrifice is completed, eternal can only refer to the result of the action, not the act itself. Just as in Hebrews 9 once the redeeming has taken place, the redemption remains, so also in Matthew 25 once the punishing has taken place, the punishment remains.

The Pauline literature is easily treated under the plea simply to take language in its ordinary sense. When Paul says the wicked will 'perish', 'die', be 'corrupted' or be 'destroyed', he means what any person usually means when he uses these words. The rest of the New Testament gives similar teaching, exemplified by Jude 7 which speaks of the sinners of Sodom as 'set forth for an example, suffering the vengeance of eternal fire' (KJV). Says Fudge: 'the passage *defines* "eternal fire". It is a fire from God which destroys sinners totally and forever. Sodomites illustrate it, and the ungodly had better take note of his warning.'[37] But what about Revelation? The lake of fire in Revelation 19 and 20 'clearly means annihilation and cessation of existence... the context twice suggests it by explaining the lake of fire as the "second death"'.[38]

Fudge's examination of the scriptural witness, when combined with his insistence that immortality is not a gift of creation but rather a gift of the resurrection of Christ, seems compelling, but it contains serious weaknesses. First, Fudge's book is methodologically flawed since, when interpreting the New Testament passages, he overemphasizes the Old Testament background at the expense of the intertestamental literature. Fudge's thesis that the New Testament *language* shares the background

---

[37]   *Ibid.*, p. 287.
[38]   *Ibid.*, p. 307.

of apocalyptic writings, but not its *ideas,*[39] will not stand scholarly scrutiny. Such an approach makes no historical sense since apocalyptic as a literary genre does not arise until about the second century B.C., after the Old Testament period, and the New Testament was written in an environment 'saturated in the conceptions and the imagery of the Apocalyptic writings.'[40] The word Gehenna which Jesus uses frequently to describe hell, for example, is a term not found in the Old Testament. Where did this word come from? According to Joachim Jeremias the name Gehinnom came to be used for the eschatological hell of the last judgment 'in apocalyptic literature from the 2nd c. B.C.' Jeremias also argues that to understand the New Testament properly a distinction between Hades and Gehenna should be kept in mind:

> This distinction is ... that Hades receives the ungodly only for the intervening period between death and resurrection, whereas Gehenna is their place of punishment in the last judgment; the judgment of the former is thus provisional but the torment of the latter eternal (Mark 9:43 and parallels; 9:48).[41]

One of the references which Jeremias cites is Sibylline Oracles 1:103 in which the 'watchers' (a term used for the angels who sinned through their physical involvement with women in Genesis 6) are judged by being sent to 'the

---

[39]   *Ibid.,* p. 122.

[40]   C.W. Emmet, 'The Bible and Hell,' in B.H. Streeter, ed., *Immortality* (London: Macmillan, 1917), p. 172. Emmet's very important essay is surprisingly not mentioned a single time in Fudge's book.

[41]   Joachim Jeremias, 'Gehenna', in G. Kittel, ed., G.W. Bromiley, trans., *The Theological Dictionary of the New Testament* (Grand Rapids: Eerdmans, 1964), Vol. I, pp. 657-658. Jeremias is one of many to have noted the New Testament distinction between Hades and Gehenna; *cf.* for example, R.C. Sutherland, Jr., 'Medieval English Conceptions of Hell as Developed from Biblical, Patristic and Native Germanic Influences', University of Kentucky PhD, 1953, p. 17.

dread house of Tarturus' where they will suffer
'retribution' in the Gehenna 'of terrible, raging, undying
fire'. Another reference is to Sibylline Oracles 2:290ff.
where sorcerers and sorceresses are judged by being sent
to Gehenna 'where there is immeasurable darkness',
where there will be 'burning in much fire' and where 'they
will all gnash their teeth'.[42] For a scholar of the stature of
Jeremias to see both intertestamental language *and* ideas

---

[42] James H. Charlesworth, ed., *The Old Testament Pseudepigrapha*
(London: Darton, Longman and Todd, 1985), Vol. I. Fudge
believes that the Sybilline Oracles consistently teach the final
destruction of the wicked which is simply not true (Fudge, *op.
cit.*, pp. 135ff.). The footnote of J.J. Collins on Sibylline
Oracles 2:290ff. is worth quoting: 'The idea of a place of
punishment in the netherworld was prominent in Orphism. The
destruction of the wicked by fire is prominent in Persian belief
about the end, but it is not an eternal punishment in the
netherworld. The idea of a fiery hell seems to be a Jewish
development. It is suggested by Isaiah 66:24, but the passage
does not imply that the wicked will be alive to feel the flames.
The fallen 'watchers' are consigned to a fiery abyss consistently
in 1 En. 10:13; 18:11, *etc.*, and this punishment was extended
to sinful humans (90:23f.; *cf.* 54:1f.). A place of fiery eternal
punishment is presupposed in the Qumran scrolls (*e.g.* 1 QS 2)
and is ubiquitous in later apocalypses (*e.g.* Rev. 19:20, 20:14f.)'
(Charlesworth, Vol. 1, p. 352). The conviction that a
development between the testaments of the idea of an afterlife
punishment for the wicked forms a crucial background for
understanding the New Testament may be frequently found in
the literature. The Revd George Montague, former general
editor of the *Catholic Biblical Quarterly*, may serve as an
example. In a paper which he delivered in the fall of 1991 for
the Catholic Theological Alliance, Father Montague said 'from
the second century B.C. onwards in the apocalyptic literature,
the fires of "the accursed valley" [of Hinnom] became a symbol
of the last judgment and the eschatological fire of hell, and the
texts seem to imply an ongoing experience of pain' (The Revd
George Montague, 'Whatever Became of Hell', working
manuscript, p. 6, quoted with Father Montague's kind
permission).

behind the New Testament apocalyptic passages means that Fudge's approach must be strongly questioned.[43]

Fudge's flawed methodology is well exemplified by his treatment of the passage in Revelation 14:10,11, a text which in my view is the most horrific in all of Scripture. John describes the fate of him who worships the beast and its image as follows: 'he shall also drink the wine of God's wrath, poured unmixed into the cup of his anger, and he shall be tormented with fire and sulphur in the presence of the holy and in the presence of the Lamb. And the smoke of their torment goes up for ever and ever; and they have no rest, day or night, these worshippers of the beast and its image, and whoever receives the mark of its name' (RSV). Fudge agrees that this text speaks of 'conscious suffering' and yet insists that 'its figures *must* still be interpreted in the light of the Old Testament.'[44] But this causes a fundamental problem for Fudge, because John speaks clearly of conscious suffering under the image of people being 'tormented with fire'. If, as Fudge has argued, the New Testament only uses Old Testament *ideas*, but Fudge finds in this text the idea of fire as an image for suffering, then what Old Testament passage is the source on which Fudge is drawing for this idea? There are no Old Testament texts which speak of torment in fire, so Fudge is actually admitting an idea which came from somewhere else; in fact it comes from the intertestamental

---

[43] It is important to stress here that I am not saying (a) the Old Testament background is not crucial to understanding the New Testament texts, because it is, and (b) the intertestamental literature is not diverse but instead is uniform in its support of the traditional view of hell, which is not true. What should be emphasized is that by Jesus' day there were not only Old Testament texts but also traditions of how these texts were understood; even though these traditions were not uniform, they do form an important source for New Testament interpretation, both in terms of language *and* ideas.

[44] Fudge, *op.cit.*, p. 301, my emphasis.

apocalpytic literature, as many of the commentators point out.

A second weakness of Fudge's work is exegetical: he often introduces a chronological lapse of time in New Testament passages which is not there in the texts themselves. It is crucial to see how this move fits in with Fudge's exact position, which he defines as 'penal suffering culminating in total extinction'.[45] If a text speaks of 'penal suffering' Fudge will claim that this is the agony which *precedes* final destruction. If a passage, however, describes final ruin or loss, Fudge will maintain that this *is* ultimate annihilation. Again and again Fudge introduces this sense of duration. In commenting on Hebrews 6:2 which talks about 'eternal judgment', for example, Fudge writes: 'The act of judging will certainly not last forever. But we notice that the text speaks of jud*gment* (*krimatos*) and not jud*ging*. There will be an act or process of judging, and *then* it will be over.[46] Then in analyzing Paul's description of those who will be 'punished with everlasting destruction' at Jesus' coming, Fudge claims: 'This retribution will be *preceded* by a penal suffering exactly suited to each degree of guilt by a holy and just God, but that penal suffering *within itself* is not the ultimate retribution or punishment. There will be an act of destro*ying*, resulting in a destruction that will never end.'[47] Or later Fudge argues that in Matthew the phrase 'weeping and gnashing of teeth' describes the *anticipation* of the execution of God's sentence, after which comes the sentence itself.[48] These kinds of comments even come into Fudge's discussion of the evidence from church history. In speaking of second century statements which describe the wicked suffering 'grievous torments in unquenchable fire',

---

[45] *Ibid.*, p. 364.
[46] *Ibid.*, p. 45; the 'then' is my emphasis.
[47] *Ibid.*, p. 47; the 'preceded' is my emphasis.
[48] *Ibid.*, p. 172.

Fudge makes the following revealing assertion: 'these statements all may be reconciled with annihilation *so long as it is preceded* by a period of conscious suffering.'[49]

The clearest example of Fudge's time lapse occurs in that ghastly text of Revelation 14:10,11, which describes the ungodly being tormented in the presence of the holy angels and the Lamb. There is no doubt that 'the victims' here 'suffer', but the question of chronology has to be introduced: 'Actual torment is meted out according to the mixture of God's cup. *Then*, as the next image points out, it is forever memorialized in the smoke that remains.'[50] So for Fudge it is the smoke which rises forever, but not the torment that lasts forever. Why then does John describe the wicked as those who 'have no rest, day or night'? According to Fudge this refers to the kind of time involved: 'the action described is not a day-time action, nor is it a night-time action. It happens either and both.' John is therefore saying that those who suffer 'have no guarantee of relief, whether day-time or night-time, so long as the suffering lasts.'[51] There is continuous suffering and *then* final extinction which is endlessly memorialized by smoke.

The commentators simply do not agree with Fudge's special pleading. R.H. Charles says bluntly: 'the third angel proclaims a doom of everlasting torment for adherents of the imperial cult.'[52] Henry Barclay Swete makes a similar comment: 'The partial punishments under the trumpets have given place to a judgment which is final and without time limits.'[53] Even those scholars who are

---

[49]   *Ibid.*, p. 315, my emphasis.

[50]   *Ibid.*, pp. 297-298, my emphasis.

[51]   *Ibid.*, p. 300.

[52]   R.H. Charles, *The Revelation of St John* (Edinburgh: T. & T. Clark, 1920), Vol. II, p. 15.

[53]   H.B. Swete, *The Apocalypse of St John* (London: MacMillan, 1907), p. 186.

repulsed by this text admit that it points to everlasting suffering. J. Massyngberde Ford, in her Anchor Bible Commentary, says 'the torment is shown to be continuous' and goes on to insist that 'the allusion to the lamb is embarrassing for the Christian'.[54] Thomas F. Glasson claims that verse 11 is 'sub-Christian' and 'impossible to reconcile with the teaching of Jesus'.[55] William Barclay comments similarly: 'We may dislike this line of thought; we may condemn it as sub-Christian – and indeed it is. But we have no real right to speak until we have gone through the same sufferings the early Christians did.'[56] As with Revelation 14:10,11, so with other passages: Fudge is unsuccessful in his attempt to chronologise these apocalyptic texts; he is introducing a time lapse which is simply not there.[57]

---

[54] J.M. Ford, *Revelation* (Garden City, New York: Doubleday, 1975), pp. 237, 249.

[55] Thomas F. Glasson, *The Revelation of John* (Cambridge: Cambridge Univ. Press, 1965), p. 86.

[56] William F. Barclay, *The Daily Study Bible: The Revelation of John* (Edinburgh: St Andrew Press, 1976), Vol. 21, p. 113.

[57] There are numerous other exegetical problems with conditionalism which space requirements precluded me from mentioning. Two of the most important are: (1) Fudge's exegesis of Matthew 25:46 seems to do violence to the parallelism of the text itself which places eternal punishment and eternal life side by side by implying that in one half of the verse it is talking about eternal *effects* (for believers) whereas in the other half it refers to eternal *causes* (for unbelievers) (*cf.* David Wells' article 'Everlasting Punishment' in *Christianity Today*, October 20, 1987, p. 41); and (2) to argue that the New Testament language of destruction means simply 'cessation of existence' misses the sense of God's progressive revelation from the Old Testament to the New in this area. As Karl Barth writes: 'It may surprise us that the ideas of man's being in death are not mitigated or even displaced in the New Testament as compared with the Old. We might have expected this now that the 'glad tidings' are proclaimed. But in fact they are accentuated as never before. Instead of the negative picture of a shadowy existence of departed 'souls', we now have a

The third shortcoming of Fudge's book follows closely on the heels of the second: he fails to understand that the apocalyptic images used for the final doom of the ungodly have a single referent, and instead claims that different images refer to differing aspects of the wicked's final fate. C.S. Lewis' literary sensitivity enabled him to see what many have missed, namely that the New Testament uses three images to portray hell, punishment, destruction, and 'privation, exclusion or banishment',[58] and that these three images point in the same direction. For Fudge, God's final sentence *begins* with banishment, *continues* with a period of conscious suffering, and *ends* with destruction. In fact, not a single New Testament passage teaches exactly this sequence. Instead, some texts speak of personal exclusion, some of punishment, and others of destruction, and these images need to be understood as giving us hints at the same eschatological reality. Fudge not only chronologises these images, but he also emphasises one to the exclusion of the other two: destruction dominates while punishment and exclusion fall into the background. Indeed, the latter image is hardly discussed.

An analysis of Matthew 24 and 25 may serve to illustrate this point. Beginning with Matthew 24:45 we have in this gospel a collection of four different pericopes

---

picture of human existence in 'hell'. Hell means punishment of a very positive kind.... The church of Jesus Christ [was] precluded from understanding man's existence in death merely as an existence in unwelcome but tolerable neutrality. On the contrary, they had to understand it positively as intolerable suffering. And they had to do this because it was the only way they could understand the being of Jesus in death' (*Church Dogmatics*, (Edinburgh: T. & T. Clark, 1960), III/2, E.T., pp. 602-603).

58   C.S. Lewis, *The Problem of Pain* (Glasgow: Collins Fount reprint of the 1940 edition, 1977), pp. 113-114.

each of which ends with an image of judgment: the question of the faithful or unfaithful servant (Matthew 24: 45-51), the parable of the wise and foolish virgins (Matthew 25:1-13), the parable of the talents (Matthew 25:14-30), and the parable of the sheep and the goats (Matthew 25:31-46). At the end of Matthew 24 Jesus warns that the wicked servant will be taken by his master and 'cut in two' (the language seems very similar to the Qumran Manual of Discipline and may instead indicate being 'cut off' from the faithful), he or she will be put out with the hypocrites where 'men will weep and gnash their teeth'. Here the images are of destruction and conscious suffering. Then in the parable of the virgins the unrighteous are shut out when the bridegroom comes; they knock but he replies, 'truly, I say to you, I do not know you' (Matthew 25:11). The image here is of exclusion and of not being known. The third pericope, the parable of the talents, ends with the worthless servant being cast into outer darkness where 'men will weep and gnash their teeth.' The image is of banishment, gloom and suffering. Then finally there is the harrowing description of Jesus' judgment on the nations, which ends with the threat that those on Jesus' left hand will be cast into the 'eternal fire prepared for the devil and his angels' (Matthew 25:41); they are later said to be sent into 'eternal punishment'. Here the image is clearly punishment, especially drawing on the recurring theme in apocalyptic literature of the unending suffering of the devil and his followers. All four of these passages use different images to point to the same horrible reality: God's eschatological judgment on the impenitent. These images are intended to have the same referent *not* different referents – it is not that there is penal suffering and *then* annihilation – but that destruction, darkness, exclusion, not being known, agony and punishment are all windows through which to see the same truth.

In summary, then, Fudge's case is *methodologically flawed* since he fails to see the importance of the intertestamental literature for the New Testament texts, it is *exegetically flawed* since he introduces a lapse of time into texts which fails to let the texts speak for themselves, and it is *hermeneutically flawed* since he fails to treat apocalyptic images with a similar referent as having the same referent. More than anything else, conditionalism looks like an attempt to evade difficulties in the apostolic witness by wrapping up these problems in a neater package than that in which they came.

But if conditionalism's doctrine of hell is inadequate, this immediately raises the question of what a proper understanding of hell should be. Here we enter into murky waters because the New Testament, in sharp contrast to the apocalyptic literature, does not describe the nature of hell in detail, but merely hints at it. I believe a great deal of the perversion and corruption of the doctrine of hell in church history may be attributed to the simple principle that nature abhors a vacuum, and since the New Testament says so little about the specifics of the ultimate fate of the wicked, many non-biblical images and details had to be supplied.[59]

---

59   Some of the best examples of the addition of non-biblical details to the description of hell may be found in the Christian apocalypses, especially the *Apocalypse of Peter*, dating perhaps from the first half of the second century A.D. and very widely circulated in various versions throughout the early church, and the much later *Apocalypse of Paul* (possibly from the late fourth century A.D.). See the work of Montague R. James, *The Apocryphal New Testament* (Oxford: Clarendon Press, 1955 reprint of the 1924 edition), or Edgar Hennecke, ed., Wilhelm Schneemelcher, *New Testament Apocrypha* Vols. I and II (London: Lutterworth Press, 1965), E.T. I will reproduce two examples to give a flavour of these works. From the *Apocalypse of Peter* the Akhim Fragment 23-24 reads: 'And there was a great lake full of flaming mire, wherein were certain men that turned away from righteousness; and angels,

I further insist that the way toward an understanding of
hell in the late twentieth century is to return to the
scriptural imagery again and to try to find a middle ground
between letting the apocalyptic language say too much
and letting it say too little.[60] A fully biblical theology of hell
must do justice to all three images for hell to which C.S.
Lewis draws our attention – punishment, destruction and
exclusion. And here is where the traditional view may be
faulted, because it focuses too much on punishment and
leaves little room for the other two pictures. At this point
the conditionalists' critique of traditionalism should be
heard when they insist that some New Testament texts
do not speak of eternal torment but instead use different
language.

The one image which is so terribly neglected in the
debate between conditionalists and traditionalists, and
which has been inadequately considered in church

---

tormentors, were set over them. And there were also others,
women, hanged by their hair above that mire which boiled up;
and these were they that adorned themselves for adultery. And
the men that were joined with them in the defilement of
adultery were hanging by their feet, and had their heads hidden
in the mire and said: we believed not that we should come to
this place' (James, *op. cit.*, p. 509). In a similar vein the
Apocalypse of Paul 35 reads: 'And I saw not far off another
old man whom four evil angels brought, running quickly, and
they sank him up to his knees in the river of fire, and smote
him with stones and wounded his face like a tempest, and
suffered him not to say: Have mercy on me. And I asked the
angel and he said unto me: He whom thou seest was a bishop,
and he fulfilled not well his bishopric...' (*Ibid.*, p. 543). The
particularly horrifying sections may be found in James, pp.
508-510, 514 (Peter), and pp. 542-548 (Paul).

60   In this connection, *cf.* the very helpful essay by Karl Rahner
entitled 'The Hermeneutics of Eschatological Assertions',
Theological Investigations (London: Darton, Longman and
Todd, 1975), Vol. IV, E.T., pp. 323-346.

history,[61] is that of *personal exclusion*. It may be argued that the scriptural support for this image is the slightest, but there is more than is often realized. At the end of Matthew 7 Jesus refers to the coming day of judgment when many will say to him, 'Lord, Lord, did we not prophecy in your name and cast out demons in your name, and do mighty works in your name?' And the response is: 'I never knew you; depart from me, you evildoers' (Matthew 7:22,23; *cf*. Luke 13:25, 27). This striking juxtaposition of personal language (I... you... me... you) with the moment of judgment is repeated at the end of the parable of the ten virgins in which the foolish virgins who are shut out beg to be let into the kingdom, and to whom the master replies, 'truly, I say to you, I do not know you' (Matthew 25:12). Even in the parable of the sheep and the goats, the language of personal exclusion is present when the Son of Man says to those on his left hand: 'depart from me, you cursed...' (Matthew 25:41).

Paul uses similar terminology to describe the day of judgment when he says that those who 'do no know God... shall suffer the punishment of eternal destruction and exclusion from the presence of the Lord' (2 Thessalonians 1:9); the verb 'exclude' needs to be supplied to the Greek which literally reads only 'from the face of the Lord'. If, as Seyoon Kim has persuasively

---

61   The idea of hell as a privation of the vision of God is a minor theme in the patristic literature. In an essay entitled 'The Fathers of the Church in the Face of the Problems Posed by Hell', Gustave Bardy does not find the notion clearly formulated until St Chrysostom (*c*. 347-407), of whom he writes: 'Without doubt this is the first time that we find a very explicit mention of that which later theology will call the pain of damnation' (*L'Enfer*, (Paris: Collection Foi Vivante, 1950), p. 169, my translation). Bardy fails to note, however, Origen's clear teaching that the primary suffering of hell is the deprivation of God (George W. Butterworth, trans., *Origen on First Principles*, (New York: Harper Torchbooks, 1966), 2:10.7.).

argued in his treatise *The Origin of Paul's Gospel*, [62] the apostle's experience on the Damascus road of personally encountering Christ is at the heart of his whole theology which speaks so often of salvation as being 'in Christ',

---

[62]   Seyoon Kim, *The Origin of Paul's Gospel* (Tubingen: J.C.B. Mohr, 1981). In his conclusion, Kim writes: 'It is most important to ascertain that *Paul received his gospel from the Damascus revelation of Jesus Christ*. We submit that *only when this insistence of Paul is taken seriously can we really understand Paul and his theology*' (p. 335, Kim's emphasis). Kim's argument only focuses on the significance of Paul's conversion experience for Paul's Christology, ecclesiology and soteriology. I believe my suggestion that the same event influenced Paul's eschatology is a valid derivation from Kim's profound insight into the apostle.

Two aspects of the significance of Romans 9:3 for the debate about the New Testament teaching on the question of hell should be underlined. First, one of the interesting facets of the argument for universalism is the inversion of the old nineteenth century liberal case that Paul is the corrupter of the religion of Jesus; now Paul is seen to have crucial insights into the higher truth of final restoration, whereas Jesus is the one who speaks of an ultimate double destiny. Universalists insist that many Pauline texts teach universal salvation and they also maintain there are few if any texts in which Paul could be construed as believing in hell (D.E.H. Whiteley, for example, claims that 'the only passage in the Pauline writings which gives a possible basis for supposing Paul believed in hell [is 2 Thessalonians 1:9]' ('Liberal Christianity in the New Testament', *The Modern Churchmen* Vol. XII, New Series, No. 1 October 1969, p. 18. Of course, many today would dismiss even 2 Thessalonians as non-Pauline.) But here in Romans 9 Paul is alluding to hell, and there is still virtual unanimity that Romans is Pauline. Romans 9:3 therefore should be an additional piece of evidence used to show that Paul did believe in a final double destiny (*contra* Whiteley, there are many passages in addition to 2 Thessalonians 1:9 which show this as well).

Second, of all the supposedly universalistic texts in Paul, one of the most frequently cited is Romans 11. But if Romans 9-11 is seen as a unit, and if Romans 9:3 is an allusion to hell, then this universalist argument needs to be strongly challenged.

then we can argue that here Paul envisions the eschatological antithesis of that experience, of being told by Christ on the last day 'depart from me, I never knew you'. This idea gains further credence when we consider another Pauline text which is rarely touched on in its implications for the doctrine of hell, Romans 9:3. In this passage Paul is in anguish about the spiritual situation of his fellow Israelites and he says, 'I could wish that I myself were accursed and cut off from Christ for the sake of my brethren, my kinsmen by race.' Listen to C.E.B. Cranfield's comments on this verse:

> With these words [*i.e.* 'cut off from Christ'] the full horror of ['I could wish myself accursed'] comes to expression. *Nothing less than the eschatological sentence of exclusion from Christ's presence is involved.* In itself [the 'I myself'] serves to emphasize the intensely personal nature of the self-sacrifice which is contemplated... and, placed thus in immediate juxtaposition to ['from Christ'], it brings out the poignancy of the separation this self-sacrifice signifies'.[63]

This neglected image of eschatological personal exclusion[64] points to three aspects of hell. First and most

---

[63]   C.E.B. Cranfield, *The Epistle to the Romans* (Edinburgh: T. & T. Clark, 1979), Vol. II, p. 458, my emphasis.

[64]   Seeing hell as eschatological personal exclusion by Christ provides part of the answer needed, I believe, to the universalism of John Hick as it is formulated in his book *Evil and the God of Love* (London: MacMillan, 1st edition, 1966). One of Hick's strongest criticisms of the Augustinian theodicy is its tendency to view God's relationship to the world in subpersonal terms, an inclination which Hick contrasts with the incarnational emphasis in much recent theology which sees God '*personally* combating human suffering in Christ's healing acts, *personally* accepting and absorbing the onslaught of moral evil in his death, and *personally* proclaiming in his resurrection the coming triumphant completion of his creative work, despite the powers of sin and death' (p. 256, my emphasis). I believe

basically, hell is being cut off from the Son of God and the
kingdom of God (the 'from me'). This is what the
scholastic theologians referred to by the *poena damni*, the
spiritual agony of exclusion from the beatific vision. As St
Augustine writes:

> To be lost out of the kingdom of God, to be an exile from
> the city of God, to be alienated from the life of God, to
> have no share in that great goodness which God hath
> laid up for them that fear Him, and hath wrought out for
> them that trust in Him [a reference to Psalm 31:19]
> would be a punishment so great, that, supposing it to be
> eternal, no torments that we know of, continued through
> as many ages as man's imagination can conceive, could
> be compared with it.[65]

John Donne eloquently spoke on the same theme centuries
later:

> When all is done, the hell of hels (*sic*), the torment of
> torments, is the everlasting absence of God, and the
> everlasting impossibility of returning to his presence...
> to fall out of the hands of the living God, is a horror
> beyond our expression, beyond our imagination.... What
> Tophet is not Paradise, what Brimstone is not Amber,
> what gnashing is not a comfort, what gnawing of the
> worme is not a tickling, what torment is not a marriage
> bed to this damnation, to be secluded eternally,
> eternally, eternally from the sight of God?[66]

A second aspect of hell to which personal exclusion
points is that hell is God's judgment in completely giving

Hick is reacting to the neglect in Western Christian thinking of
the idea of God as the personal judge, an example of which
would be the lack of reflection on this image of hell as being
personally banished from Christ by Christ.

[65]   Augustine, *Enchiridion* CXII, in *The Works of Aurelius
Augustine* (Edinburgh: T. & T. Clark, 1873), Vol. IX, p. 254.
[66]   John Donne, Sermons IV, 86, as cited by C.A. Patrides,
'Renaissance and Modern Views on Hell', *Harvard Theological
Review* 57 (1964), p. 225.

over the sinner to himself (the 'depart'). Augustine emphasised that the heart of the first sin was the evil choice by Adam and Eve to seek satisfaction in themselves and not in God:

Our first parents fell into open disobedience because already they were secretly corrupted; for the evil act had never been done had not an evil will preceded it. And what is the origin of our evil will but pride? For 'pride is the beginning of sin'. And what is pride but the craving for undue exaltation? And this is undue exaltation, when the soul abandons Him to whom it ought to cleave as its end, and becomes a kind of end to itself. This happens when it becomes its own satisfaction.... The devil, then, would not have ensnared man in the open and manifest sin of doing what God had forbidden.... By craving to be more, man became less; and by aspiring to be self-sufficing, he fell away from Him who truly suffices him.[67]

This idea of man as *homo in se incurvatus*, man curved in upon himself, may then be combined with the view of God's judgment in Romans 1 wherein God judges sinners by giving them over to their sinful choices ('God gave them up' is repeated three times in Romans 1:24, 26, 28). In the *eschaton* the sinner who desires to live apart from God is given over to the full implications of this decision by being completely turned over to seek satisfaction in himself, a final doom of eschatological incurving well captured by the Russian theologian Berdyaev:

Hell is the state of the soul powerless to come out of itself, absolute self-centredness, dark and evil isolation, *i.e.* final inability to love. It means being engulfed in an agonizing moment which opens upon a yawning abyss of infinity, so that the moment becomes endless time. Hell creates and organizes the separation of the soul from God, from God's world, and from other men. In hell the soul is separated from everyone and everything,

---

67   Augustine, *The City of God* in *The Works of Aurelius Augustine*, *op. cit.*, Vol. II., pp. 26-27.

completely isolated and at the same time enslaved by everything and everyone.... Hell is nothing other than complete separation from God. The horror of hell... is to have my fate left in my own hands.... Hell really means... that man ...is finally abandoned to his own devices.[68]

Not being known by God is a third and final element of hell to which these passages of personal exclusion point us (the 'I do not know you'). Luke brings this truth out when he writes about the narrow door (Luke 13:22-30), a text in which, after the householder shuts the door, those outside try to enter and twice receive the response 'I do not know where you come from' (verses 25, 27). Part of the message of salvation which has eluded our generation because of our persistent anthropocentrism is this: the joy of the gospel is not so much that we can know God but that God in Christ has decided to know us. Recall the striking words of Paul in Galatians 4:9, 'but now that you have come to know God, *or rather to be known by God.*' The terrible nature of sin makes human beings so inwardly

---

[68]   Nicholas Berdyaev, *The Destiny of Man* (New York: Harper, 1960) E.T., p. 277. The problem with Berdyaev's understanding of hell is that he completely subjectivizes it and claims that hell has no reality for God. In keeping with much twentieth century theology, Berdyaev refuses to involve God in judgment or retribution in any way, a view which is not easily reconciled with the New Testament witness which speaks of *God's* wrath and fury being stored up for the day of judgment (Romans 2).

C.S. Lewis reflects a similar understanding to that of Berdyaev when he says of those in hell: 'They enjoy forever the horrible freedom they have demanded, and are therefore self-enslaved' (Lewis, *op. cit.*, p.101). Lewis imaginatively pictures this idea through the characters of the dwarfs in the seventh book of the Chronicles of Narnia, *The Last Battle* (London: Collins, 1956). They are described as self-focused in chapter 7 and repeat the saying 'the dwarfs are for the dwarfs' like a liturgical chorus until finally in chapter 13 they curve so far in on themselves that they have Aslan right in front of them and they can't even see him (pp. 138-140).

focused that we need an external referent which will remain fixed who knows us and names us. This is precisely what God offers us in Christ, so that when we love God we are known by him (1 Corinthians 8:3). But those who are lost remain unknown to God throughout this life and then, horror of horrors, when the apocalypse takes place and Christ is unveiled for who he is in all his majesty, holiness, power and great glory, not only are they banished from his presence, not only are they given over to themselves, but they are also not known by God and they *know that they are not known,* for Christ has looked them in the eye and told them.[69,70]

---

69   It is interesting to note the similarities and contrasts between this idea of hell and that in one of the most profound twentieth century explorations of hell, Jean Paul Sartre's play *Huis Clos* ('No Exit'). Sartre is plagued by the existential trauma that man, uniquely, is given existence but must discover his essence. The only way to try to understand who one is is through others who act like a mirror and begin to reflect who we are. This knowledge is always incomplete and frustrated by the fact that other people, rather than seeking to know us, are using us to try to understand themselves. Thus, in Sartre's famous line, 'hell is other people,' that is, hell is life here on earth where we are all locked in this impossible game of gaining a sense of our true selves through others, a game which only results in existential frustration for all involved.

Sartre is right in thinking that one needs an external referent outside oneself to know and understand one's true destiny. In keeping with the anthropocentrism which has characterised so much of Western thought since the Enlightenment, however, Sartre looks at the problem through the eyes of the knower who is seeking to know his essence through others, whereas true salvation comes in being known by the God who informs us of our essence which is to glorify God and enjoy him for ever. In this sense Sartre has it exactly backwards: hell is not the frustration of being unable to know oneself, but rather the judgment of being unknown to God; hell is not other people, it is finally being turned over by God to yourself.

70   Underneath the debate about the New Testament teaching on the final fate of the wicked is the issue of language and the way in which imagery is to be interpreted. It may be noted, for

Like so many other doctrines, hell is finally best understood in the light of the cross. There, certainly, Christ was punished. There Christ was ruined and destroyed. But there also Christ, in a mystery beyond all comprehension, was so personally excluded from his Father who knew him in the intimacy of the Godhead that he cried out 'My God, My God, why hast thou forsaken me?' (Matthew 27:46). May our thoughts on this darkest of doctrines be only for the purpose St Chrysostom said it should ever be focused upon: 'To remember hell prevents our falling into hell.'[71]

---

example, that the picture I have chosen to stress here, that of exclusion, seems difficult to reconcile with Revelation 14:10 which speaks of those who worship the beast being tormented *in the presence of* the saints and the Lamb. This apparent difficulty also occurs whenever any of these images are pressed woodenly in comparison with the others, *i.e.* how can we speak of hell as the 'outer darkness' when it is the place of 'eternal fire,' *etc.* The crucial point is that the different images each refer to a single reality and that combining different images is not like putting together the pieces of a jigsaw puzzle, but rather like letting the sunlight reflect through a diamond and seeing each ray's colours as pointing toward a single eschatological truth.

[71]   John Chrysostom, *Homilies on Romans* XXXI, in *A Library of The Fathers of the Holy Catholic Church* (Oxford: James Parker and Co., 1877, 3rd edition with a revised translation), p. 497.

The Atonement
The Singularity of Christ and the Finality
of the Cross: The Atonement and the
Moral Order

Thomas F. Torrance

'The Son of Man came not to be served but to serve and to
give his life a ransom for many' (Matt. 20:28; Mark 10:48).
'This is good and it is acceptable in the sight of God our
Saviour, who desires all men to be saved, and come to the
knowledge of the truth. For, there is one God, and there is
one Mediator between God and men, the man Christ
Jesus, who gave himself a ransom for all' (1 Tim. 2:5f).
'And he is the expiation (or propitiation) for our sins, and
not for our sins only but for the sins of the whole world' (1
John 2:2). 'He has delivered us from the dominion of
darkness and translated us into the kingdom of his
beloved Son, in whom we have redemption, the
forgiveness of sins. He is the image of the invisible God,
the firstborn of all creation, for in him all things were
created, in heaven and on earth, visible and invisible,
whether thrones, or dominions, or principalities or
authorities – all things were created through him and for
him. He is before all things and in him all things hold
together. He is the head of the body the church; he is the
beginning, the firstborn from the dead, that in everything
he might be pre-eminent, for in him all the fullness of God
was pleased to dwell, and through him to reconcile to
himself all things, whether on earth or in heaven, making

peace by the blood of his cross' (Col. 1:14-20). 'He
entered once for all into the holy place, taking not the
blood of goats and calves but his own blood, thus securing
an eternal redemption.... Therefore he is the mediator of a
new covenant, so that those who are called may receive
the promised inheritance, since a death has once occurred
which redeems them from the transgressions under the
first covenant' (Heb 9:12 &15).

I have selected these verses from many in the New
Testament which tell us of the singularity of Christ as
Mediator and Saviour, the finality of his atoning sacrifice,
and the range of his redeeming and reconciling work that
extends through the whole created order of visible and
invisible reality. This applies, as the Epistles to the
Colossians and to the Hebrews tell us, even to the realm
of heavenly realities, powers and authorities, for they too
need to be reconciled and cleansed by the blood of Christ
(Col. 1:20; Heb. 9:23f).

The Singularity of Christ

By the singularity of Christ is meant not just his concrete
particularity in the space and time of history, but the one
unrepeatable particularity of his incarnate reality as God
and man, Creator and creature, indivisibly united once and
for all in one Person. It is the absolute singularity of Jesus
Christ who is at once the First and the Last, the Alpha
and Omega of all God's ways and works.

Until recently 'singularity' was a dirty word in science.
It was not that the concept of singularity or uniqueness
was baffling, but that it was utterly offensive to the
classical scientific mind and to the way of thinking built
into the rationalism of the Enlightenment. The reason for
this was that it conflicted with the habit of thought derived
from ancient Greece of equating the scientific with the
universal. Scientific thinking was thinking *more
geometrico*, that is, thinking in terms of necessary

timeless universal relations and forms in which the singular or particular had no rational place. Thus in modern classical science all events in time and space were interpreted within a preconceived framework of Euclidean geometry, that is, the geometry of rigid relations independent of time and motion. Natural laws were reached by generalising from particulars to reach universal timeless necessary truths, which gave rise to a rigidly determinist view of the universe. Hence within that scientific outlook a sharp distinction was drawn between necessary truths of reason and accidental truths of history, so that no historical event could be given rational consideration except as a transient particular manifestation of what is universally, timelessly and necessarily true. The same principle was applied by Kant to the moral realm through his use of the universal maxim. Within this outlook Christianity was regarded simply as one religion in a universal class of religions with rejection of any claim to uniqueness as contrary to reason, while any specific divine interaction with us in the world of time and space such as the incarnation or a miracle was ruled completely out of court as an unacceptable violation of universal natural law.

Now of course natural law must be comprehensive for it must apply to all our everyday experiences, but the concept of natural law as timelessly, necessarily, universally true has now been shattered by relativity and quantum theory. When we penetrate more deeply and accurately into the behaviour of nature, as in microphysics or astrophysics, it does not hold. This is not only because we find that nature behaves in a subtle dynamic way that cannot be formalised in logico-necessary patterns of thought, but because in nature we come across the stubbornly *unique* and absolutely *singular*, not just as exceptions but as belonging to the fundamental structure of all space-time reality in the universe. I have in mind here not only the absolute singularity of the so-called original black hole or incredibly dense state from which modern science holds the universe to have expanded, but the absolute specificity of the speed of light which moves at 186,000 miles a second. We now hold that all bodies in motion in the universe are defined by reference to space and time, and space and time are defined by reference to the invariant movement of light, while light itself is not defined by reference to anything else within the universe. Light has a unique metaphysical and physical status, an absolutely singular place in the universe. Light is the one ultimate *Constant* upon which everything else both in nature itself and in our knowledge of it depends. If the speed of light were to vary, the whole universe would be disorderly and chaotic and would not be rationally or scientifically apprehensible. It is thus ultimately by reference to the mathematical properties of light that all our knowledge of the universe is gained, for light signals, the fastest messengers in the universe, are laden with information, so that all that we know about the universe microphysically or macrophysically is gained through deciphering the mathematical patterns of light. Thus *singularity* has been found to belong to the fundamental structure of the created universe and the *concept of singularity* has become inalienably lodged in the foundation and rational structure of scientific knowledge.

I have given some attention to this radical change in the rational structure of scientific knowledge for two reasons. 1) It has brought about a new openness within the scientific world toward the uniqueness of Jesus Christ and the absolute singularity of the incarnation. 2) This change needs to be emphasised today for in religious studies within our so-called multi-faith and multi-cultural society there has been taking place a lapse back to the Enlightenment idea that Christianity is only one religion in a universal class of religions, which discounts the uniqueness and finality of the Christian revelation. Christian understanding of the incarnation is not and can never be based on natural science, but the change which, under God, has come over our scientific grasp of the intelligible nature of the created universe and its space-time structure, enables us to speak to the modern world more freely about the 'centrality of the incarnation' and the 'scandal of particularity' which lie at the heart of the Gospel of God's saving self-revelation in the Lord Jesus Christ. The singular or the unique cannot be expressed in the language of abstraction for abstract generalisation abrogates both the concretely real and the temporally real, which are properly to be understood only out of themselves.

The supreme truth of the Christian faith is that Jesus Christ, born of the virgin Mary, crucified under Pontius Pilate and resurrected from the tomb of Joseph of Arimathea, is our Lord and Saviour. In him God himself has become man within space and time (without of course ceasing to be God), so that Jesus Christ as God and man in his one Person constitutes the real ground and the controlling point for all our authentic knowledge of God and of his creative and redeeming activity toward us. He is the way, the truth and the life, and there is no way to the Father apart from him. There is only one Lord God, and only one incarnation of the one Lord God that has once for all taken place in Jesus Christ in space and time – that is the absolute singularity and exclusiveness of the one Lord Jesus Christ.

There are several aspects of this supreme truth on which I would like to focus our attention here.
1. As the Word of God become flesh, the only begotten Son of God become man, Jesus Christ is, as the Creed expresses it, 'true God of true God'. This is something we cannot adequately understand or express, but in Jesus Christ God has revealed not just something about himself but his very self, in such a way that he is identical in his divine-human Person with God's self-revelation, and in

such a way that there is an unbroken relation in being and act between what God is in himself and what he is toward us in Jesus Christ. In him God and man are perfectly and wholly one, so that there is no God behind the back of Jesus Christ, and no activity of God other than the activity of the eternal Son or Word of God incarnate in Jesus Christ. From the time of Cyril of Alexandria Christian dogmatics has sometimes spoken of this unique, singular union of God and man, divine and human nature, in the one Person of the Lord Jesus Christ in terms of the theological couplet *'anhypostasis / enhypostasis'*. The term *anhypostasis* refers to the fact that in the incarnation there was *no* independent human hypostasis or personal reality adopted to be the Son of God, and the term *enhypostasis* refers to the fact that nevertheless in the incarnation the human nature of Christ was given a real hypostasis *in* the hypostasis of the eternal Son of God. In other words, the incarnation was brought about through the grace of God alone, without any human cooperation, yet in such a way that through the sheer act of divine grace the human nature of Christ, the incarnate Son, was given complete authentic reality as human nature in inseparable union with his divine nature. This gives expression to the singular 'logic of grace' embodied in the incarnation: 'all of grace' involves 'all of man'. Instead of discounting human nature the downright act of God's grace incarnate in Christ creates and upholds human nature.

2. In the Lord Jesus Christ the Creator himself, the Word by whom all things that are made were made, has become a creature, without ceasing to be Creator. Hence it is now as man and God united in one Person that Jesus is held to be Creator. Thus St Paul could speak of Jesus as he 'in whom all things were created in heaven and on earth, visible and invisible, whether thrones or dominions or principalities or authorities – all things were created through him and for him. He is before all things and in him all things hold together' (Col. 1:16-17). If it is in God, then

it is in God incarnate in Jesus, that all human beings live and move and have their being. As the Creator Word made flesh Jesus Christ even in his human nature thus constitutes the creative ground of every human being. The indivisible oneness of God and man, Creator and creature, in the Person of the Lord Jesus Christ will not allow us to contemplate any disjunction between what Christ does in his divine nature and what he does in his human nature – to do that would be a form of Nestorian heresy. This oneness of the Creator and the creature in the Lord Jesus is an essential part of his absolute singularity and lies at the heart of the universal range of his activity as the incarnate Son inseparable from that of God the Father Almighty, Creator of heaven and earth and of all things visible and invisible.

3. The fact that it is none other than God himself who became incarnate in Jesus Christ tells us not only that what God is in Jesus Christ he is inherently in himself, but also that what he does in Jesus Christ he is inherently in himself. His being and his act inhere in one another. This dynamic nature of God is made very clear by the revelation that in Jesus Christ 'the Word became flesh and dwelt among us, full of grace and truth' (John 1:14). The incarnation of the Son of God was certainly an event that took place once for all and as such is not repeatable, but it was not the kind of event that when it has taken place comes to a halt in its movement or passes over into a static state of affairs. On the contrary, the Word became flesh in the divine freedom of God's grace in such a way that in his becoming and having become flesh, he did not and does not cease to be free and sovereign but remained and remains the free sovereign Lord of his becoming flesh. The incarnation is the living movement of the Word become flesh which must be apprehended as such. The singular nature of this divine event in the fullness of time is not easy for us to put into words, but we must think of the becoming it involved not as a becoming on the way

toward being or completion, but rather as the living movement that flows from being, as being in action in time as it continuously becomes what it really is. Just as in his becoming man God does not cease to be God, so in his incarnate becoming the Word does not surrender his eternal being as the Word. God was not eternally incarnate, for the incarnation was something new even for God, but on the other hand although the incarnation took place once for all, it is not to be thought of as just something that God once did in the past, for he remains God incarnate for ever and is unceasingly present and active as God incarnate. It is precisely as such that we must think of him in all his creative and redeeming activity in Jesus Christ, the ever-living and ever-acting Lord God who reveals himself as *'I am who I am / I shall be who I shall be.'*

4. It belongs to the ineffable singularity of Christ as God incarnate that his Person, his Word and his Act are one and undivided. This does not hold good of us creaturely human beings; our persons and our words and our acts are not unrelated, but they are all disparate. We speak but have to exert additional power to bring about what we say in deeds. We act, but our acts are not personal in themselves. Our speech and our action do not coincide in the unity and power of our person. With us act and person, word and person, word and act are all distinct. With God this is not the case, and so we must beware of projecting our finite differences into Deity – that would be a form of mythological thinking. Hence we must think of God meeting us in Christ as One whose Word and whose Act belong to the self-subsistence of his Person. What he utters in Word take place of itself, for it is filled with the power of his Person, the power by which he is who he is and by which he lives his own personal life in absolute self-sufficiency and freedom. His power is not other than the power of his Person or the power of his Word. He is in Person identical with his Word, and his Word is itself his

Act. What God the incarnate Son does, he is in his own Person, and the Word he utters he is in his own Person; in him Person, Word and Act coinhere indivisibly in one another. Jesus Christ *is* Act of God in his own personal being, and he *is* Word of God in his own personal being. Hence we must think of the incarnation as the eternal Word and the eternal Act of God become human word and human act without ceasing to be divine, moving and operating creatively and redemptively within the space and time of our world in the acutely personalised form of the Lord Jesus Christ. It is surely in this way that we are to understand the teaching of the New Testament that the Lord Jesus Christ *is himself* our *justification, redemption, mediation and propitiation; he is himself the resurrection and the life* – he who is, who was and who is to come, the incarnate *I am* of the ever-living God. His incarnate life as the one Lord and Saviour of the world and his atoning work on the cross and in the resurrection cannot be separated from one another. Incarnation and atonement intrinsically locked into one another constitute the one continuous movement of God's saving love for the world. Therein lies the absolute singularity of Christ, but therein also lies the absolute finality of the Cross.

The Finality of the Cross
In refuting Origen's idea of the creation as timelessly concomitant with the being of God and eternally coexisting with him, and in distinguishing between the eternal generation of the Son by the nature of God and the creation of the world by the will of God, Athanasius pointed out that while God was always Father, he was not always Creator. Of course God the Father always had the power to create, but actually to create the universe was to do something absolutely new, new even for God, even though the creation was in the mind of God before he actually brought it into being. It derived from the overflowing of his eternal love and its rational order was grounded in his eternal Word, so that although the

creation was something quite new it was by no means
unrelated to the eternal will of God upon which it was
unceasingly contingent. Once brought into being it is
unceasingly upheld within the creative embrace of God's
eternal presence, so that although the beginning of the
creation was a once for all event, once brought into being it
is continuously sustained in its contingent reality within
the covenant of God's eternal love and grace. As such the
creation is one of the eternal works of God. This relation of
the beginning of the creation, and of time along with it, to
the eternal power of God is quite beyond our ability to
conceive. Athanasius also pointed to the fact that the
incarnation itself was a new event, new even for God, for
the Son of God was not eternally incarnate, but became
man in a new decisive event, new even for God, and yet it
flowed out of the eternal love of God the Father, the Son
and the Holy Spirit. This relation of the eternal and the
historical in the birth and incarnate life of Christ as God
incarnate in space and time belongs to the astonishing
singularity and finality of Christ.

It is in a similar way that we must think of the cross of
Christ for it is the intersection of the divine and the human,
the eternal and the temporal, the act of God himself and
the act of man, in the cross that gives it its absolute
finality. Although it was a once for all particular event in
the space-time continuum of the empirical world, it was
also a once and for all event in an absolutely decisive
sense. Far from being a merely transient event within
time, the cross derives from and is grounded in the eternal
love of God. This point is clearly made by St Paul when in
the Epistle to the Romans he wrote: 'He who did not
spare his own Son but gave him up for us all, will he not
also give us all things with him?'(Rom. 8:32). For St Paul
the sacrifice of Christ on the cross revealed the eternal
heart of the Father, for it flowed from and is grounded in
the ultimate transcendent love of God who in freely giving
up his dear Son for our sakes, showed (as H.R.

Mackintosh once expressed it) that God loves us even more than he loves himself. The fact that the Lord Jesus Christ is God's Son means that in him God the Father himself was actively and personally present in the crucifixion of Christ, intervening redemptively in our lostness and darkness. Indeed in and behind the cross, as Karl Barth once said, it was primarily God the Father who paid the cost of our salvation: *God* was in Christ reconciling the world to himself. Since it was as God and Man in one indivisible Person who was crucified, God himself was crucified for us in Christ. It is the oneness of the sacrifice of God the Father with the sacrifice of his incarnate Son that stamps the cross with its decisive and ultimate finality. It was at once eternal and historical in its once-for-all character – that is why the New Testament can speak of the Lamb of God who bore our sins on the cross as slain before the foundation of the world. The atoning sacrifice offered on the cross was a downright act of God to which nothing can be added – that is what stamps the sufficiency and completeness of the cross as God's finished work: *Tetelesthai* (John 19:38) not only on earth but in heaven, not only in time but in eternity.

'There is one God, and one Mediator between God and men, the man Christ Jesus who gave himself a ransom for all' (1 Tim 2:5f). This does not mean that Jesus Christ mediated between God and man as a third party, for he was of one and the same being as God and of one and the same being as man. His mediation took place, therefore, both within his ontological relations with God and within his ontological relations with mankind. The Lord Jesus Christ was and is God and Man in one Person, for in him divine and human nature were and are hypostatically and for ever united. Hence just as we must think of the incarnation of the eternal Son of God as taking place within the one being of the triune God, so we must think of his mediating work as taking place within the life of the triune God. Hence, as we shall see, the doctrines of the

atonement and of the Holy Trinity cannot be held apart
from one another. At this point, however, I wish to focus
attention on the truth that the atonement took place not
outside of but within the incarnate constitution of the
Mediator who is at once true God of true God and true
Man of true man. Behind this, of course, also lies the
cognate truth that the Person and the Work of Christ, his
Being and his Act, are uniquely one, so that we must think
of his incarnate life and his redeeming activity as
completely interwoven from his conception and birth to his
crucifixion and resurrection. It was from the very beginning
of his incarnate existence that the Lord Jesus began to pay
the price of our redemption.

The atoning mediation of Christ is thus to be expounded
in terms of the *internal* relations between Christ and God
and between Christ and all mankind. The expiatory and
propitiatory activity of the Mediator, while deriving from
the innermost being of God, is fulfilled within the
ontological depths of our fallen, enslaved, depraved and
guilt-laden human existence, that is, in and through the
oneness of God with us in our actual condition embodied in
the incarnate existence of the Mediator. In Jesus Christ
God the Creator of us all has entered personally and
directly into the very foundations of our creaturely being,
as he only can, in order to heal and save it through taking
it upon himself and setting it upon a wholly new basis. It
is important for us here to take absolutely seriously,
without any reservations, the truth of *Immanuel*, 'God
with us'; that is, the fact that in Jesus Christ God himself,
while not ceasing to be God, really became one of us and
one with us as we are. He assumed from the virgin Mary
our actual human nature in such a way as to make our sin,
our guilt, our death and our judgment, our plight and our
agony his own. He took upon himself our twisted, lost and
damned existence, with all its wickedness, violence and
abject misery, and substituted himself for us in the
deepest and darkest depths of our perdition and

godlessness, all in order to save and redeem us through the atoning sacrifice of himself whereby he expiated our guilt in taking our just judgment upon himself, wiped away our sin and debt in making the restitution which we are utterly unable to make, thereby cancelling all our debt and blotting out all accusations against us and justifying us in himself. Such is the unfathomable nature and extent of his substitutionary and vicarious work in giving himself freely for us, acting from beginning to end in our place, on our behalf and in our stead. And such is the astonishing grace of the Lord Jesus Christ who, though he was rich, for our sakes became poor that we might be made rich in him – the blessed reconciling exchange summed up in the New Testament term *katallage*.

Let me now direct attention to several features of this atoning work of the Mediator.

1. In order to deal with sin God sent his Son into our actual existence and made him one with us in the concrete likeness of our flesh of sin (*en homoimati sarkos hamartias*), yet in such a way as not to sin himself but by his holiness to condemn sin in the very flesh which he took from us and made his own (Rom. 8:3). St Paul put this even more strongly when he wrote that, sinless though Christ was, God made him sin for us (*hyper hemon hamartian epoiesen*) that we might be made the righteousness of God in him (2 Cor. 5:21). He even wrote to the Galatians that since the works of the law are under a curse, Christ has redeemed us from the curse of the law, in being made a curse for us (Gal. 3:10, 13). The soteriological principle involved here was formulated by the early Church in various ways: 'the unassumed is the unhealed', 'what Christ has not taken upon himself has not been saved'. The crucial question was whether Christ took upon himself our fallen humanity with its alienated mind, and thereby laid hold of the root of our sin lodged in it, in order to redeem, heal and sanctify it in himself within

his own holy life and activity as the incarnate Mediator, or whether he acted redeemingly upon our fallen existence through some kind of external activity, as if he were merely an instrument or intermediary in the hands of God effecting our salvation. Thus the issue at stake was whether in his incarnation Christ took some neutral humanity upon himself, or whether he actually became what we are in order to make us what he is. Latin theology took the view that in becoming flesh the Son of God took, not our actual nature, but a human nature untouched by sin and guilt, which gave rise to the notion of the immaculate conception, and to a doctrine of atoning transaction expounded in terms of moral and juridical external relations between Christ and ourselves. Eastern theology, however, rejected that anti-Pauline dualist approach and insisted that in the incarnation the Son of God took upon himself our actual sinful existence subjected to his own judgment, but in such a way that his assumption of that was also and from the very beginning a redeeming, healing and sanctifying of it. In Christ our fallen Adamic humanity was recreated and through his vicarious obedience as the Son of God become man it was restored to perfect filial relation to the Father.

The difference between the two approaches is considerable. In the Latin view the atoning sacrifice on the cross deals only with actual sin, so that in addition to the expiatory sacrifice offered on the cross, although on the ground of what it accomplished, infusions of grace are provided to deal with original sin. In the Greek view, however, it is the whole incarnate life of Christ vicariously and triumphantly lived out from his birth to his crucifixion and resurrection in perfect obedience to the Father within the ontological depths of his oneness with us in our actual fallen existence, that redeems and saves us and converts our disobedient alienated sonship back to filial union with the Father. That is the grace of the Lord Jesus Christ. The cardinal issue here, then, is the all-important truth of the *vicarious humanity* of Jesus Christ as Lord and Saviour of mankind. This carries with it a rejection of any idea that the humanity of Christ played a merely instrumental role in some kind of external legal transaction in the hands of Almighty God, and gives it an essential and integral place in indivisible oneness of agency with that of the Father and the Holy Spirit. In this way the atonement, downright act of God though it was, is to be regarded not as something done over our head but as something made to issue out of the depths of our actual existence through the incredible oneness which Christ forged with us in his vicarious humanity.

2. Whenever the incarnation and the vicarious act of Christ on the cross are held apart, the atonement is inevitably thought of as an external transaction between God and man and between Christ and man, in which divine and human agency in Christ are held apart, which inevitably calls in question the inseparable conjunction in him of divine and human natures. In that event the doctrine of atonement loses its intrinsic coherence and wholeness as set forth in biblical revelation and tends regularly to break up into different theories. As I understand it, however, the concept of atonement running through the New Testament Scriptures is given expression by way of Christological reinterpretation of the redemptive acts of God in the deliverance of Israel from Egyptian bondage. The main Old Testament terms and images used to speak of that (from the Hebrew roots *kpr, ga'l, pdh*), reminted under the impact of the Gospel and translated into Greek, carried the central forms of thought traditionally used by the Church in expressing something of the indescribable mystery of Christ's passion and the ineffable truth of atonement in its various but profoundly interrelated aspects. These aspects had to do with the mighty acts of divine salvation through deliverance from oppression and judgment, through expiatory sacrifice offered in atonement for sin and in propitiatory reconciliation with God, and through

redemption out of destitution and debt in virtue of a bond of affinity or covenant love. I think of them as the dramatic or dynamic, the cultic or priestly, and the ontological aspects of atonement.

The great prophets adapted these various conceptions to speak of the ultimate redemption of God's people through his anointed Servant who is afflicted with the judgments of God as he bears their iniquities on himself, makes himself an offering for sin, intercedes for the transgressors, and mediates a new covenant between God and his people. Those evangelical oracles were appropriated by Jesus from the Old Testament to speak of himself who came not to serve but to serve and give his life a ransom for many, and were taken up and developed by the Apostles to fill out their teaching about the atoning significance of Christ's vicarious life and passion especially as he had interpreted it in the Holy Supper. It was his whole life, and above all that life poured out in supreme sacrifice of death on the cross, that made atonement for sin, and constituted the price of redemption for all mankind.

Early Christian theology did not make systematic use of these various ingredients in the apostolic teaching of the atonement handed down in the deposit of faith. Nor did it distinguish them explicitly from one another in their particular emphases, for they naturally ran into each other and modified each other within the Church's kerygmatic presentation of the saving passion of Christ, but all the characteristic points were given their due place in a realist and holistic doctrine of atonement, the dramatic, the priestly and the ontological. Sometimes the dramatic aspect of redemption is prominent, that is the mighty act of God's saving deliverance out of the power and oppression of evil and the judgment of God upon it. Closely interlocked with this is the priestly aspect of redemption through atoning sacrifice for the expiation of sin and guilt whereby God incarnate in Christ draws near to us and draws us near to himself, cleansing us through his blood, sanctifying and healing us by the power of his Spirit, ransoming us from servitude to the world, delivering us from slavery into liberty, from darkness to light, thereby constituting us as a new priesthood and a special people belonging to himself for ever. The third main aspect of atonement as redemption out of destitution or forfeited rights, perdition and death is more ontological in character, for it depends on the divine-human nature of the Redeemer who stands in for us in our need and makes our desperate condition his own on the ground of his incarnate oneness with us. In the Old Testament such a redeemer was known as the *go'el*, who claims the cause of another as his own, and stands in for him when he cannot redeem himself. That was applied in the prophecies of the book of Isaiah to God's advocacy of Israel, not only in its deliverance from Egypt as his first-born son, but to the messianic redemption of Israel in the future into unbroken communion with himself. It was only such a redeemer who could deliver people from the ultimate destruction of death and the pit. What was thus prefigured in God's relations with his ancient people was found to be fulfilled in the Gospel with the actual coming of the Son of God in the flesh and the physical reality of Christ's saving life and passion. In this aspect of redemption the emphasis is on the incarnate Person of the Redeemer, the one Mediator between God and man, who in his oneness with us sums up and is intensively in himself all that he undertakes in atoning activity on our behalf. It is in virtue of this incarnational identification with us in our destitution, perdition, damnation and death that he makes our cause his own and claims for us the salvation he has achieved in invading the tyranny of sin and judgment and death to which we are subjected, destroying their hold on us, and thereby setting us free for fellowship with God the Father through himself and his gift of the Holy Spirit. It is in and through this incarnational or ontological aspect of redemption that all the ingredients and features of God's atoning work are knit together in one dynamic whole. Apart from it the other two aspects tend to fall apart in our understanding.

3. Through the incarnation the atonement is established and anchored in our human existence, but it is also anchored in the transcendent being and love of God from whom it derives and to whom it restores us in the communion of his reconciling love. This is where we must consider the relation of atonement to the Holy Trinity. We may take as our guide here what St Paul has to say about reconciliation as the movement whereby God the Father draws near to us and draws us near to himself through the blood of Christ and thereby gives us access to himself (Eph. 2:13ff). St Paul has in mind in this passage the fact that surrounding the temple in Jerusalem a barrier had been erected beyond which neither Gentiles nor excommunicated Jews (the 'publicans and sinners' of the Gospels) might pass in order to draw near to God in worship. That is the middle wall of partition, as he called it, which has now been broken down for the enmity between man and God has been abolished through the cross of Christ, with the result that both Jews and Gentiles may have access by one Spirit to the Father. What we have presented there is atoning *propitiation* whereby God draws near to us and draws us near to him through the blood of Christ. Propitiation has nothing to do with propitiating God as though he needed to be placated in order to reconcile us to himself, but with the two-way movement on the part of God who in his prevenient love freely draws near to us in order to draw us near to himself on the ground of the atoning self-sacrifice of Christ offered for us. In propitiation God acts from both sides of the barrier of enmity between us, from the side of God toward us sinners, and from our side toward himself, thereby effecting reconciliation between us, and bringing us into

communion with himself, so that through Christ the one Mediator we are given access in one Spirit to the Father.

The New Testament tells us that it is only on the ground of the reconciliation with God effected through the cross that the Holy Spirit is mediated to us, and it is only as Christ himself is mediated to us through the presence of the Spirit that we may be united to Christ in his vicarious humanity and participate in the fruit of his saving and redeeming work. It was only after Christ had been lifted up on the cross and after he was glorified that the Holy Spirit was given. Calvary and Pentecost belong integrally together, for the pouring out of the Holy Spirit upon us belongs to the fulfilment of God's reconciliation of the world to himself. And St Paul tells us that it is only through atoning propitiation through the blood of Christ that we may draw near to God and be given access to knowledge of him as he is in himself as Father, Son and Holy Spirit, so that apart from that access we may not know God in the inner relations of his triune being, but only in the undifferentiated oneness of his unnameable being as is claimed in Judaism. It is not too much to say, then, that the proper understanding of God as Father, Son and Holy Spirit takes place only within the movement of atoning propitiation whereby God himself draws near to us and draws us near to himself and thereby enables us to have communion with him in his inner trinitarian relations, for it is only within that two-way movement of divine reconciliation that God's self-giving and self-revealing to mankind achieve their full end. Through Christ and his cross alone do we have access by one Spirit to the Father, and so our reconciliation and communion with God through the atoning mediation of Christ are ultimately grounded in the triune being of the one eternal God. We may express this in another way: since the Lord Jesus Christ the only-begotten Son of God is of one being with the Father, and since he is God and Man inseparably united in his incarnate Person, the atoning work of the incarnation falls

within the inner being and life of the Holy Trinity. This
trinitarian grounding of atonement in the eternal being of
God also belongs to the absolute and eternal finality of the
cross.

4. What are we to think, then, about the range of atoning
redemption if it flows from and is anchored in the nature
and being, and the love of the Father, the Son and the
Holy Spirit? It cannot but be commensurate with the
eternal nature, being and love of the Blessed Trinity, for to
limit the range of atoning redemption would be to limit the
range of the nature, being and love of the Father, the Son
and the Holy Spirit. Since God *is* love, to limit the range of
his love would be tantamount to imposing limits upon the
ultimate being of God and to call in question the universal
nature of the communion inherent in his triune reality as
God. Let us focus our attention, however, upon the fact
that it is the divine-human nature of Christ that
determines the nature and range of his redeeming work.

We recall that in Jesus Christ the eternal God himself,
God the Creator, God the Word by whom all things have
been made, became man: and recall that in him divine
nature without any diminishment and human nature
without any diminishment have been hypostatically and
indivisibly united in his one incarnate Person. We may not
think, therefore, of any separation in Jesus Christ between
his divine and his human nature, or therefore of any
separation between his divine and his human activity.
Since it is in God by whom we have been created that we
live and move and have our being, it is in God become
man, in the Lord Jesus, that we live and move and have
our being – every human being is ontologically bound to
him. It is in Jesus Christ the incarnate Creator, then, that
the being of all men, whether they believe or not, is
creatively grounded and is unceasingly sustained. By his
incarnate constitution as the Mediator between God and
man who is at once Creator God and creaturely man, Jesus

Christ as Man represents all mankind: in him all men have the creative and sustaining source of their being. He cannot but represent in his death all whom he represents in his incarnate constitution. Atonement and incarnation cannot be separated from one another, and therefore the range of his representation is the same in both. If in his incarnation Christ the eternal Son took upon him the nature of man, then all who belong to human nature are involved and represented – all human beings without exception. It is for all and each that Jesus Christ stood in as substitute and advocate in his life and in his death: as such he died for all mankind and made atonement for their sins. Let it be emphasised that this involves and applies to everyone without exception, for to limit the range of his activity as God and man in his incarnate life, death and resurrection, would be to introduce a limitation into his eternal being as love, and a schism or contradiction into his incarnate Person as God and man. To hold that some people are not included in his incarnate and redeeming activity is to cut at the very root of his reality as the Creator incarnate in space and time, as he in whom all things in the universe, visible and invisible, were created, hold together and are reconciled by the blood of his cross (Col. 1:15-20).

It is commonly argued by some people that if Jesus Christ died for all people then all people must be saved, but if some people go to hell then he did not die for them. And this is sometimes tempered by the proposition put forward by Alexander of Hales in connection with the Augustinian and scholastic notion of irresistible causal grace, that while the death of Christ was sufficient for all people it was efficient only for some. This implies a restricted and partial notion of God's incarnate assumption of our humanity and of its burden of sin, guilt and judgment, and therefore a merely partial and not a total notion of substitution. Of course if God really became man and took upon himself the whole burden of guilt and judgment, then such an arbitrary view would be impossible. If we really hold that it is God himself who bears our sins in Jesus Christ, God himself who in becoming man takes man's place and stands with man under his own divine judgment, God himself the Judge becoming the man judged, then we cannot allow any divorce between the action of Christ on the cross and the action of God. How is it at all possible to think of the divine judgment in the cross as only a partial judgment upon sin, or a judgment only upon some sinners, for that is finally what it amounts to if only some sinners are died for, and only some are efficiently implicated in atonement? The concept of a limited atonement thus rests upon a limitation of the very being of God as love, and a schizoid notion of the incarnation, *i.e.* upon a basic Nestorian heresy.

At the heart of this Halesian argument, appropriated by Theodore Beza and injected into Calvinism, there is posited a logico-causal relation between the atoning death of Christ and the forgiveness of our sins. If that atoning death applies to all men then logically and causally all men must of necessity be saved: but if some men actually go to hell then logically and causally the efficacy of that atoning death does not and cannot apply to them. It is in that way that the case for either universal salvation or limited atonement is usually made. However, there are at least two fatal inter-connected errors in this argument upon which it shatters completely.

On the one hand, it operates with a logico-causal relation between the vicarious death of the Lord Jesus and the forgiveness of our sins, but that is falsely to project into the atonement a kind of connection which obtains between finite events and statements about them in our fallen world, and to substitute it for the transcendent kind of connection that is revealed in the creative and redeeming activity of God himself. As we have already noted, our finite distinctions between word, act and person cannot be projected into Deity, for the power and operation of God are of quite a different kind, the power and operation of his transcendent presence in which his being and act and Person are integrated in the power of his triune being. That is the kind of connection made manifest in the virgin birth of Jesus or in his bodily resurrection from the dead, but also in the miracles when by the Spirit of God Jesus healed the sick, gave sight to those born blind, fed thousands of people from a few loaves and fish and raised the dead. Jesus Christ *is* the resurrection and the life, and that cannot be construed within a system of this-worldly logico-causal relations. The kind of connection that obtains in the atoning death of Christ was demonstrated in the resurrection of Jesus. The connection between the atoning death of the Lord Jesus and the forgiveness of our sins is of an altogether ineffable kind which we may not and cannot reduce to a chain of this-worldly logico-causal relations. To do that comes very near to sinning against the Holy Spirit.

On the other hand, the argument for universalism or for limited atonement is one that involves a rationalisation of evil in attempting to say why some men are finally saved and why some men are finally not saved, by resorting to an explanation in terms of a logico-causal continuity. Whatever else evil is, it involves a fall of man from fellowship with God and a breach in all moral relations between man and God and man and man. Evil involves a radical discontinuity which cannot be explained in terms of continuity without explaining it away. By its irrational nature, the mystery of iniquity, as the New Testament speaks of it, cannot be explained for the discontinuity it involves is absolutely unbridgeable. Evil is so bottomless or abysmal that to deal with it, do away with it or overcome it, nothing short of the direct presence and power of the eternal and infinite God was needed. In order to redeem us from the enormity of evil God 'had to' become incarnate in our mortal existence and penetrate into the chasm of our sinful and guilty separation from himself, which he freely did on the cross out of his unlimited and unstinting love. Conversely, the fact that God himself, God incarnate, penetrated into our damned existence and death in order to save us, reveals the bottomless chasm and the irrational, inexplicable nature of evil by which we are separated from him. If then anyone thinks he can explain why the atoning death of Christ avails efficaciously only for some people but not for all through offering a logico-causal explanation, he is really putting forward an argument which is tantamount to doing despite to the infinite agony of God Almighty at Calvary, for he does not consider the fearful nature of sin and evil which cost God the sacrifice of his own beloved Son. In the nature of the case, why some people do not believe in Jesus Christ as Lord and Saviour, and go to hell just cannot be explained – here, as John Calvin so often wrote, we have to do with something quite inexplicable that may only be construed as happening 'accidentally' – *per accidens* or *accidentaliter* – that is, irrationally and inexplicably. 'How God condemns the impious and also justifies the impious is shut away from human understanding in incredible secret'(*De aet. pred.* IX.3). It cannot be said that Calvin was always consistent, but he did remark that even if a man goes to hell it does not mean that Christ did not shed his blood for him. And he explicitly rejected the proposition that Christ suffered sufficiently for all, but efficaciously only for the elect (*Ibid.* XI.5).

It should now be clear that universalism and limited atonement are twin heresies which rest on a deeper heresy, the recourse to a logico-causal explanation of why the atoning death of the Lord Jesus Christ avails or does not avail for all people. Any such an attempt at logico-causal explanation of the efficacy and range of the atonement is surely a form of blasphemy against the blood of Christ.

The Atonement and the Moral Order

The universal range of the redemptive work of Christ takes in not only all humanity, but the whole created universe of space and time, including all things (*ta panta*) visible and invisible, earthly and heavenly alike. This is an aspect of Jesus Christ's triumphant work to which St Paul referred again and again, as in the Epistles to the Romans, Ephesians and Colossians, for the dimensions of divine reconciliation have such an universal sweep that there is nothing anywhere that can separate us from the love of God which is in Christ Jesus our Lord. Everything centres in Christ, and the whole created universe holds together through relation to him as its Head, for it pleased the Father that in him all the fullness of God should dwell, and it is by him and through the blood of his cross that all things are reconciled to God, whether they are things in earth or things in heaven. It is not too much to say, therefore, that the atonement is so profound and inclusive that it takes in the rational and moral order of the whole universe of time and space, and integrates it on the basis of a heaven and an earth redeemed in Christ and sanctified in the resurrection of his body, the firstfruit of the new creation.

My particular concern here is with the bearing of the atonement on the moral order, for by and large in Western theology, Roman and Protestant alike, the doctrine of atonement is formulated within the parameters of the moral law as it stands, without any recognition that the whole moral order had to be redeemed and be set on a new basis through the atonement. The origins of this go back to a dualist way of understanding and interpreting the message of the Gospel according to which, as it became very clear to the Nicene Fathers in their struggle with Arianism, the relation between the incarnate Son and the Father was merely one of an external and moral kind contingent upon the divine will, and not a relation internal to the being and life of the Godhead. Correspondingly it operated an external relation between the saving work and the Person of Christ, so that his atoning sacrifice was expounded merely in moral and juridical terms, that is, within the parameters of a moral and legal order of an intermediate kind not directly grounded in God although ultimately dependent upon his will like the created order of things in the cosmos. This dualist way of thinking inevitably disrupts any unitary approach to the Person of Christ or any coherent understanding of the Gospel of salvation, for if Jesus Christ is not the incarnation of the only begotten Son who is eternally in God, then he constitutes no more than a created and temporal centre ontologically distinct from God within the immanent moral and rational order of the created cosmos. In that event all relations between Jesus Christ and God could be construed only in external moral and rational terms without any unifying centre in the Person of Christ who as the Creator Word made flesh, who as God and Man, is the one Mediator between God and man. That is to say, the atoning sacrifice of Christ would then be understood not as a divine-human act which penetrates into the ontological depths of human nature and life or bears savingly upon the distorted and corrupt condition of man's actual human existence. It was largely due to this way of thinking that the doctrine of the atonement, in spite of the Church's rejection of Arianism, tended to become detached from the incarnation and thus from its unifying hypostatic centre in Jesus Christ who is of one being and agency with God the Father and the Holy Spirit, with the result that interpretation of the various aspects of Christ's death in terms of external relations could not but break up into different 'theories of the atonement' – which unfortunately is what has regularly happened in Western theology.

However, if the atonement is understood in terms of the inner ontological relation between Christ and God, on the one hand, and in terms of the inner ontological relation between Christ and mankind, on the other hand, then no account of it can be offered merely in terms of a moral or legal framework external to the incarnation, for that is itself part of the actual state of affairs between man and God that has suffered disruption and needs to be set right. This is in fact the very point of St Paul's doctrine of *justification* in which he faced up to the astonishing fact that God is both just and the justifier of the ungodly. Somehow the law, deriving as it does from God, is found to be the strength of sin and does not and cannot deal with the root of sin, but paradoxically serves to maintain sin in its strange contradictory existence. Somehow the moral or legal order, while having absolute divine sanction, itself belongs to the separation between man and God, and even shields the sinner from direct relation to God, for the law in its refracted form in the fallen world stands between man and God and keeps God at a distance from him. This is why the dialectic of sin always leads to legalism. Such is the tangled and contradictory state of affairs that had to be set right through the expiatory and propitiatory blood of Christ, but in and through which God himself is justified in justifying the ungodly, and the ungodly are justified not through the law but through the justification of God. As St Paul presented it, then, justification by the grace of God alone is the free righteous act of God in the atoning life and death of Christ, which takes place both 'under the law' (*hypo ton nomon*) and 'apart from law' (*horis tou nomou*).

We may express the problem St Paul faced in this way. The moral relations between man and God that obtain in our fallen world have to do with the unbridgeable rift between what we *are* and what we *ought* to be, for no matter how much we try to be what we ought to be we can never transcend that deep rift in ourselves. It belongs to our fallen humanity and the very root of our sin that we are trapped within that rift – that is why all our free will is finally a form of our self-will. That is the very state of affairs, the fall from God lodged in our actual being, that needs to be done away, for even what we call morally 'good' in fulfilment of what we ought to do before God, needs to be cleansed by the blood of Christ. This applies also to the judgments of our human conscience, for it too needs to be sprinkled by the blood of atonement – that is surely why at Holy Communion as we partake of the body and blood of Christ we feel shame for our whole being, for our good as well as our evil.

The problem is that the very moral order itself has been compromised and distorted and needs to be put right. Within the moral order as it stands the substitutionary death of Christ would be judged morally wrong. Gregory of Nyssa once pointed this out, when he showed that judged by the accepted moral criteria it would be wrong for one person to take the place of another or die in another's place, for no one can represent another within his moral responsibility, and no one therefore can be a responsible substitute for another from within his guilt. The morally inexplicable fact that God in Christ has actually taken our place, been judged in our place and died the just for the unjust, made it very clear that the whole moral order as we know it in this world needed to be redeemed and set on a new basis, but that is precisely what the justifying act of God in the atoning sacrifice of Christ was about. Thus while in St Paul's phrase Christ subjected himself 'under the law' to redeem those that are under the law, nevertheless his act of grace in justifying us freely through redemption was 'apart from law'.

Such is the utterly radical nature of atoning mediation perfected in Christ, for it involves what might well be called 'a soteriological suspension of ethics' in the establishing of a new moral life that flows from grace in which external legal relation is replaced by inner filial relation to God the Father. This radical change is to be grasped, as far as it may, not in the light of abstract moral or legal principle, nor in terms of the works of the law, but only in the light of what Christ has actually done in penetrating into the dark depths of our twisted human existence where moral obligations and duties conflict with one another, in doing away with the unbridgeable rift with which the moral nature of human being has been bound up since the fall. That is the profound regeneration (*palingenesia*) in the very roots of human existence which Christ brought about in his healing and sanctifying assumption of our Adamic humanity, when through his vicarious life, through the holy perfection of his obedient Sonship, and through the cleansing power of his atoning sacrifice in death and resurrection, he redeemed the very moral and spiritual world to which human beings belong from the compromise and ambiguity with which it had been distorted. This is an altogether new way of life for us resulting from our being translated out of the bondage of law into the freedom of the children of God. Through the presence of the Holy Spirit poured out upon us on the ground of Christ's atoning triumph, this new life of ours in him is inwardly ruled by the indicatives of God's love rather than externally governed by the imperatives of the law.

Quite true to this change was the way in which John Macleod Campbell and Hugh Ross Mackintosh sought to offer an account of the atonement mainly from within the context of the inner relation between God the Father and his incarnate Son, which puts a very different construction upon the Christian life and behaviour. This by no means rules out the propriety of forensic, juridical or penal relations in a doctrine of the atonement, but they are intensified, deepened and refined in their import through what took place in the ontological depths of our Lord's atoning life and death. As such they were transformed under the impact of the holy love of the Father revealed and incarnated in the obedience of his beloved Son, and brought to bear upon Christian thought and life through the Spirit of the Father and the Son. Here the ultimate ground of the moral order in God is no longer a detached imperative bearing down abstractly and externally upon us, for it has now been embodied once for all in the incarnate Person of the Lord Jesus Christ and takes the concrete and creative form of new righteousness that transcends the split between the is and the ought, the righteousness of our Lord's obedient Sonship in which our human relations with our Father in heaven have been healed and reconciled. We are now made through justification by grace to share in the righteousness of God in Christ. Thus we are made to live in union with him and in the communion of his Holy Spirit who sheds the love of God into our hearts, and informs our life with the very mind of Christ the obedient Son of the Father. This does not represent merely a conceptual change in our understanding of the moral order, but a real ontological change resulting from the interlocking of incarnation and atonement in the depth and structure of our human existence and the translation of the Son/Father relation in Christ into the daily life of the children of God. The atonement is so profound that it transforms the fundamental moral framework of thought and constitutes the very parameters within which it is rightly to be understood. Hence we go back on the atonement if we seek to understand and interpret it within the parameters of the unredeemed moral order.

What all this involves cannot be spelled out here, but it will be sufficient to bring this discussion to a close with two remarks.

First, the renewal of the moral order by God belongs to the cosmic sweep of atoning reconciliation in which, as we have seen, all things visible and invisible, not only earthly but heavenly realities, are cleansed and sanctified. The whole creation with its immanent rational and moral order has been laid hold of in Christ the incarnate Creator, and included in his triumphant victory over corruption and his bodily resurrection from the dead. The vast created order of space and time now centres in Christ and revolves round the axis of his cross and resurrection. He is the First and the Last. What the Saviour has done once for all penetrates back through the ages of the world into the very beginning of creation, undoing the calamity of the fall, breaking the chain of irreversible sin and guilt, in the redemption of time and existence as they are gathered up in Christ. But it also pierces through the present into the future and opens wide the gates of human existence and history toward the new heaven and the new earth which altogether transcend the first heaven and the first earth, although in ways that elude human comprehension and expression. Whenever divine revelation speaks of beginnings or ends and the ultimate victory of God over the forces of evil and darkness, it makes use of apocalyptic language and imagery which fragment in their using and which we are quite unable to master through any kind of conceptual parsing, but must respect as fleeting enigmatic glimpses given us by God of the consummation of all things over which Christ is enthroned as the Lamb that has been slain but behold he is alive for evermore.

Second, let me point to the fact that in the ancient liturgy of atonement that took place annually in the ancient tabernacle or temple, the climax came when the blood of the atoning sacrifice was carried by the high priest beyond public gaze through the veil into the Holy of Holies where it was sprinkled upon the mercy-seat overspread by the wings of the cherubim who cover their faces before the holy presence of God. It was not otherwise in the fulfilment of that ancient liturgy, when the Lord Jesus Christ, as both High Priest and Lamb of God, died on the cross, rose again from the grave and ascended into heaven, as he offered himself in atoning sacrifice once for all through the eternal Spirit, and ever lives to make intercession for us. Thus divine revelation makes it clear that the consummation of the atonement was carried out in the transcendent realm of the triune God altogether beyond the perception and understanding of mankind. By its intrinsic nature the atonement is infinitely greater and profounder than we can ever conceive or express, so that in thinking and speaking of it we cannot but clap our hands upon our mouth and fall down before the Lord God in worship. Like the Holy Trinity the atonement is infinitely more to be adored than expressed, so that appropriate and faithful thought and speech about it cannot but break off in sheer wonder, reverence, thanksgiving and praise.

Are They Few That Be Saved?

Paul Helm

You will recall that when the question 'Are they few that be saved?' was originally asked, no direct answer was given. The question was answered by a command or exhortation. So there is the strongest precedent for not providing a direct answer to the question, and I intend in this paper to follow that precedent. But I shall make one important assumption that lies behind both the question and Christ's answer, the assumption that not all will be saved.

I

Part of the terribleness of the biblical teaching on hell is that it is a condition of separation from the love and mercy of God that is without boundary or limit. Another part of its terribleness is due to the surging feeling, whenever the subject of hell is mentioned, that such a fate is both unnecessary and unjust. Thus Charles Darwin:

> I can hardly see how anyone ought to wish Christianity to be true; for if so, the plain language of the text seems to show that the men who do not believe, and this would include my Father, Brother, and almost all my best friends, will be everlastingly punished.
> And this is a damnable doctrine.[1]

---

[1]   Quoted by Galen Strawson, *The Independent on Sunday Review*, 24th June, 1990, p. 27.

Such a feeling may not only be prompted by a belief in the indiscriminate and limitless benevolence of God, but also by the purest evangelical conviction that if any are saved this is due to an act of pure, unmerited divine favour. The question that then surges is: If some are saved by pure grace, why are not all saved?

But perhaps the questioner forgets that since the fact that any are saved is an act of pure unmerited favour the question ought to be: Why are any saved? This reminds us that Christian salvation is not a right but a gift, and a gift can perfectly consistently be given, or withheld, as the giver sees fit. But why should anyone with unlimited resources wish to withhold the gift?

Hell also seems unjust to many because the punishment does not seem to fit the crime. Can anyone deserve such a fate? Can the merest peccadillo deserve the unremitting punishment of hell? It is hard to accept the fact that, however terrible hell is, divine justice reigns there. Yet any other conclusion than this would be unthinkable. But if justice reigns in hell as well as in heaven, then the Christian may rest content. One important reason for a Christian accepting that hell is a place of justice is because Christ, whose moral understanding was not warped or twisted as ours is, and who fully represented the moral character of God, saw no injustice in hell. As for sin, we forget too easily that sin can never be merely a peccadillo, but that it is essentially a state of hostility to God and rebellion against him. If peccadillos are not that, then they will not be punished in hell.

But there is another aspect of the biblical teaching about heaven and hell which for many is impossibly difficult to bear. The biblical teaching implies that the human race is to be forever divided by a great gulf. For anyone who places supreme value on the human personality or the human race, on 'One World', that thought of an eternal division must be an intolerable one. In view of this it is not surprising that one of the great driving forces behind the attack on the doctrine of hell in modern times has arisen from humanism and from humanistic versions of Christianity. Quite consistently so, for the doctrine of hell cuts clean across such humanism because it shows that however important human beings are, and however worthwhile the social and political goal of human harmony and solidarity may be, there is a value that is superior to it, the will and character of God himself.

These comments all have to do with the *particularism* of heaven and hell. Linked with this, though not strictly implied by it, is the *exclusivism* of these conditions; the stark fact that according to Scripture one's location in either heaven or hell depends only upon one's relationship to Christ. If biblical particularism is replaced by some version of universalism, the view that all people are to be saved, then a way has to be found of justifying universalism. One way is to deny to Christ any saving power. Another is to soften the exclusive claims that Christ makes for himself, and to hold that Christianity is but one of several or of many roads to the Celestial City.

In the remainder of this paper I wish to examine several of the more interesting and attractive arguments which, if successful, serve to weaken the exclusivism and hence the particularism of the gospel. These arguments have arisen from within Christendom, and therefore pay some attention to the authoritative place of Scripture in Christian theology. Later I shall take up one of these arguments and develop it, endeavouring to persuade you of its reasonableness.

II

As we have noted, exclusivism is closely linked with the particularism of the Christian faith. There is not a logical connection, for it is quite conceivable that, had God intended it, everyone could have been saved through Christ. Paradoxically, in these circumstances the exclusivism would have had universal benefits. Yet while not logically connected, in the Bible exclusivism and particularism are closely intertwined. In the same way that attempts are made to avoid biblical particularism so, as already noted, attempts are made to water down Christ's exclusive claims by adopting one or other form of *syncretism*, the idea that the various major religions of the world – Buddhism, Hinduism, Islam and so on – each form different but equally valid and reliable ways to God. John Hick provides a very clear example of such syncretist thinking.

Hick presents his case against exclusivism in two phases. In the first phase he discusses the historic exclusiveness of the Christian faith embodied in the claim that apart from faith in Christ there is no salvation. This claim has sometimes been expressed, especially in Roman Catholicism, by the words 'no salvation outside the church'. While by 'the church' here is usually, though not always, meant the Roman Catholic Church, there is another sense of 'church' in which that formula could be acceptable to a Protestant, who holds that membership of the true church is founded on faith in Christ as Saviour. But however this principle is expressed it clearly places Christ at the centre as the sole revealer of God's saving grace, as the only Saviour, without the knowledge of whom no rational adult can be saved.

But, as Hick correctly points out, over the generations such a simple, clear-cut principle has been made increasingly complicated. Roman Catholics, in particular, have watered down this exclusivism by their doctrine of the 'baptism of desire' and by claiming that a person who is ignorant of Christ may nonetheless implicitly desire the salvation which Christ alone provides. And some Protestants have said something similar, as we shall see.

What such qualifications amount to is the claim that although there is no salvation outside Christ yet a person may be savingly related to Christ even though he has never heard of him. Even here Christ is at the centre, though in a less overt way.

Hick proposes, in the second phase of his argument, to sweep all such qualifications away. As Copernicus propounded a revolutionary theory which placed the sun and not the earth at the centre of the universe, so Hick proposes a similar shift in religion. A shift

from the dogma that Christianity is at the centre to the realisation that it is *God* who is at the centre, and that the religions of mankind, including our own, serve and revolve around him.[2]

So as Hick sees it our view of the religions of the world should be *theo*centric rather than *christo*centric, and Christianity should be seen as but one aspect of the many other aspects of world religion.

Such a proposal contains an immediate difficulty, as Hick recognises, namely that most religions, and certainly Christianity, make exclusive claims for themselves. So although Hick may propose the view that all religions provide valid ways to God, the religions themselves do not view things this way at all.

Hick's reply to this is that since the ultimate divine reality transcends the human mind, 'the different encounters with the transcendent within the different religious traditions may all be encounters with the one infinite reality, though with partially different and overlapping aspects of that reality'. According to Hick no-one knows enough about God for it to be otherwise. More

---

2   'The Copernican Revolution in Theology' in *God and the Universe of Faiths* (London, 1973), p. 131.

than this, God is unknowable, and the various ways of approaching God to be found in the major religions are each equally valid ways of approaching the inapproachable.

So Hick rests his syncretism on a foundation of religious relativism. Like all relativistic positions it is hard, if not impossible, for such a position to be held consistently. Hick claims, somewhat dogmatically, that the infinite God cannot be known, while at the same time believing that all religious positions are partial insights into one infinite whole. But how can Hick confidently claim this about God while at the same time claiming that God cannot be definitely known by anyone? If God is unknowable how can it be known that anyone or anything is related to him? How can Hick know this much?

This question is not a mere debating point, for it takes us to the heart of the matter. There is an unreasoned, dogmatic principle at the centre of Hick's position – the principle that God cannot be known. But it is precisely this that Christianity denies, claiming not only that God can be known but also that he is self-revealing in the natural world, in Scripture and supremely in the Incarnation.

In addition, we can see that Hick's initially attractive analogy of the Copernican revolution replacing the Ptolemaic picture of the universe is not in the least convincing. In order for the analogy to hold it must be possible to say that a religion can be God-centred without being Christ-centred, because Hick wishes to maintain that the major non-Christian religions are as God-centred as Christianity is. For all religions are attempting the same impossible feat, in Hick's eyes, that of encompassing the unknowable God in human thought.

But no Christian who wishes to follow the New Testament at this point could allow the idea that God is not knowable. Nor could he allow that God saves other than through Christ. The God-centredness that the Christian recognises is also a Christ-centredness.

At one point Hick says something which qualifies his relativism. For it becomes clear that he does not hold that just any conception of God is valid, still less that all are equally valid. Rather he says:

> Every conception of the divine which has come out of a great revelatory religious experience and has been tested through a long tradition of worship, and has sustained human faith over centuries of time and in millions of lives, is likely to represent a genuine encounter with the divine reality.[3]

So on this view Buddhism would be a valid encounter with the divine, but the Moonies would not be. This certainly modifies Hick's relativism, because it cuts down the number of acceptable religions, yet a strong relativism remains. Moreover although Hick makes this qualification we may wonder whether, consistently with his own position, he is entitled to make it. For if all religions are varied attempts to represent the infinite divine reality in symbolic language, it is impossible to say that one religion *is truer than* another, and so it is impossible to say that one religion is more likely to represent a true encounter with the divine reality than another.

So there is reason to think that Hick's attempt to draw a picture of world religions in which none of them is exclusive fails because he cannot develop it without falling into inconsistency. But more to the point, the Christian will wish to insist, as has already been noted, that the

---

3   'The New Map of the Universe of Faiths' in *God and the Universe of Faiths* (London, 1973), p. 141. Hick has developed his ideas further in *God Has Many Names* (London, 1980) and *An Interpretation of Religion* (London, 1987).

New Testament itself cuts across the idea of there being many valid religions, many different ways to God.

It does so in ways which almost precisely anticipate the distinctive manner in which Hick attempts to draw a new map of the universe of faiths. And so we find, for example, that Christ claims to be the light of the world, its sun, the Copernican centre (John 8:12). He claims to be the exclusive revealer of the Heavenly Father (John 14:6), and the apostles proclaimed the name of Christ as the only name given under heaven among men whereby we must be saved (Acts 4:12). According to the New Testament there is no need to re-draw the map, even if we could, because Christ is already at the centre of it, as the sun and light of the world. And it is a person's relation to Christ that determines the outcome of the judgment to come.

The exclusiveness of the Christian faith is not that of a snobbish clique or club. It is not based upon birth, or money or position. The exclusiveness of the Christian gospel is the exclusiveness of grace. It is because God-in-Christ himself makes exclusive claims as the revealer of God and the Saviour of men that the church herself proclaims 'no other name'.

So what it is necessary to insist upon is not the exclusiveness of a religion, or of groups or associations of people, but the exclusiveness of Christ and of salvation through him. Such salvation may, in exceptional circumstances, be enjoyed by someone who is not in fellowship with any church but who lives in isolation. It is not that church membership is necessary; it is rather that there is no salvation outside Christ.

Sometimes it is held that there are suggestions in the Scripture itself that salvation is not exclusively through Christ. There is the case of Melchizedek, and the example of Cornelius the centurion is cited. When talking to Cornelius Peter said, 'Of a truth I perceive that God is no respecter of persons; but in every nation he that feareth him, and worketh righteousness is accepted with him' (Acts 10:34-5).

Many have taken these words to mean that any sincerely religious person, no matter what religion he professes, is accepted by God, and that Cornelius himself was an example of such a person. But this appears to be an incorrect interpretation. What Peter is saying is that Cornelius is a 'God-fearer' (as Acts 10:2 states), a Gentile who had adopted the Jewish faith. As a God-fearer Cornelius trusted in the promises of God, and Peter was sent to show him that those promises had been fulfilled in Christ. But cases such as Melchizedek and Cornelius raise the question of the extent to which a person may be reconciled to God and not know it because he is ignorant of Christ. We shall consider this matter later.

In saying, with the New Testament, that there is salvation in none but Christ, and that Christ must be preached for salvation, it is not implied that non-Christian religions are valueless and utterly pernicious. The New Testament does not teach this. Rather it teaches that those who are adherents of other religions can sometimes speak the truth in their religious beliefs, as we see, for example, from the way in which Paul cited Aratus while preaching to the Greeks in Athens (Acts 17). Scripture also indicates that those who are outside Christ may nevertheless exhibit traits of character which are admirable and worthwhile, as did the barbarians of Malta who showed no little kindness to Paul and his companions (Acts 28:2).

So, to continue our theme, the exclusivism of Christianity is not an exclusivism of truth, for there are truths known quite independently of a knowledge of God's special revelation. Nor is it the exclusivism of morality, for there are acts of generosity and kindness (for example) which are not prompted by a conscious awareness of the saving grace of God. Rather it is, as we have already noted, the exclusivism of salvation. For Christ and Christ alone is the mediator of God's saving grace to men and women, and salvation is through faith in him and in no other.

III

So much, in this paper at least, for attempts to argue for universalism by denying Christian exclusivism. An effort will now be made to try to answer the particularistic question more directly by examining what Scripture says in the light of the views of two well-known Reformed theologians, B.B. Warfield and W.G.T. Shedd, whose position is nearer to mainstream biblical Christianity than is that of John Hick. The first question we shall have in mind is, 'Does particularism entail parsimony?'

In a number of writings[4] B.B. Warfield developed a theological view which can be called 'Calvinistic Universalism'. Warfield was concerned to draw out the full implications, as he saw them, of the biblical assertion that Christ is the Saviour of the world (John 3:16) and that he is the last Adam (1 Corinthians 15:45). Warfield held that it is a consequence of the teaching of John 3:16 that those for whom Christ provided a definite and fully-effective atonement are the majority of the human race. To him it was unthinkable that Christ should be the Saviour of the world and yet not save the majority of people. For

---

4   For example, 'Are They Few That Be Saved?' in *Biblical and Theological Studies* (1952), pp. 334-50; 'God's Immeasurable Love' in *The Saviour of the World* (London, n.d.), pp. 103-30; 'Jesus Christ the Propitiation for the Whole World' in *Select Shorter Writings* ed., John E. Meeter, Vol. 2 (Nutley, New Jersey, 1970), pp. 167-77; *The Plan of Salvation* (1915).

although 'the world' as used in Scripture does not mean 'every person' it does, for Warfield, carry with it the idea that Christ is the Saviour of the bulk of humanity. Those who are not saved are the exceptions and they constitute the anomalies of God's saving work. The answer to 'Why does not God save everyone?' is that God willed it so; the answer to the question 'Why does God save most people? (as Warfield believed that he does) is to be found in the depth and width of the divine mercy.

The election of the church and her predestination to glory do not imply, Warfield argued, that the redeemed are a minority, though they do imply that salvation is utterly gracious and undeserved. In Warfield's view God's saving purposes widen through history, rather as a ripple in a pool. By a process of development, first Israel and then the Christian church, which is the 'internationalised' Israel of the New Testament era, enlarge the circle of God's saving grace until it embraces the vast majority of men and women, 'the world'. The lost are 'the prunings' as Warfield put it.

> For not the individual merely but the world-fabric itself is to be redeemed in the 'regeneration when the Son of Man is to sit on the throne of His glory'. During the process there may be much that is discarded: but when the process is completed, then also shall be completed the task which the Son of Man has taken upon Himself, and the 'world' shall be saved – this wicked world of sinful men transformed into a world of righteousness.[5]

To Warfield's mind the definiteness of the atonement and the need for personal regeneration both together signify that God's grace is particular; it comes to definite individuals, the very individuals to whom God intends it to come, and to no other, and it comes efficaciously to them. Those doctrinal constructions from the biblical teaching

---

5   *The Saviour of the World*, p. 128.

which are sometimes known by the names of 'definite atonement' and 'regeneration' are ways of safeguarding, in human thought and in the life and experience of the church, that biblical teaching. But by themselves these particularistic doctrines do not carry any implications about either the number or the proportion of the saved.

> It must be borne well in mind that particularism and parsimony in salvation are not equivalent conceptions; and it is a mere caricature of Calvinistic particularism to represent it as finding its centre in the proclamation that there are few that be saved.[6]

Warfield proceeds to state that only the Calvinist can be a true universalist in the sense of believing that the world can be brought into personal communion with God.

> Calvinism thus is the guardian not only of the particularism which assures me that God the Lord is the Saviour of my soul, but equally of the universalism by which I am assured that he is also the true and actual Saviour of the world.[7]

To argue whether 'the world' in John 3:16 means 'all men' or 'some men', (the 'world of the elect') and whether, if it means some men, it means 'few men', completely misses John's meaning. For John is emphasising, in using that expression, the quality or degree of the divine love. God loves *the world* in all its rebellion, hatred and filth. And John is also bringing out the fact, by his deliberate use of that expression, that Christ's redemption is directed to the organic totality, the world, and not merely to scattered individuals within that organism. Just as a person might dig up a tree, while leaving scraps of root in the ground, and replant it successfully elsewhere, so Christ saved the world, even though there are individual people who are not saved.

> In saving men (Christ) came to save mankind; and therefore the Scriptures are insistent that he came to

---

6   *The Plan of Salvation*, p. 97.
7   *Ibid.*, p. 99.

save the world, and ascribe to him accordingly the great title of the Saviour of the world. They go indeed further than this: they do not pause in expanding their outlook until they proclaim that it was the good pleasure of God 'to sum up all things in Christ, the things in the heavens, and the things in the earth.'[8]

So Christ saves the world in the way in which the Fire Service saves the building. Some planks and beams and brickwork might be lost in the fire, but the structure remains, the building is saved.

In sketching this 'Calvinistic universalism' attention has been concentrated upon B.B. Warfield. But others can easily be cited. For instance Charles Hodge held that 'the number of the finally lost in comparison with the whole number of the saved will be very inconsiderable.'[9] W.G.T. Shedd likewise held that 'the Bible teaches that there will always be some sin, and some death in the universe. Some angels and men will forever be the enemies of God. But their number, compared with that of unfallen angels and redeemed men, is small.'

The purpose in citing these views is to demonstrate that historic, biblical Calvinism has on occasion felt the pull of universalism while not advancing so far as to embrace total universalism (as it might be called). How justified such a view is is a matter to be considered shortly.

In a similar way some Calvinists, perhaps in response to the pull of universalism, have felt the need to soften the exclusivism of the Christian faith. Not that they have wavered from maintaining that Christ is the only Saviour from sin but they have held, or suggested, that the saving benefits of Christ might be enjoyed outside the bounds where God's special revelation is known. They have held

---

8   *Ibid.*, p. 100.
9   *Systematic Theology* III, pp. 879-880.

that an adult may be regenerated, and thus saved, without ever hearing of Jesus Christ. In some cases, at least, the connection between special revelation in Scripture and the Spirit of God is broken.

The most forthright exponent of this view among Reformed theologians is W.G.T. Shedd. In his *Dogmatic Theology* he writes of those adults whom God is pleased to regenerate without the written word, making it clear that he does not refer only to those who are intellectually incapable of grasping even the simplest statement. According to Shedd, God the Holy Spirit is able to produce the disposition of faith in an intelligent adult who has never heard of Christ.

> It is evident that the Holy Ghost, by an immediate operation can, if he pleased, produce such a disposition and frame of mind in a pagan, without employing as he commonly does the preaching of the written word.[10]

Shedd stressed that

> the pagan cannot be saved by good works, or human morality, any more than the nominal Christian can be. Pagan morality, like all human morality, is imperfect; and nothing but perfection can justify... the most virtuous heathen has an accusing conscience at times, and must acknowledge that he has come short of his duty.[11]

In a later work, *Calvinism Pure and Mixed,* Shedd writes:

> that this work is extensive, and the number of saved unevangelized adults is great, cannot be affirmed. But that all adult heathen are lost is not the teaching of the Bible or of the Westminster Confession.[12]

---

[10] *Dogmatic Theology*, (1888), Vol. 1. p. 437.

[11] *Ibid.*, Vol. 1., p. 440.

[12] *Calvinism Pure and Mixed* (1893), p. 61. Page references are to the 1986 reprint (Edinburgh). Warfield refers to Shedd's view as an 'erroneous opinion' ('Are They Few That Be Saved?' p. 350).

Shedd also appeals to other Reformed theologians in support of his position. He quotes Zanchius

National reprobation does not imply that every individual who lives in an unevangelized country, must therefore unavoidably perish forever: any more than that every individual who lives in a land called Christian is therefore in a state of salvation. There are no doubt elect persons among the former; as well as reprobate ones among the latter... it is not indeed improbable that some individuals in these unenlightened countries, may belong to the secret election of grace, and the habit of faith may be wrought in them.[13]

He also cites the Second Helvetic Confession (1566):

We recognise that God can illuminate whom and when he will, even without the external ministry, for that is in his power.[14]

And Richard Baxter:

I am not much inclined to pass a peremptory sentence of damnation upon all who never heard of Christ, having some more reasons than I knew of before to think that God's dealings with such is much unknown to us.[15]

And he could also have quoted Zwingli. In his 'Sermon on the Providence of God' Zwingli has this to say:

Nothing prevents God from choosing from among the heathen men to revere Him, to honour Him, and after death to be united to Him. For His election is free.

I certainly, if the choice were given me, should prefer to choose the lot of Socrates or Seneca, who, though they knew not the one Deity, yet busied themselves with serving Him in purity of heart, than that of the Roman Pontiff who would offer himself as God if there were only a bidder at hand, or the lot of any king, emperor or prince, who serves as defender of such a little tin god. For though those heathen knew not religion in the letter

---

[13] *Dogmatic Theology*, Vol. I., p. 437.
[14] *Ibid.*, pp. 436-7.
[15] *Ibid.*, p. 441.

of it and in what pertains to the sacraments, yet as far
as the real thing is concerned, I say, they were holier
and more religious that all the little Dominicans and
Franciscans that ever lived.[16]

But the chief question, as Shedd recognises, is not what
has been said by theologians or confessions of faith, but
what the teaching of Scripture is. He is at pains to
emphasise, as we have already seen, that Scripture
teaches that salvation is *ordinarily* through the word. But
Shedd says that the disposition to believe in Christ, (the
habit of faith), without there first being any knowledge of
Christ is to be found in John 9: 36-38 ('Who is the Lord,
that I might believe on him?') and in the cases of the
Ethiopian eunuch and of Cornelius already cited. Shedd
also holds that Matthew 8:11 teaches that there are
individuals from outside Israel, the contemporaries of
Abraham, Isaac and Jacob, who will be saved.

In going back beyond human authorities we cannot
afford to neglect what Scripture *may* teach. For the history
of the Church has shown that the conflict, or apparent
conflict, between Scripture and experience has often led to
a more comprehensive understanding of Scripture and so,
in turn, to a firmer faith in God's revealed truth. And it
would be most unfortunate to allow prejudice or tradition,
however hallowed, which may strongly dispose us to
believe that there are few that are saved, or that a
knowledge of Christ is indispensable to salvation, to
prevent a true appreciation of the biblical data.

Are Warfield and Shedd correct in the account they give
of what the Scriptures teach?

---

[16] English Translation in *On Providence and Other Essays,* ed.
for S.M. Jackson by W. J. Hinke (1922, repr. 1983 Durham
N.C.).

Warfield claims that texts such as Matthew 7:14, Luke 13:23 and Mark 20:16 are ethical rather than prophetic in their intent. They are concerned with changing people's attitudes rather than with predicting the final numbers or proportions of the saved and the lost. How could Luke 13:23 be interpreted otherwise, Warfield asks, when it is found alongside parables which teach the inexorable growth of the kingdom of God throughout the world? He thinks that it is important, in addition, to note that in Matthew Christ never answers the question 'Are they few that be saved?' directly but uses it to issue a personal warning and a challenge.

In defending this interpretation Warfield says:
It is, in other words, not the number of the saved that is announced, but the difficulty of salvation. The point of the remark is that salvation is not to be assumed by any one as a matter of course, but is to be sought with earnest and persistent effort.[17]
We may grant that Christ uses the question to make a direct, personal application. But is this all that the text teaches? Christ does not only say outright that many will be saved, he also says that many will seek salvation and will not find it. While 'many' does not mean 'most', could there be any point in Christ saying what he did if many are saved and many lost, or if few are lost and most are saved? It could be argued further that by his words Christ is underlining, by implication, the fewness of the saved, by showing that many are not saved even though they earnestly desire salvation.

Had Christ wished merely to stress the arduousness of gaining salvation there are other ways in which this might have been done, and were in fact done, as the Gospels record. One prominent example is the passage about the taking of the kingdom of God by force (Matthew 11:12).

---

17 'Are They Few That Be Saved?' p. 341.

In the passage under discussion Christ does not merely say that it is an easy thing to miss salvation, but that many are missing it, and that comparatively few are finding it. It is not merely narrowness against roominess that is being stressed, but the few against the many. The very least that can be said is that Christ's language places a burden of proof on those who hold that the teaching of Scripture is, overall, that most men and women will be saved. This burden of proof Warfield seems unable to discharge when he says, rather lamely:

> that there are many who enter in by the one road and few who find the other is presented as merely the result of differences in the roads themselves – that the one is inviting and easy, the other repellent and difficult.[18]

But even if it is a consequence of the width of the road that many find it, it is scarcely a significant consequence, since the over-riding fact, according to Christ, is that many do find the way to destruction, while few are found on the road to life.

But to say that there are weaknesses with Warfield's exegesis is not to say that his case is overthrown. One suspects that the chief reason Warfield had for maintaining these views was his commitment to post-millennial eschatology. If post-millennialism is correct, then there must be some way of reconciling Christ's words with that eschatology, even if Warfield's exegesis is not that way.[19]

It is always important to distinguish what is abstractly possible from what one is warranted in believing. Perhaps there is some abstract sense in which it is possible for people to be saved in ignorance of the revealed truth of

---

18 'Are They Few That Be Saved?' p. 342.
19 In discussion, Professor Henri Blocher suggested that these verses might be interpreted as referring to impenitent Israel.

God. This is, after all, how God is believed to convey his salvation to those who die in infancy and for all we know, to those adults who live and die demented. But is there any warrant from Scripture to believe that God has in fact conveyed his grace to rational adults in such a way?

What of Shedd? Shedd claims that there may be the habit of faith without the exercise of faith in the case of some who have no knowledge of special revelation, basing his claim upon texts such as John 9:36-38. But is one warranted in making such a claim by appealing to the evidence of those individuals who did in fact come to active faith in Christ? In order to establish his claim Shedd surely needs to be able to identify cases where the habit of faith was present in an individual who is ignorant of Christ, and as far as one can see he does not do this.

IV

Warfield and Shedd are considering two separate questions: Are any saved by the Holy Spirit using means which do not causally arise out of God's revelation of himself in Scripture? Are there more saved than lost? An affirmative answer to the first question by Shedd is then used as some evidence in favour of an affirmative answer to the second question. In closing this paper I wish to keep these questions separate and to try to offer a defence and further elaboration of Shedd's view that the Holy Spirit may use means other than Scripture in converting adults who remain ignorant of Jesus Christ.

Consider, for a moment, the properties or attributes of God. God has *essential properties*, properties such that if he lacked any of them he could not be God. *Goodness* is, presumably, one such property. A being who lacked goodness could not be God, any more than could a being that lacked mercy or love. But of course while God has goodness, he is not the only being that has goodness; saints and unfallen angels are also good.

Besides essential properties which God may share with some of his creatures, there are essential properties which he does not share, properties which perhaps he cannot share. *Being underivedly good* is one such property, presumably. Such a property is essential to God; moreover, only God has such a property. It is therefore *individually essential* to him. So God has *individual essential properties*.

So *being underivedly good* is an essential property that God alone possesses and could possess, an individual essential property of God. Are there any more individual essential properties which God has than the example already given? There are lots of them. Most general essential properties, with an appropriate adverbial qualifier, generate divine individual essential properties. Thus

> *being underivedly just*
> *being supremely good*
> *being infinitely wise*

are all examples of properties which God has essentially and which only God has.

How, you may ask, does this metaphysical machinery, fascinating as it is, help us in the case of particularism and exclusivism? Perhaps in the following way: suppose that a person, ignorant of God's special revelation in Scripture, were to pray using words which mean any of God's individual essential properties. Suppose he were to say, 'O most merciful one, have mercy upon me'. If the description 'most merciful one' is necessarily true of God and is true of God only, then it would appear to follow that in using such an expression the speaker successfully refers to God. For God is essentially most merciful, and only God can be.

If the speaker refers successfully to God, he does so whether or not he believes that in using the expression he is referring to the God and Father of our Lord Jesus Christ. Moreover, he succeeds in making such a reference no matter from what source the terms he uses have come, whether from special revelation, natural theology, metaphysical speculation, or from some tradition of piety whose pedigree is not clear. In other words successful reference of this sort does not require an intact causal link from God's special revelation in Scripture to what the person believes. The answer to the question, 'From where has such a person gained his belief?' need not necessarily be 'From Scripture'.

Suppose, then, a person with little or no acquaintance with special revelation, but in deep personal need and despair, who cries out 'O most merciful one, have mercy on me'. I suggest that this is a prayer that is sincerely addressed to God and sincerely addressed to the only true God, even though the one who is speaking may not realise the fact. And I, for one, find it hard to imagine that such a prayer could not or would not be answered.

John Stott has put the matter this way:
Jesus Christ is the only Saviour, and that salvation is by God's grace alone, on the ground of Christ's cross alone, and by faith alone. The only question, therefore, is how much knowledge and understanding of the gospel people need before they can cry to God for mercy and be saved. In the Old Testament people were 'justified by faith' even though they had little knowledge or expectation of Christ. Perhaps there are others today in a similar position, who know that they are guilty before God and that they cannot do anything to win his favour, but who in self-despair call upon the God they dimly perceive to save them. If God does save such, as many

evangelical Christians believe, their salvation is still
only by grace, only through Christ, only by faith.[20]

Perhaps it is possible to press the point further than we
have so far pressed it. There are properties which God has
which, though not essential to him, nevertheless he alone
has, and which he alone can have. Let us call these *unique
properties*. For example, the property of *being the Creator
of the universe* is a unique property of God. Anyone who,
in prayer, addresses 'the Creator' is in fact addressing the
only true God. And anyone who, in addressing the
Creator, pleads for his mercy, is in fact casting himself on
the mercy of Christ.

The so-called atheist's prayer 'O God, if there is a God,
save my soul, if I have a soul' is often the subject of some
merriment. No doubt such a prayer can be offered in a
cynical and God-defying way. But what if it were to be the
cry of someone who despairs of himself? Is there any
convincing reason to think that that prayer will not be
answered?

Let us take it for granted that Christ is the only Saviour,
that there is no other name under heaven given among
men whereby we must be saved. How is this exclusivism
to be understood? The way in which it is usually
understood is that Christ brings men and women to
knowingly confess him as Saviour and Lord. Let us call
this *transparent exclusivism*. But it is possible to think of
the Saviour exercising his exclusivism through bringing
some men and women to unwittingly confess him as
Saviour and Lord, by worshipping Christ in ignorance. Let
us call this *opaque exclusivism*. Is there any reason to
think that Scripture teaches the doctrine of opaque
exclusivism? There may be. Did Paul, when he declared to
the Athenians 'Whom ye ignorantly worship, him declare I

---

20   *The Authentic Jesus* (London, 1985), p. 83.

unto you' (Acts 17:23) mean that prior to his preaching of the gospel they were engaging in true worship? Did someone who believed his words move from religious opaqueness to religious transparency, from trusting Christ unknowingly to trusting him in full knowledge? And did Cornelius, and the Ethiopian eunuch? We shall glance at these cases as we conclude by considering certain objections to what I have been arguing.

V

I shall consider six objections:

Are you saying that there are many ways to God? Not if by that question is meant that there are many ways to God prescribed by God. But here, as elsewhere, it is necessary to distinguish between what God prescribes and what in his sovereignty he brings to pass. What he prescribes in Scripture is clear; there is no other name, and salvation is to be had only through faith in Christ alone. But of course such a prescription only comes to one who is acquainted with Scripture or part of Scripture. It can hardly apply to others. And it may be that in his sovereignty God regenerates such and enables them to trust in himself. Such regeneration is the fruit of Christ's work even though it results in saving faith that is ignorant of him.

Are you saying that all religions worship the same God? No, far from it, as earlier remarks ought to have made clear. But it is possible to distinguish between religions and individuals within those religions, and my argument has to do with individuals – few or many – within other religions than Christianity, where the message, or the full message of the gospel, is not known.

What evidence do we have that what you are suggesting ever takes place? As we have seen Shedd and others appeal to Scripture to answer this question; to the case of the blind man in John 9, of the Ethiopian eunuch, of Cornelius and so on. But there is a difficulty with such an appeal, namely that each of these individuals came in fact to a full and conscious faith in Christ. It seems unacceptedly abstract and hypothetical to say, what Shedd's argument implies, that (for instance) if Cornelius had not met Peter he would have been saved. Scripture does not invite us to break up the causal nexus of events as revealed and to speculate about each link in the chain. For it might be counter-argued that the Holy Spirit produced the desire for Christ in each case as a first stage in their actually coming to Christ.

I am less interested in arguing that such cases do in fact take place; rather, I wish to maintain that if they do I can find no convincing reason why they are not instances of saving faith.

But is this case truly Copernican? It certainly attempts to preserve God at the centre, both as the one who sovereignly grants his grace, and who is the true object of saving trust. It does this by asserting both that God can be known (he is not merely an unknowable thing-in-itself, as Hick claims); and that he can be known in ignorance of the fact that he is the God and Father of our Lord Jesus Christ. Are not both these biblical positions?

But could such a person be said to trust Christ? Why not? Is not Christ God? In laying aside the divine glory Christ did not lay aside his divine nature; the Son of God is God and, in becoming incarnate, continues to be God. So that if Christ is divine then the attributes of divinity are his. If God is essentially merciful, then so is Christ. If God is, while not essentially the Creator, nevertheless the only one who could create, then so is Christ; 'all things were created by him, and for him' (Colossians 1:16).

Are you saying that Scripture is not necessary? I am certainly not asserting this; rather I am saying that if there are cases such as those that I have sketched then

Scripture is not necessary. But it remains necessary for those who have some knowledge of it; in this sense increasing knowledge of the Scripture brings with it increasing responsibility.

If such cases of saving faith in the absence of special revelation, cases of opaque exclusivism, do occur, they qualify, though in a quite marginal way, the exclusivism of the Christian faith. For they provide instances not of people being saved apart from Christ, but of being saved by Christ apart from the knowledge of Christ. Whether they qualify the particularism of the faith in a significant way, and give us reason for thinking that a majority of humankind will be saved, depends upon how many such cases there are. In the nature of things the answer to that question is, at present, known only to God.

10

Everlasting Punishment
and the Problem of Evil

Henri Blocher

We all perceive the difficulty which John Hick magnifies: *the doctrine of hell*, as it is commonly called, *seems to aggravate the problem of evil*. 'It renders', he writes, 'any coherent Christian theodicy impossible by giving the evils of sin and suffering an eternal lodgment within God's creation.'[1] The argument that God eventually brings good out of evil 'is completely vitiated in its Augustinian context by the proviso that this divine activity of drawing good out of evil is to operate only in a minority of cases and that the great majority of mankind is eternally to sin and eternally to suffer torment.'[2] He sees the same basic flaw in Thomist thought and in Calvinism.[3] Whereas his restraint and courtesy lend so great a charm to his writing generally, bitterness infiltrates his prose when he broaches the topic, and vehemence breaks the fluidity of his style: 'We shall find incredible and even blasphemous the idea that God plans to inflict perpetual torture upon any of His children.'[4] Pusey 'could with a good conscience attribute to God an unappeasable vindictiveness and

---

1.   *Death and Eternal Life* (Basingstoke & London: MacMillan, 1990 rep. of 1985 ed. [1st ed. Collins, 1976]), p. 201.
2.   *Evil and the God of Love* (London: Fontana Library, Collins, 1974, 3rd pr. [1st ed. MacMillan 1966]), p. 95.
3.   *Ibid.*, pp. 116f. and 129.
4.   *Ibid.*, p. 382.

insatiable cruelty which would be regarded as demonic if applied analogously to a human being.'[5]

These words provide us with a mere sample of a contemporary theologian's expression – Professor John Hick being chosen both on account of his well-deserved renown in the English-speaking world and of his special interest in the problem of evil. Parallel statements from other pens would not be hard to find. The late John A. T. Robinson did not entertain any doubt: 'Judgement can never be God's last word, because if it were, it would be the word that would speak his failure,'[6] and also: 'In a universe of love, there can be no heaven which tolerates a chamber of horrors, no hell for any which does not at the same time make it a hell for God.'[7] Even such a moderate theologian as the highly revered John Baillie could vent similar feelings and charge the old orthodox view with ultimate dualism: 'What the doctrine of eternal punishment does, then, is to make evil an eternal element in the universe, no less positively real than the good itself.'[8] Surely, to revert to the way John Hick puts the accusation, 'hell, understood as Augustine... understood it, must be accounted a major part of the problem of evil,' or, even, 'the largest part' of it.[9]

It is possible, we suggest, to reach such *a renewed understanding of the old dogma* that will relieve some of

5   *Death and Eternal Life, op. cit.*, p. 200.
6   *In the End God* (London: Fontana Library, Collins, 1968 rev), p. 130.
7   'Universalism – Is It Heretical?' *Scottish Journal of Theology* 2 (1949), p. 155, as quoted by Jon E. Braun, *Whatever Happened to Hell?* (Nashville & New York: T. Nelson, 1979), p. 36.
8   *And the Life Everlasting* (London: Oxford University Press, 1934), p. 244.
9   *Evil, op. cit.*, pp. 95 and 377.

the tension – although our main motive in our search should not be to obtain this apologetic advantage, but more rigorously, and intelligently, to appropriate Scriptural teaching!

Underlying Convictions
Space allows but a sketch of the positions we tend to assume in our proposals, a brief description of the base for our building attempts.

On *evil*, we have argued elsewhere[10] that the various 'explanations', that purport to tell its *whence* and *why*, all fail to satisfy. The theoretical solutions that have been offered, whether they invoke universal order (Leibniz, Thomism), independent freedom (with the so-called 'free-will defence'), the requirements of human character-training (Hick), or the power of dialectics (Hegel, and even Barth in his own way), are found lacking in Biblical support. We may expose them as diverse forms of a strategy of *denial*: the implications draw the evilness out of evil, evil is denied as truly and finally evil. Rational schemes bring evil back into harmony with the rest, with creation, and, thus, they open the road to the excusing, or justification, of what should excite unmitigated horror and indignation. They plead overtly for *theodicy*; they work covertly for *kakodicy*.

In Scripture *only* have such strategies of evasion and excuse been resisted totally. A miraculous chastity! Scripture never dodges the issue, but it reveals with superabundant attestation three pillars of truth: *the evil reality of evil* – 'Woe to those who call evil good and good evil' (Isa. 5:20) – it never slides into the *felix culpa* paradox or speculation; *the all-embracing sovereignty of the Lord* – who 'works all things after the counsel of his

---

10   Henri Blocher, *Evil and the Cross*, trans. David G. Preston (Leicester: Inter-Varsity Press, forthcoming in 1992).

will' (Eph. 1:11); *the perfect goodness of God and of his work* – 'and behold! it was superlatively good' (Gen. 1:51).

Although we would claim that these three cannot be shown, in the strictest logical analysis, to be incompatible, how difficult it is to hold them together! We speak of *the thorn in the flesh of reason*, even reformed, believing, reason. Yet, these three stand immovably sure. We find them intertwined *on the cross*, 'an evil than which no greater can be conceived,'[11] which, nevertheless, 'the hand and purpose of God had predestined to occur' (Acts 4:28), the very *locus* of the revelation of Goodness, goodness infinitely greater than any goodness we are able to conceive....

We find no rational solution of the riddle. We cannot understand why the Sovereign Lord of all Goodness ever decreed that there should be offences against him. *But we can understand that we cannot understand*: the radical singularity of evil, its otherness which is other than any created otherness, is defined thereby. And the reverse side of the absence of a theoretical solution is the assurance of the *practical solution*. Because there is no answer to the question *why?*, there is one to the question *how long?*, the weightier question after all. The three pillars of Biblical witness support the *hope* that does not disappoint. Evil shall be defeated. Evil *has been* defeated. On the cross, God was in Christ triumphing over all evil; it is finished, for ever.

On *hell*, we would see no escape from the main tenets of traditional orthodoxy. We dare not disregard the authority of the greatest doctors in Christian, especially Evangelical, history. We cannot but take to heart Charles Hodge's warning: 'Any man... assumes a fearful

---

11   Hick's apt phrase, *Evil, op. cit.*, p. 279.

responsibility who sets himself in opposition to the faith of the church universal.'[12] The decisive reason, however, is conformity with Scripture itself, interpreted philologically-historically, according to the analogy of faith. Biblical doctrine includes that some, at least, impenitent sinners to the end of their lives, shall undergo eternally and consciously a punishment inflicted by God's judgement. Jesus emphasized that several, among the sons and daughters of men, shall know that awful fate: it is the most solemn fact of the case. Saint Augustine shows the right reaction before our Lord's dreadful phrases in Mark 9:43-48: 'Who would not tremble, hearing from divine lips such a repetition and so vigorous a declaration of that punishment.'[13] Sober conviction here, we may add, does not entail blanket approval of all the theses and the manner of defence which champions of the dogma have put forward. We confess some uneasiness, for instance, with the way of W.G.T. Shedd's recently republished and significant treatment: it appears sometimes to indulge in peremptory exegesis and to impose authoritarian dilemmas on the reader.[14] But imperfections in advocates should not obscure the balance of the textual data: Scripture does seem to teach everlasting punishment.

Annihilationist arguments, even set forth in Edward W. Fudge's full and careful recapitulation,[15] come short of the proof needed. It remains unlikely that 'death' and 'destruction' in Biblical parlance should be construed as the extinction of existence, the adjective *aiônios* taken to

---

12   *Systematic Theology* (Grand Rapids: Eerdmans, 1986 repr.), p. 871.

13   *Civitas Dei*, XXI, ix (1): Quem non terreat ista repetitio et illius poenae commendatio tam vehemens ore divino?

14   W[illiam] G. T. Shedd, *The Doctrine of Endless Punishment* (Edinburgh: Banner of Truth, 1990 repr. [1st publ. 1885]).

15   *The Fire That Consumes. A Biblical and Historical Study of Final Punishment* (Houston: Providential Press, 1982).

mean only 'final', or to apply to the *effect* of retribution
rather than to the *act*, not to 'the punish*ing*' but to 'the
punish*ment*.'[16] The language of Scripture, with its
stereotyped metaphors, and in the role it plays, seems to
insist on the durational, permanent character of the state
of torment, and to exclude any later change, anything
beyond the outcome of the *last* judgement. One can sense
a paradox in the concept of permanence in destruction
which the Bible itself expresses when it speaks of '*second
death*,' 'undying worm,' and tradition sharpens, *e.g.* in the
words of Saint Gregory the Great: 'a deathless death, an
endless end, a ceaseless cessation, since [the] death
lives, the end always begins, and cessation knows not
how to cease.'[17]

Jean Cruvellier's extensive (and intensive) examination
of the conditionalist-annihilationist case, a few decades

---

16   *Ibid.*, p. 44.
17   *Moralia in Job*, IX, lxvi/100: Fit ergo miseris mors sine morte,
     finis sine fine, defectus sine defectu, quia et mors vivit, et finis
     semper incipit, et deficere defectus nescit (Migne, *Patrologia
     latina*, 75, 915). Braun, *Whatever Happened to Hell, op. cit.*,
     pp.77f., quotes these words from the Sermon of Agobard of
     Lyons, in 829 or 830, as found in *Early Medieval Theology*,
     trans. G.E. McCracken & Allen Cabaniss (London: SCM Press,
     1957) p. 354, which refers to Gregory's *Moralia in Job 9.48*.
     But one does not find the words when one looks up this
     reference, which is also given by Migne with the text of
     Agobard, *PL* 104, 282B. We have found it, however, in chapter
     66, with the cue, there, that an older numbering (not Migne's)
     made it chapter 48. A fine illustration of the way of academic
     work! Migne also refers to the notes added to Book III of *De
     Gubernatione Dei s. Salviani, PL* 53, 65; Faustus of Riez (a
     fifth century bishop) is quoted for a similar paradox: Tali
     morte punientur, ut eis mori in dolore non liceat, morituri
     vitae, et morti sine fine victuri. An even earlier instance, we
     have found in Saint Augustine's *Enchiridion* xxiii, 92: Ubi
     autem infelix mori non sinitur, ut ita dicam, mors ipsa non
     moritur.

ago, has stood the test of time.[18] It is noteworthy that many scholars, who show little concern for dogmatic conformity, authorities like Oepke or Gnilka,[19] do not take the side of annihilationists. Actually, not a few, among those who *reject* 'the awful dogma', do recognize its presence in Scripture. Shedd was able to quote from Davidson [Samuel, if we are not mistaken], 'the most learned of English rationalistic critics':

...if a specific sense be attached to words, never-ending misery is enunciated in the Bible. On the presumption that one doctrine is taught, it is the eternity of hell-torments. Bad exegesis may attempt to banish it from the New Testament Scriptures, but it is still there, and expositors who wish to get rid of it, as Canon Farrar does, injure the cause they have in view by misrepresentation.[20]

Adversaries are not gifted, necessarily, with superior, and unprejudiced, lucidity; yet, their witness is less vulnerable to *a priori* suspicion!

Similarly, we are constrained to a *non possumus* answer if we are asked to embrace final restorationism, the doctrine of the *apokatastasis pantôn*, or to leave it as an open possibility. Orthodox tradition, we feel, has not paid enough attention to the grand proclamation of *fullness* in the New Testament, recapitulation and universal reconciliation; we shall develop this point in a moment.

---

18 'La Notion de châtiment éternel d'après le Nouveau Testament,' *Etudes Evangéliques* (Aix-en-Provence) 14 (1954), pp. 60-99, 160-191, 240-265, and 15 (1955), pp. 81-118. The summary in Stewart D.F. Salmond's *The Christian Doctrine of Immortality* (Edinburgh: T. & T. Clark, 1897), pp. 594ff. is still worth consulting.

19 A. Oepke, 'Apollymi, apôleia, Apollyôn,' *Theological Dictionary of the New Testament*, I, 394-397; J. Gnilka, 'Hoelle. Die Aussagen der Schrift', *Lexikon für Theologie und Kirche* (Freiburg: Herder, 1960²), V, especially 446.

20 *The Doctrine of Endless Punishment, op. cit.,* p. 118.

Warnings against the snare of symmetry, we receive as
timely indeed.[21] We confess being moved deeply by
Tennyson's *In Memoriam*:
  I stretch lame hands of faith, and grope,
  And gather dust and chaff, and call
  To what I feel is Lord of all,
  And faintly trust the larger hope.[22]
But *is* what Tennyson felt to be the Lord of all *truly* the
Lord of all? The teaching we have received from the Lord
of all rules out what appears to us, in our human,
truncated, perspective, 'the larger hope' – in faith, not
sight, we *trust* that it must be smaller and poorer than the
true Biblical hope.

We shall not rehearse the reasons that deter us from
subscribing to *apokatastasis* universalism.[23]
Theologically, in front of the all-sufficiency of Christ's
work, we remember that transferring men and women from
the headship of Adam to the headship of Christ belongs to
the ministry of the Holy Spirit, through the faith he
creates. This the Holy Spirit does in 'the day of salvation,'
'as long as it is called today,'[24] before it is called 'too
late'. Regarding the simple exegesis of New Testament
texts, by and large, universalists no longer hold the field.
Even John Hick concedes: 'I would not in fact claim with

---

21   As given by John W. Wenham, *The Enigma of Evil. Can We
      Believe in the Goodness of God?* (Leicester: Inter-Varsity
      Press, 1985 [1st ed. under other title 1974]), p. 32 note 7,
      quoting from U. E. Simon; also by H.U. von Balthasar,
      followed by John R. Sachs, 'Current Eschatology: Universal
      Salvation and the Problem of Hell', *Theological Studies* 52
      (1991), p. 240.
22   Quoted by Braun, *Whatever...*, *op. cit.*, p. 50.
23   See Henri Blocher, 'The Scope of Redemption and Modern
      Theology', *Scottish Bulletin of Evangelical Theology* 9.
      2.(1991), p. 80.
24   *Cf.* Salmond, *The Christian Doctrine*, *op. cit.*, p. 658.

confidence that [Paul] was a universalist.'[25] They have
shifted their ground, and they have adopted a second
degree strategy: they focus on hermeneutics, and argue
from the existential-kerygmatic intention of the texts
against their use in a predictive doctrine. This stance is
not rare, and prevails among Roman Catholic theologians.
Karl Rahner's mighty influence has swayed academic
opinion: 'What Scripture says about hell, in conformity
with the eschatological character of the threat-discourses,
is not to be read as an anticipatory report [*Reportage*] on
something that will happen some time, but as unveiling
the situation in which the man who is addressed truly
finds himself now.'[26] Even Ratzinger could write (he was
not yet a Cardinal): 'The dogma of hell does not wish to
provide man primarily with some information *from* beyond,
but to address him kerygmatically *for* his present life.'[27]
This strategy agrees with the modern, post-Kantian,
mind-set. But it is not entirely new. Saint Augustine
himself explains that the more liberal, or laxist, teachers
on hell felt free to take what is said in Scripture as
terribilius quam verius, more as a threat than as a true
prediction.[28] In the present situation, this hermeneutical
choice hardly combines with a high view of Scripture; it
easily entails sour comments denouncing 'literalism' or
'fundamentalism' in those who care to disagree.[29]

The existential emphasis also helps to bear the one
sore tension in the universalist's soul. As he zealously
espouses the values of our surrounding culture, he is not
only concerned for universal acceptance; he is strongly

25   *Death...*, *op. cit.*, p. 248.
26   'Hoelle,' *Sacramentum Mundi. Theologisches Lexikon für die
     Praxis* (Freiburg: Herder, 1968) II, 736.
27   'Hoelle. Systematisch', *Lexikon für Theologie und Kirche* V,
     448 (our trans.); theology is not to develop 'Faktizitaeten.'
28   *Enchiridion*, xxix, 112.
29   See, for instance, Sachs' article, 'Current Eschatology', *op. cit.*,
     pp. 227,232,254.

attached to autonomous, indomitable, *unforeseeable* freedom. How can the two be reconciled? This antagonism obviously embarrasses John Hick[30] and John Sachs;[31] in spite of clever efforts, they have not solved it, not even (we surmise) to their own satisfaction.

Current Orthodox Apologies

How do traditionalists, on the other hand, defend the dogma, especially in view of theodicy?

The older emphasis falls on the claims of justice, the need and right of retribution: appeal is made both to Scripture and to conscience. Shedd attains to eloquence as he exclaims: 'When examples of great depravity occur, man cries: 'How long, O Lord, how long?' The non-infliction of retribution upon hardened villany [*sic*] and successful cruelty causes anguish in the moral sense.'[32] Ajith Fernando, in his warm little book on our topic, recalls how Norway felt obligated, in 1945, to restore the death-penalty in order that Quisling be adequately punished.[33] Together with Saint Augustine, the classical line insists that punishment, in truth, is no evil added, but the balancing *cancellation* of evil, the moral order repaired, the good vindicated.[34] C.S.Lewis refines the argument: 'In a sense, it is better for the creature itself,' who is being punished, rather than 'eternal continuance in (the) ghastly illusion' of sinful pleasure.[35] Fernando proclaims: 'Judging sinners not only enhances the glory of God, it also restores goodness of creation. This is why we say that

---

30   *Evil, op. cit.*, pp. 379f.
31   'Current Eschatology,' *op. cit.*, pp. 234,241,246ff.
32   *The Doctrine, op. cit.*, p. 145.
33   *Crucial Questions About Hell* (Eastbourne: Kingsway Publications, 1991), p. 102.
34   Hick, *Evil, op. cit.*, pp. 93f.,112,201.
35   *The Problem of Pain* (London: Geoffrey Bles, 1940), p. 110.

judgement is essentially a benevolent act': he speaks as
the heir of all orthodox ages.[36]

But what about God's love and mercy? God displays
them on the other side, in them that inherit eternal life.
Beyond that simple answer, champions of the traditional
view have little to say. We are left with the mystery of the
divine choice. Love is a matter of choosing: *electio* goes
with *dilectio*. This need not be considered a weakness....
Even John Hick has seen fit to warn (although not when
dealing with precisely the same point): 'We must not
abandon our professed agnosticism by assuming that what
we should regard as loving coincides with God's unknown
will.'[37] How wise!

The same writer also notes, correctly, that the problem
with God's love remains, though it may be felt to be less
acute, if the final fate of many is annihilation or
extinction.[38] The orthodox could argue that even
universalists have to face it: should all suffering cease,
having suffered shall never be abolished![39] John Hick
himself, when he thinks of Auschwitz and of 'the more
extreme and crushing evils,'[40] takes refuge in the
unknown: 'The only appeal left is to mystery.'[41]

Some orthodox writers would carry further the last
consideration, and argue from God's permission of evil in
history to the propriety of the same in eternity: if it is

---

[36]   *Crucial Questions, op. cit.,* p. 101.
[37]   *Death, op. cit.,* p. 24.
[38]   *Evil, op. cit.,* p. 378.
[39]   As Hick reminds us, quoting Léon Bloy's aphorism, *ibid.,* p.
       386.
[40]   *Ibid.,* p. 365.
[41]   *Ibid.,* pp. 369f.; p. 371: 'a real mystery, impenetrable to the
       rationalizing human mind.'

compatible with divine love and holiness *now*, it must be *for ever* also.[42] A.H. Strong elaborates:

> As benevolence in God seems in the beginning to have permitted moral evil, not because sin was desirable in itself, but only because it was incident to a system which provided for the highest possible freedom and holiness in the creature; so benevolence in God may to the end permit the existence of sin and continue to punish the sinner, undesirable as these things are in themselves, because they are incidents of a system which provides for the highest possible freedom and holiness in the creature through eternity.[43]

Strong also introduces the thought that hell may be needed as 'a matter of instruction to all moral beings. The self-chosen ruin of the few may be the salvation of the many,' and he explains:

> Through the punishment of the lost, God's holiness may be made known to a universe that without it might have no proof so striking that sin is moral suicide and ruin, and that God's holiness is its irreconcilable antagonist.[44]

Saint Augustine also intimates that the reality of God's vengeance, *veritas ultionis*, by some necessity, *had* to appear.[45]

Many, however, wish to avoid the impression of dualistic symmetry. In order to affirm the victory of God and good, they minimise the part of hell and the number of reprobates. Says Shedd: 'Sin is a speck upon the infinite

---

[42] Hodge, *Systematic Theology, op. cit.*, p. 879; Augustus H. Strong, *Systematic Theology* (Philadelphia: the Judson Press, 1907, 20th pr. 1958), p. 1053.

[43] *Loc. cit.*

[44] *Ibid.*, p. 1052.

[45] *Civitas Dei*, XXI, xii.

azure of eternity; a spot on the sun. Hell is only a corner of
the universe.'[46]

Among the modern, the most popular argument, the very
soul of most apologies for the possibility of hell, refers to
human *freedom*. Since the nineteenth century, one notices
a systematic effort at *discharging* God from the
responsibility of punishment. With typical frankness and
terseness, Shedd states: 'The existing necessity for hell-
punishment is not chargeable upon God'; and he adds:
'Almightiness itself cannot forgive impenitence, any more
than it can make a square circle.'[47] Again, he insists:
'Pardon may be proffered by God, but *penitence may
become impossible through the action of man* – penitence,
not only forgiveness.[48] Salmond concurs: 'The question is
not what God imposes on us in the other life, but what we
take with us into it. We carry *ourselves* into it....'[49]
Rahner: hell is 'not to be understood as a punishment
additionally inflicted by a vindictive God';[50] Ratzinger: it
shows God's 'unconditional respect before the free
decision of man';[51] Hayes: 'The possibility of hell is the
most radical theological statement about the nature of
human freedom';[52] all agree, in spite of their universalistic
sympathies. Fernando follows the path, as he stresses

---

[46]   *The Doctrine, op. cit.,* p. 159. Similarly, Hodge, *Systematic
       Theology, op. cit.,* pp. 879f.; Strong, *Systematic Theology, op.
       cit.,* p. 1052; Fernando, *Crucial Questions, op. cit.,* pp. 67f.
[47]   *Ibid.,* p. 165.
[48]   *Ibid.,* p. 169.
[49]   *The Christian Doctrine, op. cit.,* p. 668; already p. 666.
[50]   'Hoelle,' *op. cit.,* col. 738 (our trans.).
[51]   'Hoelle, Systematisch', *op. cit.,* col. 449: Es laesst uns
       einerseits den bedingungslosen Respekt vor der
       Freiheitsentscheidung des Menschen wissen (our trans.).
[52]   Zachary Hayes, *Visions of a Future: A Study of Christian
       Eschatology* (Wilmington, Del.: Glazier, 1989), p. 182, as
       quoted and approved by Sachs, 'Current Eschatology' *op. cit.,*
       p. 234.

that God did not make us 'robots'[53] – a familiar tune. Even James I. Packer quotes approvingly C.S. Lewis' saying 'that the doors of hell are locked on the *inside*', though he is careful to preserve the truth of infliction by God, at the same time.[54]

The sharper edge of the argument is the idea that sinners, such being the power of their freedom, will persevere in hatred against God, for ever and ever. Here lies the strongest rationale of hell. Shedd tells us that 'wicked will intensifies itself perpetually';[55] 'the guilty free agent reaches that dreadful condition where resistance to evil ceases altogether, and surrender to evil becomes demoniacal.'[56] 'Sin,' he goes on to say, 'ultimately assumes a fiendish form, and degree. It is pure wickedness without regret or sorrow, and with a delight in evil for evil's sake.'[57] Hence Shedd's assurance: the finally lost could not tolerate God's presence and will *prefer* hell.[58] Many writers agree with Shedd, Charles Hodge included – who foresees, in hell, the 'unrestrained dominion of sin and sinful passions'[59] – together with Strong[60] and others.[61] This view plays a major role in C.S. Lewis' apology, with the intriguing idea that the damned could enjoy an abominable 'black pleasure' in hell.[62] Lewis unequivocally accepts that God is ultimately defeated by

---

53   *Crucial Questions, op. cit.*, pp. 92f.
54   James I. Packer, 'The Problem of Eternal Punishment', *Crux* 26 (1990) note 7, p.25, related to p. 22.
55   *The Christian Doctrine, op. cit.*, p. 147.
56   *Ibid.*, p. 150.
57   *Ibid.*, p. 155.
58   *Ibid.*, pp. 153f.
59   *Systematic Theology, op. cit.*, p. 868; *cf.* pp. 877f.
60   *Systematic Theology, op. cit.*, pp. 1048f.
61   Sachs, together with Hayes (and Bernanos as a great novelist, 'Current Eschatology', *op. cit.*, p. 235).
62   *The Problem of Pain, op. cit.*, p. 114.

the free choice of evil on the part of some of his creatures.[63]

Opinions differ somewhat on the infinite gravity of sin. Fernando cites Jonathan Edwards, but declines taking sides.[64] For Shedd, sin is an infinite evil while 'the suffering of man is only relatively infinite,' and 'that of the God-man is absolutely infinite.'[65] This distinction enables him to justify the endlessness of gehenna-suffering, while Christ's lasted only hours.

A Tentative Appraisal of the Same

The classical affirmation of retributive justice, with penal infliction upheld as the good restoration of the cosmic moral order, should be maintained against all contrary winds. John Hick's criticisms stem from his characteristic presuppositional antimony: the opposition of juridical objectivity and personal-ethical relationships.[66] Scripture does not warrant such a separation, which reflects the humanistic 'ground motive' (to use *dooyeweerdian* language), the antinomy of Nature and Freedom. Evangelical theology may boldly defend one of its cardinal tenets and face modernistic attacks upon the retributive principle: it has abundant ammunition, and, in recent decades, it has used them to good effect.[67]

The real difficulty arises when we think of God's *love*. Some advocates, at least, of the doctrine of hell, do sound strangely insensitive.... Remembering God's mercy upon

---

63 *Ibid.*, p. 115.
64 *Crucial Questions, op. cit.*, p. 104.
65 *The Doctrine, op. cit.*, p. 196, note 43.
66 *Evil, op. cit.*, pp.112, 201.
67 Cf. Henri Blocher, *La Doctrine du péché et de la rédemption* (Vaux-sur-Seine: Fac-Etude, 1982) pp. 45-48, for a treatment of the penal principle (against Paul Ricoeur; with the benefit of the groundwork reestablished by scholars like Leon Morris and James I. Packer).

his elect does not wipe away tears over loved ones impenitent – and *all* men should be to us 'loved ones.' Our confession is of weakness, of naked trust, while reason in groping darkness 'gathers dust and chaff.' As people under the Word, we *believe* that justice and love are one in God, the same fire of holy passion. We cannot yet *see* that truth. We do not know how to reconcile the perfection of divine mercy, the bliss of the redeemed, and the torment of the lost. But we do not presume to teach the Lord lessons of love. But we know *him*. Our disarmed faith knows God, and it suffices.

The stumbling-block is none other than the opaque mystery of evil. Why did God sovereignly permit sin to happen – now the special, unforgivable, sin of hardened unbelief, which must be punished? Scripture offers no other answer than the sharp apostrophe of Romans 9:20f., the thorn in the flesh of reason. To utter that conviction is obviously to steer away from Strong's confident explanation of sin, endless sin, as 'incident to the system'. *Mè genoito*! Such a logic is not attuned to the Biblical horror of sin; it trifles with tragedy, that tragedy that pervades the whole of Scripture. If we share God's revealed abhorrence of the smallest sin, we shall consider it a vicious slander that the 'system' of God's dealings should incidentally entail the slightest trace of evil.

We rejoice rightfully in the thought that the redeemed may far outnumber the lost – but should it be our reply to anguished questions concerning permanent evil and total wickedness continuing throughout eternity? It would be turned into cheap comfort. How can numbers and percentages matter when the *absolute* sovereignty of love is at stake? Annihilationism is not required for one to share in John Wenham's distaste for this kind of mathematics! If a single fly is enough to spoil the whole bottle of perfume (Eccles. 10:1), will not a single hater of God spoil the final state of creation? Dostoevsky was more sensitive than some theologians: *one* lost soul is enough to create the problem; even if Judas were alone in hell, we could not reassure ourselves by saying that his 'own place' is but a small corner in the universe.

We may inquire into the divine reasons behind the decision to permit sin and hell, but Strong's speculative proposal about the need of 'moral instruction' fails to carry much conviction. Why would sinless spirits need such a gruesome object-lesson, as they see everything in God's own perfect light? And, once sin has entered the world: is not the cross a sufficient proof, even stronger than hell, of God's holiness and of sin's heinousness?

Would it be normal for God to allow for sin to go on for ever since he allows it now? That logic appears to by-pass entirely the Biblical theme of divine *patience*. Is not the point that God tolerates at present what he will *no longer* when his patience comes to an end?

Apologetes sometimes do a disservice to the causes they would defend!

We shall excuse ourselves of all calculus of infinities, and hide behind a quotation from Charles Hodge (Hodge always above his peers!): 'Men are apt to involve themselves in contradictions when they attempt to reason about the infinite. The word is so vague and so comprehensive, and our ideas of what it is intended to express are so inadequate, that we are soon lost when we seek to make it a guide in forming our judgments.'[68] So we press on and meet the main apologetic argument frontally: *freedom*.

There is a sense, Biblically, in which the unrepentant sinner draws upon himself the punishment he deserves; as

---

68   *Systematic Theology, op. cit.*, p. 878.

he reaps what he has sown, he is a true
heautontimôroumenos, as Strong puts it.[69] Yet, the
Biblical picture of the wrathful Lord and Judge of all hardly
suggests a mere passive role. There is something
suspicious in the zeal to exonerate God of responsibility in
judgement – theodicy built on insignificance?

At any rate, many statements on human freedom have a
strong Pelagian flavour. If one stresses God's
powerlessness in front of impenitent hearts, what about
the king's heart like water in God's hand, which he (the
Lord!) directs wherever he pleases (Prov. 21:1)? What
about dependence, *not* on he who wills or he who runs, but
on God who has mercy (Rom. 9:16)? What about John 6:45
(and 65), and so many other texts? John Hick frankly
voices his misgivings when he reads the Gospel of John:
'In the Fourth Gospel the notion of a free human response
to Christ upon which men's eternal destinies depend is
obscured and indeed undermined by the disconcerting idea
that mankind is already irrevocably divided into two
races...,'[70] he means, by those passages which teach 'a
predestination involving a fixed and impassable gulf...'.[71]
There is a touch of caricature here, but, at any rate, Hick's
witness to Johannine doctrine cannot be suspected of
sympathy!

In spite of his anti-predestination bias, Hick does
perceive in part the inadequacy of the pure spontaneity
view of freedom; he discerns that freedom is nothing if it
does not express the constancy of a nature, or character;[72]

---

69   *Systematic Theology, op. cit.*, p. 1041; Strong's allusion to
      Terence's title is affected by a small misprint
      [heauto͟utimôroumenos] which has gone uncorrected through
      many printings!
70   *Death, op. cit.*, p. 246.
71   *Ibid.*, pp. 246f.
72   *Evil, op. cit.*, p. 311.

twice, he puts forward the analogy of psychotherapy to suggest that freedom may stand in need of liberation.[73] Rahner, at least in one exceptional remark, and Sachs who follows him, show a much deeper metaphysical sense.[74] They are aware of the shallowness of the autonomy-concept. But they dare not denounce it openly; the foundational and fulfilling role of Being which they wish to honour is still a far cry from Biblical Lordship.

Explaining evil, with hell in its train, as the unavoidable risk of freedom, presupposes an ultimate dualism: for the nature of freedom as involving the real possibility of rebellion is a Necessity, a metaphysical law or principle, which confronts God from the outside (it is *not* found in his own being!). It also tends to make evil 'natural', not so abhorrent after all, if it is the price to be paid for the emergence of that supreme value, free-will. This amounts to dodging the evilness of evil, and denying the horror of hell.

The difficulty doubles when continuance in sin becomes cardinal in the fate of the lost. Strikingly, those who affirm that it is so do not make the feeblest attempt at any Scriptural proof. Psychological considerations on habit and hardening eclipse all other arguments. Strong *only* seeks support from a verse (the only reference): from Mark 3:29, 'he is guilty of an eternal sin.'[75] From its context and synoptic parallels, it is easy to understand this word as guilt remaining, not as sin being constantly reproduced; Beza and Bengel had discerned this natural meaning (the latter's *Gnomon* reads *Peccatum* hoc loco *reatum significat*). Hodge offers a theological reason, drawn from the lost's alienation and separation from God: since 'God

---

73   *Ibid.*, p. 381; *Death, op. cit.*, p. 253.

74   Sachs, 'Current Eschatology', *op. cit.*, pp. 234 note 28,241, 246ff.

75   *Systematic Theology, op. cit.*, p. 1034.

is the source of all holiness and happiness, separation
from Him is of necessity the forfeiture of all good,' which
entails sinfulness.[76] This reasoning, however, is not
strictly conclusive. It does not take into account the
complexity of 'separation'; orthodoxy has to maintain that
the lost, in the final state, still depend *metaphysically* on
God, and have in him their being if they are to exist at all.
Even in life, we say they are separated from God, 'without
God in the world,' and, yet, the very energy of their
sinning, at every instant, is given them of God. Hodge's
logic, then, does not envisage the possibility of *another*
relationship to God, in judgement, that will exclude both
fellowship and active sinfulness (this relationship we shall
presently call *death*; whereas 'life' is spent either in divine
fellowship or in active sinfulness, in 'death' there is
neither).

Supporting reasons being so weak, we may observe
that the thesis of sin continuing is found nowhere in
Scripture. On the contrary, the punishment refers only to
'things done through the body' (2 Cor. 5:10); Hodge has to
concede the point.[77] It is the harvest of the seeds of this
life. With all due caution, because of the parabolic genre
and because the intermediate state is in view, we may
comment that the rich man's, 'Dives', attitude in the
Lazarus story (Luke 16) does not resemble Shedd's
picture: he seems to be quite lucid on his past behaviour,
rather submissive and regretful![78] There is a fatal tension
in the thesis under scrutiny: for it affirms *both* the extreme
of vicious rebellion *and* the sinner's approval of his
judgement as just. How can Shedd both write: 'It is pure

---

[76] *Systematic Theology, op. cit.*, p. 879.
[77] *Loc. cit.*, and similarly, Strong, *Systematic Theology, op. cit.*,
p. 1039, or Shedd, *The Doctrine, op. cit.*, p. 146.
[78] *Contra* Hodge, *Systematic Theology, op. cit.*, p. 877, or Shedd,
The Doctrine, op. cit., p. 140.

wickedness, without regret or sorrow'[79] and 'The sinner's own conscience will "bear witness" and approve of the condemning sentence,' as the *Westminster Larger Catechism* specifies, 'upon clear evidence and full conviction of their consciences'?[80] Conscience is the man conscious! Conscience would be suppressed by total sin! It is not possible to associate them, as Shedd suggests, as 'brimstone and fire'.[81]

And now we come to the weightiest *datum* of all. The theory of sin forever flourishing ignores the message of Christ's perfect victory over sin and all evil. *Every* knee shall bow and *every* tongue confess...(Phil. 2:10f), those of the lost included. It cannot mean mere outward, hypocritical and forced agreement; what sense could there be in any outward show in the light of that Day, when all the secrets shall be exposed (Rom. 2:16), before the God who is Spirit? Sinners are forced, then, to confess the truth, but they are forced by truth itself, by its overwhelming evidence and spiritual authority; they can no longer refuse to see, they cannot *think* otherwise. Through Christ, it has pleased God to reconcile, *apokatallaxai*, the whole universe, including all rebellious spirits (Col. 1:20). 'Reconciliation' does not imply *salvation*, here, as independent exegetes have recognized; it means the restoration of order, of all within God's order, 'pacification,' as all are brought back into the divinely-ruled harmony.[82] Nothing could be farther removed from divine defeat and sin going on after judgement.

---

[79]   *Ibid.*, p. 155, already cited.
[80]   *Ibid.*, p. 140.
[81]   *Ibid.*, p. 151.
[82]   See already Martin Dibelius, *Die Briefe des Apostels Paulus an die Kolosser, Epheser, an Philemon* (Handbuch zum Neuen Testament III/2; Tuebingen: J.C.B.Mohr, 1912), p. 73 (*in loc.*): vom Versoehnungswerk an den Menschen ist erst 1[22] die Rede, hier handelt es sich um die Unterwerfung des Alls; note in the French *Bible de Jérusalem* (1956); 'pacification' is F.F. Bruce's

The Fire and Worm of Remorse

The main fact about everlasting punishment, the fate of the reprobates, is this: *sin shall be no more*. Such is the thesis we propose. With great wisdom, Francisco Turretin ('the Protestant Aquinas') cautions his reader, as an introduction to his paragraph on hell: 'What the punishment really is, or in what does the essence of the pains of hell consist, is not easy to define.'[83] Most Biblical indications are couched in metaphorical language, which lends itself easily to a variety of understandings.[84] Yet, the hints there are, and the main axes of the eschatological vision unfolded in Scripture, encourage us boldly to profess this assurance.

It may be *nearer* to older orthodoxy than nineteenth and twentieth century emphases. Soundings in Calvin's writings have not met a distinct affirmation that the damned would continue sinning. In the *Institutes*, III, 3, 24, commenting on Mark 3:29, he does say that those who blaspheme against the Holy Spirit will be struck by 'an eternal blindness,' but this metaphor does not necessarily imply a sinful attitude; in III, 25, 5, he stresses that 'rightfully so, the memory of their iniquity does not perish,' a formulation which could suggest that iniquity itself does not go on. Saint Augustine has a stronger statement. Speaking of the final division between the Two Cities, the

---

proposal, according to Fernando, *Crucial Questions, op. cit.*, p. 75.

[83] *Institutio theologiae elencticae* (New York: Robert Carter, 1847), locus xx, qu. 7, par. 4, vol. III, p. 519: Quid sit vero, seu in quo poenarum infernalium ratio consistat, non facile est definire.

[84] Later centuries inflated that language, with the major influence of a Peter and a Paul Apocalypse in antiquity, and the *Visio Tnugdali* in the Middle Ages: *cf.* Tarald Rasmussen, 'Hoelle. Kirchengeschichtlich', *Theologische Realenzyklopaedie* XV (1986) pp. 450f.

two categories of people, he writes: 'The former shall have no longer any desire, the latter any ability, to sin.'[85] Saint Augustine's intention, obviously, is to exclude sin being committed *on either side*. Whether the total absence of any *facultas peccandi* amounts, for him, to agreement with God, to reconciliation in the sense of Colossians 1:20, is not clear. But we would claim that it is logically entailed: for a man to disagree with God is to sin, and to do so anew at every moment; Saint Augustine has discerned that it cannot be any more, the *facultas* is no longer there. This may change our perspective more than we realize at first.

Confirmation comes as we reflect on *divine patience*. What is amazing, in Biblical vision, what is abnormal, incredible, is not that God should suppress sin – rather, that he should not do so immediately! How can it be that the LORD, in whom all men live, and move, and have their being, of whom and unto whom are all things, *endures* for so long *vessels of wrath*? How does he tolerate that creatures of dust, proud little nothings, break his law, deride his name, spit in his face? And they get away with it! And *God,* day by day, grants them the very life they so spend! It is unimaginable. Yet we confess the incredible truth of divine patience.

When the time of patience falls due, however, sin can be no more.

May we so receive the figurative language of Scripture that it can agree with this theological model? Saint Ambrose, already, we are told, interpreted the 'gnashing of teeth' as that of sinners being wroth with themselves,[86] and Klaas Schilder of their 'self-condemnation and self-

---

85   *Enchiridion*, xxix, 111.
86   According to Harry Buis, *The Doctrine of Eternal Punishment* (Grand Rapids: Baker Book House, 1957), p. 60.

loathing.'[87] This means precisely agreement with God in his reprobation of their behaviour (Hoekema speaks of the 'bitterness of remorse and hopeless self-condemnation'[88]). The unquenchable fire and the undying worm are the main symbols of the everlasting torments; although the fire also recalls God's judgement upon Sodom,[89] the fire and the worm come from Isaiah 66:24, where the key-idea seems to be that of perpetual *death* – we notice that they affect the *corpses* of rebels. Further, as used in the New Testament, both figures may easily be interpreted as the self-condemning conscience; actually, there is a spontaneous use of them, in everyday talk, for *remorse*: we all understand what a 'burning' or 'gnawing' remorse means. Turretin mentions that many 'would expound metaphorically or allegorically [these figures] of the most grievous anguish of conscience, and of despair,'[90] and he leans cautiously on that side. Isaiah 66:24 and Daniel 12:2 also speak of abhorrence (*dèrâôn*) and shame:[91] this resembles a more literal language to denote a right attitude, attuned to God's own judgement, towards the past sinful lives; all creatures will share in God's

---

87   *Ibid.*, p. 131.
88   Anthony A. Hoekema, *The Bible and the Future* (Exeter: Paternoster Press, 1979), p. 268.
89   It also recalls the fire in the vale of Hinnom (Jer. 7:31: *cf.* Isa. 30:33). Incidentally, the oft-quoted statement that the garbage of the city of Jerusalem used to be burned there is extremely late and untrustworthy; there is no witness to the tradition before David Qimhi (c. 1200 A.D.), and it seems most unlikely in itself, as demonstrated by J[oseph] Chaine, 'Géhenne,' *Supplément au Dictionnaire de la Bible*, dir. Louis Pirot, vol. III (1938) cols. 573f. Josiah's desecration does not amount at all to the same (2 Kings 23:10).
90   *Institutio, op. cit.*, p. 519: metaphorice seu allegorice exponi volunt de gravissimis angoribus conscientiae et desperatione.
91   The *Biblia Hebraica Stuttgartensia* critic, W. Baumgartner, would suppress 'shame' in Daniel 12:2 as a gloss added to explain the following word. It behoves us to be more cautious (it is found in Greek versions).

abhorrence; the lost will be ashamed, theirs will be the
ultimate 'confusion of face', as they shall be unable to
escape the truth of their past actions.

The main Biblical expressions, then, may refer to the
reaction of the moral creature, no longer able to sin, when
he or she becomes at last *lucid*. Then, impenitent sinners
appreciate the value of their lives and see them as they
are, under God's reprobation. Edward Young, the poet, did
not fall wide of the mark:
For what, my small philosopher, is hell?
'tis nothing but full knowledge of the truth....[92]
We would add: full knowledge in self-abhorrence,
condemnation, remorse.

Remorse may be the most helpful concept at this
juncture. But final remorse differs from remorse as it is
experienced in life: final remorse will be remorse-in-
agreement with God. In life, as long as it is called 'today',
only *repentance* agrees with God; remorse remains a
twisted and truncated apprehension of the truth of one's
deeds. Will not, then, final truthful remorse amount to
repentance? As a matter of fact, Saint Augustine once
used the word 'repentance,' *poenitentia*, for the lost. The
soul in hell, he wrote, 'is tormented by sterile
repentance.'[93] We would hesitate to follow him, and would
suggest that the deepest difference between remorse and
repentance is this: repentance has a *future*, it enters the
open future; remorse relates only to the *past*. The remorse
of the gnashed teeth and gnawing worm relates only to the
past.

Eternal Death
Here, we reach the other main feature of the everlasting
punishment: it is *death*, 'second', definitive, eternal death.

---

[92]   Quoted by Shedd, *The Doctrine, op. cit.*, p. 141.
[93]   *Civitas Dei*, XXI, ix (2): sterili poenitentia crucietur.

Patience comes to an end. The veil is lifted. The light of
judgement reveals the exact truth of each life. The man
who bears his guilt, and who has not been clothed upon by
Christ, can only loathe and condemn what he has done,
what he has been. *And then?* What comes next? *Nothing*.
The concept of a 'next' stage is empty and deceptive. The
life which God had given has been spent, and wasted.
Now, it is death. 'Full stop' for ever and ever. 'Abandon
all hope ye who enter here': there can be no hope when
there is no longer any future.

The Biblical idea of death does not involve non-
existence, but, indeed, the *loss of life*. Life is ability to act
and to project, life is sharing in exchanges; total death is
isolation, paralysis (no *facultas* left, to recall the
Augustinian word), non-renewal, that is *fixity*, absolute
fixity. *Rigor mortis, rigor secundae mortis*, could we say,
using the same kind of metaphor which Isaiah coined and
Jesus himself borrowed. What remains is the *corpse* of a
sinful life together with the lucid consciousness of that
truth – abhorrence – and no ground whatsoever for any
change of that final situation.

If we take the name 'second *death*' seriously, the
distance between Biblical eschatology and ideas of a
second chance of salvation, or of a limited punishment-
time, becomes manifest. They betray their lack of
penetration.

Somewhat intriguingly, we may borrow phrases or
sentences from writers whose global doctrine we
criticized, to illustrate the meaning of 'eternal death'. Karl
Rahner argues from the power of freedom to set something
definitive: 'because "eternity" is not the temporal
continuation, beyond, of the history of freedom, but the
accomplished definitiveness of history, hell is "eternal",

and, so, the manifestation of God's righteousness.'[94]
Rahner probably plays with a sophisticated idea of
eternity, a purely a-temporal eternity, which we would not
consider adequate.[95] It is not adequate for eternal life, but
it could approximately suit eternal *death*, the endless
duration of which is equivalent to a *nunc aeternum*.

We could similarly compare Karl Barth's view on man in
the final state: his emphasis is that man shall exist
eschatologically *as past*, 'one day he will only have
been.'[96] But this, in our proposal, would apply only to the
lost. C. S. Lewis exploits the word 'destruction' as used
in Scripture: 'If soul can be destroyed, must there not be a
state of *having been* a human soul? And is not that,
perhaps, the state which is equally well described as
torment, destruction , and privation? (...) What is cast (or
casts itself) into hell is not a man: it is "remains".'[97]
Lewis, then, deviates, and he interprets these words in
terms of maximum sinfulness. We would say: what is cast
into hell is not the man *living*, but the man *dead*.

We are utterly unable to *imagine* the experience of
absolute fixity, the 'feeling' of the remorse-consciousness
eternalized. As long as we enjoy a measure of life,
duration equals renewal. Knowing our inability may help

---

94   'Hoelle,' *op. cit.*, col. 738: die 'Ewigkeit' aber nicht die
     zeithafte Fortdauer hinter der Freiheitsgeschichte, sondern die
     getane Endgueltigkeit der Geschichte ist, darum ist die H.
     'ewig' und so Erscheinung der Gerechtigkeit Gottes.
95   See various contributions in Nigel M. de S. Cameron, ed., *The
     Power and Weakness of God: Impassibility and Orthodoxy*
     (Edinburgh: Rutherford House Books, 1990), including our
     'Divine Immutability', p. 9 on eternity.
96   *Church Dogmatics* III/2, G.W. Bromiley & T.F. Torrance, ed.,
     trans. Harold Knight *et. al.* (Edinburgh: T. & T. Clark, 1960),
     p. 632.
97   *The Problem, op. cit.*, p. 113.

us to disentangle our theological judgement from
emotional reactions to imagery.[98]

The model accommodates easily and *economically* other
elements of the doctrine of everlasting punishment: not
only the reference to the deeds done through the body
(with the harvest metaphor), but also the diversity in
degrees (few stripes, many stripes). There can be no
proportion more exact to guilt than that of the suffering of
seeing oneself in the light of truth. That God be glorified
and sanctified by sinners punished, as Scripture intimates
(Isa. 5:16; Ezek. 38:16) is readily perceived; that there is
a satisfaction of the order of divine law, a vindication of
God's honour and holiness, and a kind of 'reconciliation'.

Daring Questions, to Conclude

The import of the foregoing reflections for theodicy does
not appear to be insignificant. We may confidently dispel
any foolish fantasy of divine defeat. Can we make a few
more speculative steps?

If sinners ultimately glorify God, they do reach in a
paradoxical way the *telos* of all creatures as such. And
they *know* it, since they now see the truth of their lives;
they see their evil works – which they now abhor – as
included in God's plan, by his permissive will, and used for
his purposes. May this imply another side in their
remorse-consciousness? They are excluded from the
fellowship of God; they cannot 'enjoy him for ever'; here is
the tragedy, and the meaning of 'outer darkness' (they
have no share in the banquet-feast of salvation). Yet,
their thought is fixed in the knowledge that, through their
very deprivation, they glorify God and agree with him.

---

[98]   Packer, 'The Problem...', *op. cit.*, p. 25: 'Do not try to imagine
        what it is like to be in hell.'

Would *annihilation* be a better fate, objectively, and even subjectively, for the lost themselves? Salmond quotes from Plutarch:

> The idea of annihilation was intolerable to the Greek mind. If they had a choice between entire extinction and an eternity of torment in Hades, they would have chosen the latter; almost all, men and women both, would have surrendered themselves to the teeth of Cerberus, or the buckets of the Danaidae, rather than to non-entity.[99]

This pagan preference, which was also T.H. Huxley's, according to Fudge, [100] may not have been so far misguided.

Would it have been better for the lost if they *had not existed at all?* Jesus' words in Matthew 26:24 are often so understood as to imply this ultimate negativity.[101] Yet, Jesus does *not* say: 'It would have been better for him not to have been *created*'! Jesus refers to the man's *birth*. He probably recalls the laments of Job and of Jeremiah, who wish they had died in their mothers' wombs. We dare not claim that our Lord consciously implied here a doctrine of the eternal destiny, and redemption, of those who died in early infancy and of aborted fœtuses; the point of comparison in his statement, however, is the loss of the privileges of *this* life as incurred by a stillborn child (*cf.* Eccles. 6:3ff), and *not* pure non-existence. If we may cautiously trust the larger hope that the existence of the lost shall not amount to a total waste, neither for the universe, nor for God, nor for themselves, it may shed some encouraging light on the problem of evil.

That impenitent sinners should be 'reconciled' to God through the perfection of remorse, through condemnation

---

99   *The Christian Doctrine, op. cit.*, pp. 610f.
100 *The Fire..., op. cit.*, pp. 198.
101 Buis, *The Doctrine, op. cit.*, p. 38, quotes this verse against annihilation.

embraced, in 'outer darkness' and death and not in the life-giving fellowship of God, remains a tragedy. It follows from the seriousness, heinousness, of sin: the capital evil. Why God has permitted, in his wise and benevolent sovereignty, the horror of evil still deserves to be called the 'opaque mystery'. None of our considerations should push us further, to a non-Biblical *felix culpa*! Regarding the everlasting punishment, our effort aims only at keeping within the bounds of revealed truth, but *without* reading into the text misconceptions that cause many to stumble.

On all invisible things and that rise higher than our powers of understanding, we can have no assurance but by the sole Word of God. So we ought to cling to that Word, and reject everything that would be added unto it (John Calvin).[102] Amen!

---

[102] *Institutes of the Christian Religion*, III, 25, 5: we translate directly (as we have done in our previous quotations) from Calvin's French, which differs somewhat from the Latin: Or de toutes choses invisibles, et mesmes qui surmontent la capacité de notre entendement, il n'y en a nulle asseurance que par la seule Parole de Dieu. Ainsi c'est à icelle qu'il faut tenir, rejettans tout ce qu'on nous amènera d'avantage.

Index